Christ's Politics

William Moore-Ede, 1901, by James Eadie-Reid. (Shipley Art Gallery, Gateshead.)

Christ's Politics

A LIFE OF WILLIAM MOORE-EDE

Anne Spurgeon

Christ's Politics: A Life of William Moore-Ede
Anne Spurgeon

Published by Aspect Design

Designed, printed and bound by Aspect Design
89 Newtown Road, Malvern, Worcs. WR14 1PD
United Kingdom
Tel: 01684 561567
E-mail: allan@aspect-design.net
Website: www.aspect-design.net

All Rights Reserved.

Copyright © 2021 Anne Spurgeon

Anne Spurgeon has asserted her moral right
to be identified as the author of this work.

The right of Anne Spurgeon to be identified as the author of
this work has been asserted in accordance with Section 77 of
the Copyright, Designs and Patents Act 1988.

This book is sold subject to the condition that it shall not,
by way of trade or otherwise, be lent, resold, hired out or
otherwise circulated without the publishers prior consent
in any form of binding or cover other than that in which it
is published and without a similar condition including this
condition being imposed on the subsequent purchaser.

A copy of this book has been deposited
with the British Library Board

Cover Design Copyright © 2021 David Spurgeon.

ISBN 978-1-912078-05-9

In memory of Mary Jane Gray

ABOUT THE AUTHOR

Anne Spurgeon was formerly a senior lecturer in the Institute of Occupational and Environmental Health at the University of Birmingham. She now researches industrial and social history focussing on the nineteenth and early twentieth centuries. She grew up in Lancashire and also has strong family links to Tyneside. She now lives in Worcestershire. Her previous book was *Women and Children in the Factory: A Life of Adelaide Anderson*.

CONTENTS

Acknowledgements ix
1. Introducing William Moore-Ede 1
2. A (Very) Brief History of Christian Socialism 13
3. Formative Years 22
4. Alston Moor 30
5. A Peripatetic University 45
6. A Real Sheffield Blade 55
7. The Munificence of Mr Firth 65
8. Return to Tyneside 74
9. Teaching and Temperance 83
10. Stormy Educational Waters 93
11. The Gospel of Penny Pies 102
12. Industrial Matters 115
13. Abuse and Neglect 127
14. Marsden Miners 137
15. The Housing of the People 150
16. Turning Back the Tide 160
17. Worcester 168
18. For the Many Not the Few 179
19. Cradley Heath 187
20. Under the Widely Blowing Banner 196
21. The Vindication of Righteousness 203
22. Twopenny Dinners 214
23. A Garden Suburb and Gheluvelt Park 223

24. The Dean's Cowsheds 233
24. An Apostle for Peace 245
26. Black Friday and White Coal 254
27. Home Territory 262
28. Musical Passions 270
29. The Friends 280
30. The Final Years 288
Afterword 297
Bibliography 299
Index 303

ACKNOWLEDGEMENTS*

My first encounter with the name William Moore-Ede was a very brief one. Whilst researching a previous biography of a woman factory inspector I found a letter from a clergyman expressing concern about lead poisoning in Gateshead. Several years later I was one of those people William liked to encourage to 'wander around Worcester Cathedral and be drawn forward by what they saw and heard' and I noticed the small memorial window and found the booklet by Canon Graham Neville in the giftshop. Was this the same Reverend Moore-Ede I had seen quoted in the Factory Inspector's report for 1882?

My first acknowledgment, therefore, is to the late Canon Neville who produced that fascinating booklet, for it is that which provided the inspiration for this biography. It told me a great deal about William's life during his time as Dean of Worcester, and also noted that there had been a previous life in Gateshead, something he had not had the opportunity to explore fully. This present biography has emerged in a somewhat different style and format to that of Canon Neville's, but hopefully a complementary one. For I suspect that we shared a feeling that William Moore-Ede merits rather more attention than he has previously received.

My second acknowledgement is to the staff of Worcester Cathedral, particularly Cathedral librarian, David Morrison, who helped me to find so much information about William's time in Worcester and accommodated me for weeks in the library as I searched through the 'scrapbooks' that documented the various activities of the Dean. In addition, there have been numerous others who at different times have answered my queries about altar cloths, stained glass, memorials and monuments as well as about doctrine and practice. I thank them all for their time and interest.

I am also extremely grateful to the staff of the various archives around the country that contain material relating to William Moore-Ede. These include the local studies centres at Gateshead and Newcastle, the Dryden Centre in Gateshead and St Mary's Heritage Centre, (formerly Gateshead parish church), the Newcastle Literary and Philosophical Society, Alston Library, the Northumberland County Archives located at the Woodhorn Mining Museum in Ashington and the Cutlers Hall in Sheffield.

Finally, my partner and I have enjoyed visiting many churches, both urban and rural, as well as various other sites connected in some way with William Moore-Ede. We have always received a warm welcome and found a great interest in the subject. I would like to thank them all for their unfailing hospitality and willingness to give us their time.

---

* The initial research for this book, which involved travel from home, was carried out pre-pandemic in 2019 and early 2020. Due to government travel restrictions during 2020–21, however, any subsequent research relied heavily on web-based material.

Chapter One
INTRODUCING WILLIAM MOORE-EDE

On the morning of the 5 April 1882 Thomas Burt, Member of Parliament for Morpeth in Northumberland, received a worrying letter from the Rector of nearby Gateshead on Tyne. The Rector, the Reverend William Moore-Ede, wrote to express his 'grave concern about the terrible murders, for they are nothing less, that are daily being committed in the town.'[1] There was not, as might be supposed, a northern version of Jack the Ripper at large on Tyneside but a number of recent fatalities had highlighted an equal if not greater threat to the women of Gateshead. White lead, or more precisely lead carbonate, was a pigment most commonly added to house paint to give it that clean, sparkling, long-lasting quality so much prized in middle-class homes. It was not, however, its use but its manufacture that concerned William Moore-Ede, an activity carried out largely by women workers in grimy workshops scattered along the banks of the River Tyne.[2] Many of these women, it seemed, were becoming victims of lead poisoning. According to a member of the campaign group the Humanitarian League, employment in the leadworks was 'the preserve of women of the very poorest and roughest class'. This was a group, apparently, that included 'the widow who has a family to support, the wife of a drunken husband and the girl whose character will not bear

---

1. William Moore-Ede's (WME) letter to Thomas Burt (5 April 1882). NA (National Archives) HO/45/A15330.

2. For a description of white lead manufacturing see: R. H. Sherard, *The White Slaves of England* (Fifield, London, 1897).

scrutiny.'³ Meanwhile the editor of the *Daily Chronicle* took an unashamedly sensational view of this situation. In a series of articles under headings such as 'Massacre of the innocents,' 'Death in the workshop' and 'White cemeteries,' he described how, in the process of white lead manufacture, lead was 'gasped into the lungs, swallowed in the saliva and absorbed through the skin.' The symptoms of lead poisoning he noted 'progressed through anaemia, headaches, vision problems, convulsions and death.'⁴

In the 1880s there were few statistics on industrial fatalities to support these claims but a glance at the regular reports in the local press left no doubt that women were indeed succumbing to lead poisoning on a regular basis. A member of the Gateshead Board of Guardians, John Caris, had also written to Thomas Burt to express his concern. For in recent months a number of young victims, too ill to work any longer, had sought shelter in the workhouse and several had died. The Rector of Gateshead, meanwhile, said he had been 'moved to make a few remarks on the subject' in his sermon at St Mary's parish church the previous Sunday, and after the service he had become acquainted with the personal tragedy of one of his parishioners.⁵ 'Mr James Gray, a widower, sought me out,' he informed Thomas Burt. 'He told me that his seventeen-year-old daughter, Mary Jane, had died the previous week.' Apparently, Mary Jane who had always been a healthy young woman, had been employed at Foster & Blacketts leadworks for just nine months. A few days earlier she had come home feeling unwell. She had died just twenty-four hours later. The cause of death was certified by the local doctor as 'lead poisoning – epileptic convulsions.'⁶ Her father's grief had been

---

3. The Humanitarian League was a radical pressure group formed in the nineteenth century, opposed to all avoidable suffering. They wished to change attitudes towards the treatment of criminals, conditions of labour, the killing of animals for food, sport or profit and the use of natural resources.
4. 'Massacre of the Innocents'; 'Death in the Workshop'; 'White Cemeteries'. BNA (British Newspaper Archives), *Daily Chronicle*, 15, 21, 28 December 1892.
5. St Mary's was previously the parish church of Gateshead. It is now a heritage centre.
6. op cit., letter to Thomas Burt.

intensified by his inability to afford a decent funeral for his only child. Mr Gray, a general labourer of very limited means, had asked Mary Jane's employer if they would cover the cost of a coffin, but they had refused. As a father himself, the Rector's natural empathy with the feelings of Mr Gray would have been particularly intense that day, for one of his own children, Oswald, had died a few weeks earlier, shortly after birth. And he would have been painfully aware of the contrast between Mr Gray's situation and that of his own family, thinking no doubt of the tiny coffin they had provided for baby Oswald and the loving respectful service that had accompanied his burial.

Mr Gray's distress and Foster & Blackett's callous refusal was something that William Moore-Ede would never forget. Over fifty years later he referred to it again when, as Dean of Worcester Cathedral, he addressed an assembly of Friendly Societies in the Midland town of Kidderminster. 'I am aware,' he said, 'that some people sneer at the workingman's desire for a decent funeral for those who belonged to him. I hold that it is an object not to be sneered at – it is part of the spirit of independence and self-respect.'[7] It was a statement that pointed not only to the deprivations suffered by ordinary working people, but also to their inherent dignity and pride. The tragedy of Mary Jane's death would always epitomise for William Moore-Ede the blighted lives of the poor and powerless in society and the denial of the same rights and opportunities afforded to its wealthier members. He concluded his letter to Thomas Burt with two sentences, both heavily underlined in black ink. 'There has been no inquest. Make of this what you will!'[8]

Thomas Burt would have been surprised to receive such a letter from an Anglican clergyman. Described as having at most 'a rather detached interest in Unitarianism' with 'scant regard for the

---

7. WME, 'Sermon at St Mary's Church, Kidderminster,' following the Annual Parade of Friendly Societies of the District. BNA, *Birmingham Daily Gazette*, 27 March 1933.

8. op cit., Letter to Thomas Burt.

Thomas Burt, Liberal-Labour MP for Morpeth from 1874 to 1918. (National Portrait Gallery.)

Church of England,' Thomas was not a particularly religious man.[9] Having recently been elected to Parliament he had been appalled and bewildered by the amount of time MPs spent debating religious affairs. Unfortunately, he had taken up his seat just as the Public Worship Regulation Bill of 1874 was beginning its protracted and tedious journey through the House of Commons. The Bill, primarily aimed at curtailing the introduction of Roman Catholic ritual into Anglican worship, was a largely unsuccessful attempt to end a theological battle that had been going on for over forty years. 'The House devoted some of the best weeks and months of the session in deciding whether a clergyman should stand with his face to the east or to the west, or whether they should have lighted candles on their altars,' he informed an equally disgusted audience of hard-working miners.[10] Against this background William Moore-Ede's letter and its expression of concern about young victims of lead poisoning was unexpected. It suggested to him that the newly appointed Rector of Gateshead was a rather different sort of clergyman to those he had met in the past.

So who was William Moore-Ede and why does he merit a special mention in the array of Anglican clerics who populate religious history? He was not a Bishop or an eminent theologian, or even a martyr, marked out by persecution or tragedy. His significance, however, lies in his adherence to a particular interpretation of the Anglican faith which during the nineteenth century came to be known as Christian Socialism. It was a doctrine that was born and nurtured during his own early years and which attracted a significant following amongst Anglican priests in the decades that followed. Much of what we know about early Christian Socialism as it developed during this period derives from the writings and teaching of its celebrated founders, Frederick Denison Maurice, Charles Kingsley, John Ludlow and Thomas Hughes, and there

9. L. J. Satre, *Thomas Burt, Miners' MP, 1837–1922* (Leicester University Press, Leicester, 1999).
10. ibid

is a strong literary focus on the complexities of their theology and politics and how this changed and developed over time.[11] Like so many movements inspired and propagated by ardent followers, Christian Socialism has long been prone to disputes and schisms among its protagonists, such that it soon ceased to be a unified whole. Both the words 'Christian' and 'Socialist' have at different times become theologically and politically contentious amongst those who would variously dispute the claim of either to represent the true Christian faith or the ideological position of socialism.[12] William Moore-Ede was not immune to these debates, for his own beliefs had been developed within a strongly academic setting and were grounded in extensive theoretical knowledge. In his subsequent work, however, his emphasis was always on the practical application of the doctrine and its communication of this to those, both rich and poor, he encountered in the harsh industrial world in which he lived. As such his reputation was not so much that of a theological luminary but a grassroots practitioner, a significant example of how the Christian Socialist life was actually lived during the late nineteenth and early twentieth centuries. Preaching without practice, he often observed, was 'not of much value'.[13] During his lifetime he was a popular figure primarily because of his straightforward engagement with many of the social issues of the day and his equally straightforward presentation of the theology that inspired it. Educational opportunity, decent housing, safe working conditions, pension provision in old age and the alleviation of child poverty were just some of the subjects with which he concerned himself. In consideration of all these issues, he maintained, one should simply look to the teaching of Jesus Christ.

11. Maurice, Kingsley and Ludlow were ordained university professors. Kingsley was also a writer of moral fables, of which the best known is *The Water Babies*. Hughes was a lawyer and founder of the newspaper *Christian Socialist*.

12. For more detailed discussion of the development of Christian Socialism, see C. Bryant, *Possible Dreams* (Hodder & Stoughton, London, 1996); A. Wilkinson, *Christian Socialism: Scott Holland to Tony Blair* (SCM Press, London, 1998).

13. 'The Dean's Bungalows. Opening Ceremony at Worcester,' BNA, *Worcester Echo*, 14 May 1920.

Many people are repelled by the statements of theologians which they find abstruse. They regard religion as outside their comprehension, a matter for the clergy and for Doctors of Divinity, but when they tear away the web of speculation which men weave around the gospel story and get to Jesus himself and his teaching it is extraordinary how plain and simple the gospel is.[14]

Similarly, it seemed, William was impatient with the wrangling that beset the various proponents of political doctrines. He would always argue that it was unavoidable and indeed necessary for the Church to be involved in 'politics' and in later years joined those who campaigned for ordained clergy to become MPs, but this did not imply uncritical adherence to a political party.[15] Although he was often in sympathy with progressive Liberal policies and later with those of the Independent Labour movement, he avoided formal membership of either party and always maintained a degree of distance from both. For ultimately, he considered, it was the existing economic system and the values that governed the functioning of that system which needed to change and for this he turned to the precepts of Christianity. Like one of his Christian Socialist contemporaries, Henry Scott Holland, he believed that economic relationships should be 'both moralised and brought under political control.'[16] 'Many people,' said Holland, 'live as tools of the system in a state of miserable double-mindedness . . . like shuttlecocks, banded between our political economy and our Christian morality . . . oscillating between a-moral economics and individual piety.'[17] William Moore-Ede would have agreed. 'The only politics that can succeed,' he told an audience at the Church

---

14. WME, address at the Church Congress, Sheffield, October 1922. BNA, *Sheffield Daily Telegraph*, 13 October 1922.

15. Until the 'Removal of Clergy Disqualification' Act of 2001 ordained Anglican clergy were not allowed to stand for election to Parliament or to sit in the House of Commons.

16. Henry Scott Holland was a professor of divinity, University of Oxford.

17. S. Paget, *Henry Scott Holland* (John Murray, London, 1921). Quoted in Wilkinson *Christian Socialism*.

Congress in 1923, 'are Christ's politics. What is morally wrong can never be politically right.'[18]

A major part of William Moore-Ede's working life was spent in two strikingly different places, Gateshead on Tyne, where he was Rector from 1881 to 1901 and Worcester, where he was Dean of the Cathedral from 1908 to 1934. He is remembered fondly in both places, each marking his presence in their own particular style, reflecting their own specific preoccupations and those of the time. In Gateshead he was a parish priest in the far north of England where his ministry took place against a background of poverty, disease and deprivation. Here mention of his name tends to provoke references to social reform, education and, in particular, 'Penny Dinners for poor children.' In the Gateshead suburb of Dunstan, once home to a range of heavy industries and their associated social problems, William was a regular preacher at the local church, Christchurch, on Ellison Road. The building William would have known was demolished many years ago and is now replaced on the site by the more modern St Nicholas with Christchurch. Behind this church, however, there remain several rows of Edwardian terraces built immediately following his period in Gateshead. The names of these streets pay homage to various prominent public figures of the time and here, amongst an assortment of military commanders and venerated members of the English cricket team, we find Moore Avenue and Ede Avenue. Meanwhile in another suburb called Low Fell, close to the Bensham Rectory where William lived, there is another modern building called the Dryden Centre which specialises in the provision of adult education and training. One of its classrooms bears the name of William Moore-Ede. And adorning one wall there is a decorated bronze plaque featuring an engraving of him as a young man, together with a text describing his contribution to the provision of food and education for poor children of the town and his chairmanship of the Gateshead School Board. William would have been immensely

---

18. op cit., *Sheffield Daily Telegraph*, 13 October 1922.

proud to be associated with the activities of the Dryden Centre, for his commitment to educational opportunities for ordinary working people was a central part of his mission.

In Worcester, by contrast, William Moore-Ede was Dean of the Cathedral, required to involve himself, Trollope-like, in the fabric and functioning of an old traditional establishment. Here he is most often remembered as the person who founded the Friends of Worcester Cathedral, an organisation which nearly a hundred years later continues to work energetically to raise funds to help preserve

Memorial plaque to William Mooore-Ede, a pioneer of social reform, recounting his provision of 1*d* dinners for poor children. Note: correct birth date is 1849. (Dryden Centre, Gateshead. Pictured in 2019.)

the historic building and its contents. Again, William would have been delighted to know that since its foundation in 1931 the society has raised over a million pounds to fund, not only the maintenance of the building as in William's time, but its various activities such as the choir, stone masonry and numerous other groups which support its work. He loved Worcester Cathedral and took very seriously his responsibility for maintaining the beauty of its building and its services.

Adjacent to the nave of the Cathedral, within the old monastic cloisters, William is buried in a simple grave with his first wife, Eleanor Cookson, and his second, Sarah Harrison. And nearby, set into the medieval stonework of these cloisters, is a small memorial window bearing the inscription 'In Memory of William Moore-Ede DD, Dean of Worcester 1908–1934.' It is, perhaps, a relatively modest memorial for someone who was such a prominent figure during his lifetime, but one that he himself would probably have preferred. Moreover, it is not so much this window that speaks most directly of his legacy but those he commissioned on behalf of others. For on another side of the cloisters there is a series of decorated glass panels, each recounting the death of an individual young man who was formerly associated in some way with the Cathedral, and who lost his life during the First World War. In addition, there are memorial windows dedicated to the Cathedral bell ringers, members of the choir and former boys from the associated Kings School who similarly died in this conflict, each name carefully recorded. These touchingly intimate windows, together with a much larger one of three lights installed in the Cathedral's military chapel, were designed by the artist James Eadie-Reid, a close friend of William who had worked for the Gateshead Stained Glass Company during the early years of the twentieth century.[19] Earlier, in 1901, he had painted two formal portraits of the Rector of Gateshead, one of which hangs in the Cathedral's treasury while the other, commissioned by the local School Board, can be found in Gateshead's Shipley Art Gallery. An early devotee of the Arts and Crafts movement, Eadie-Reid was also a Christian Socialist, renowned for his murals and stained glass that depicted ordinary labourers or, in the case of these memorial windows, ordinary soldiers, sailors and nurses alongside representations of Christ. For many years his work had featured in numerous churches around the North of England and the Midlands and in 1921 he was commissioned to create Worcester Cathedral's own particular tribute to the dead of the war at the behest of Dean Moore-Ede.

    Meanwhile, securely stored in the Cathedral's treasury there is

---

19. The two families were linked by the marriage of William Moore-Ede's nephew, Arthur Lawrence, (the son of William's sister) to the daughter of James Eadie-Reid.

The casket containing a scroll, awarded to William Moore-Ede in 1934, conferring on him the Freedom of the City of Worcester. (Courtesy of Chris Guy, Worcester Cathedral.)

another reminder of William Moore-Ede which tells of his work beyond the precincts of the building itself. This is a little silver casket beautifully modelled in the form of the Cathedral and mounted on a base of thirteenth-century oak taken from the roof timbers of the ancient building. The casket contains a scroll that conferred on William Moore-Ede the Freedom of the City in gratitude for 'his eminent services to the people of Worcester' services which, as we shall discover, ranged widely across a large number of different social projects.

It is instructive to seek out memorials for they are important pointers to someone once considered significant within a town, a building or an institution. They are especially interesting when, as in William's case, they take such different forms in different places. As we have discovered in the twenty-first century, however, memorials can, by their very nature, provide only a brief snapshot of the life of the person they commemorate, leaving out much of their story and often raising rather more questions than answers.[20] What follows therefore

20. As witnessed by public anger directed at statues of persons who, despite being philanthropic benefactors, have also been identified as participants in the slave trade.

is an attempt to answer some of the questions that lie behind these simple reminders of William Moore-Ede, by telling a fuller story of his life and work.

During his lifetime he was a prominent public figure, locally, nationally and occasionally internationally and virtually all the information on which this account is based is derived from sources that are publicly available, much of it in local and national newspapers of which there were many at the time, each with its own particular social or political agenda. William, himself, seems to have produced little in the way of formal academic writing or correspondence, official or otherwise. One suspects that, given the range of his activities and a family life that included eight children, he had neither the time nor the inclination to do so. He was, however, a prolific deliverer of sermons and public addresses which were invariably reproduced verbatim and subsequently commented upon in the press. Added to this he was a dedicated committee man, doggedly steering his way through acrimonious gatherings of individuals who, it often seemed, were determined to sabotage his best efforts. This was not, one suspects, because he enjoyed committee meetings, but rather because they provided an avenue of influence for those who occupied only a middle rank within the rigid social class structure of the time. You must, he once warned those who might wish to emulate him, be prepared to endure the drudgery of many inconvenient meetings. His committee work is thus another facet of his life which is recorded in comprehensive detail. Taken together these reports provide an extensive resource for a biographer although, like all such resources, they demand a certain amount of selection which necessarily determines the shape of the life presented. Primarily, therefore, this is the story of William Moore-Ede's work and his response to the various environments and situations in which he found himself, but it is also a story told through a specific lens, that of Christian Socialism, for this was the doctrine that inspired him throughout his life.

Chapter Two
A (VERY) BRIEF HISTORY OF CHRISTIAN SOCIALISM

William Moore-Ede is on record as describing himself as a 'radical'. It was a term he used rather more often than 'Christian Socialist' and it was one he used in the address he gave to the civic and clerical dignitaries assembled in Worcester's Guildhall on 17 April 1934 when he received the Freedom of the City. It was an auspicious occasion and an unusual one, for William was the first member of the clergy to receive this essentially secular award. As he surveyed the great and the good of Worcester that day his thoughts travelled back, as they often did, to that other April morning half a century earlier when he had been moved by the death of Mary Jane Gray and the grief of her devastated father. Since that day, he reflected, his life had contained many twists and turns. He was unpopular, he said, when he was appointed as Dean of Worcester Cathedral in 1908. 'I was a radical. I wore a moustache, and I was a teetotaller. Today I am the same.'[1] Beneath this light-hearted remark there lurked a reference to some difficult moments as he recalled his long career in the Church of England. His unwavering commitment to temperance and his preference for a rather droopy moustache might seem innocuous characteristics in themselves, but it was what each signified that aroused suspicion in some traditional Anglican minds. For the more comfortable in the Church of England, whose life no doubt included copious quantities of fine wine, William's resolute abstinence from alcohol was, at the very least, disappointing. More importantly, however, his membership of the temperance organisation,

1. WME, address at the ceremony which conferred on him the Freedom of the City of Worcester. 17 April 1934. BNA, *Birmingham Daily Gazette*, 18 April 1934.

the Independent Order of Rechabites, was suggestive of a suspicious propensity towards Methodism, a tendency apparently confirmed by his ecumenical attitudes and frequent support for non-conformist churches and other organisations.[2] Yet his implacable opposition to alcohol was born of the human misery he had witnessed amongst the poor, who so often and so disastrously sought refuge from their miserable existence in beer and cheap gin. Dinner guests at the Deanery in Worcester, it was said, would always find plenty of pretty wine glasses on the table but, at best, these would be filled with nothing more exciting than lemonade.[3] And then there was the moustache. In 1908 it had been quietly suggested to him that he should shave it off. Even in 1934, his stubborn refusal to abandon it had provoked some wry comments in the *Church Times* which, for some reason, felt compelled to mention that he 'remained the only Dean in England with a moustache.'[4] As William seems to have suspected, the moustache seemed to linger on in conservative minds as an indelible mark of socialism, an enduring allegiance to the teaching of his mentor at Cambridge, influential economist Alfred Marshall, for whom this walrus-like appendage was the hallmark of his physical persona. Underlying all this of course was a more fundamental concern. It was William's reputation for 'radicalism' that had most worried the Worcester Cathedral clergy in 1908, for it encapsulated all the anxieties of those who feared insurgency and upheaval, not only within the established church but in society as a whole.

Since the 1930s the word 'radical' has assumed a variety of connotations, not all of which would be familiar either to William or his audience. The terms 'radical' or 'radicalisation' as popularly understood in the twenty-first century, with its connotations of cultural and religious fundamentalism and even terrorism, does not sit comfortably with the attitudes of William Moore-Ede. Rather those who espoused 'radicalism'

2. The Independent Order of Rechabites was a Friendly Society founded by a group of Methodists in 1835 as part of the wider temperance movement. Membership was conditional on total abstinence from alcoholic beverages.

3. WCL (Worcester Cathedral Library) scrapbooks. Letter from the Very Reverend Robert Jeffrey, Dean Emeritus of Worcester, to Canon Graham Neville. 25 May 2007.

4. *Church Times*, 20 July 1934.

during William's lifetime were focussed primarily on the gross inequalities that characterised nineteenth and early twentieth-century British society. Their concerns ranged over a number of social and economic injustices such as poor wages, appalling working conditions, wretched housing, hunger, inadequate healthcare and education and the lack of any provision for old age. Underpinning all of these was a lack of parliamentary democracy, the basic right of every person to cast a vote, and thereby shift the balance of power from the aristocratic elite to the people themselves. The radicalism of the second half of the nineteenth century, therefore, had its origins in the Chartist movement of the 1840s, with its demands for universal suffrage and the wholesale reform of the electoral system.[5] Such reform struck at the heart of nineteenth-century society. It would mean the abandonment of the old belief, seemingly endorsed by both church and state, that the privileged station in life of a few, which underwrote their ability to exert power and control over the rest of the population, was somehow immutably ordained. No longer would the rich man be able to dwell comfortably in his castle while the poor man lingered gratefully at his gate.[6] In non-conformist churches, which drew most of their congregations from the working classes of industrial towns, radical ideas had already taken root by the early years of the nineteenth century. The growth of Methodism, in particular, was inseparably intertwined with the growth of trade unions, cooperative societies, and demands for political representation of working people. In addition, in Scotland, 'The Great Disruption' of the early 1840s, when over a third of Scottish clergymen walked out of their parishes to form the new Free Church of Scotland, was an expression of disgust with an established church that was dominated by wealth and patronage and unconcerned with the deprivations of the poor.

Meanwhile in the Church of England the interests of property,

5. The Peoples Charter of the 1840s demanded votes for all men, equal sized electoral districts, the abolition of the property requirement for MPs, payment of MPs, annual general elections and a secret ballot.

6. The third verse, now usually omitted, of the popular hymn 'All things bright and beautiful' contained the words 'The rich man in his castle, the poor man at his gate, He made them high and lowly and ordered their estate'.

privilege and political power were firmly embedded within its institutional organisation. The Church itself was a legally established part of the realm and it maintained an indisputable stake in the processes by which influence filtered down through the social hierarchies. As the nineteenth century progressed, however, it was becoming increasingly clear that it was haemorrhaging members at an alarming rate, losing its power and influence, particularly in urban areas. The old rural parish structure with its formal appointed rituals and hierarchical social control was no longer fit for purpose in a rapidly industrialising society where the democratised atmosphere and spontaneous preaching of non-conformism held much more appeal. Many in the higher ranks of the Church of England were initially reluctant to confront the source of their declining numbers, opting to define the problem simply in terms of the physical limitations of their buildings. There were, they concluded, not enough churches to cater for an increasing population in urban areas and those that did exist were too small. It was an ill-judged response that spawned an expensive programme of church restoration and construction, bequeathing to future generations a substantial legacy of over-sized redundant buildings. Some clergy, however, were quite prepared to recognise that the established church had simply lost touch with ordinary working people. There was an upsurge of genuine outrage felt by many of those based in the densely populated towns and cities, who daily encountered the dreadful conditions in which so many people lived and worked. Increasingly they began to acknowledge the need for an engagement with social injustice that moved beyond the selective distribution of charity towards the 'deserving poor', and towards a direct practical involvement with the political aspects of society. The response of these clergy crystallised into a movement within the Church of England termed 'Christian Socialism'.

The term 'socialism' can also be a misleading one when encountered in a twenty-first-century context for, as already noted, the movement and its ideology has undergone numerous changes over the years. Christian Socialists of the mid nineteenth century were undoubtedly concerned with social justice and the redistribution of wealth and opportunity. As

William emphasised in an address in Newcastle in 1906, 'the Church of the future is the church which faces social questions … the only test of the Christian religion which the modern world will regard as adequate is its applicability to the solution of the social question.' 'The evangelistic side of the Church,' he argued, 'must be supplemented by a new and profound concern regarding environments, the social institutions and arrangements regarding the Christian ideal of the conditions in which men lived.' For William, therefore, socialism was 'the desire to adapt social arrangements so as to secure the well-being of the whole body of society.'[7] Such 'arrangements' however, have taken different forms at different times and the Labour Party of the twenty-first century would be largely unrecognisable to those who gathered together at the inaugural meeting of the Independent Labour movement in 1893 and formally agreed their stated aim, 'to secure the collective and communal ownership of the means of production, distribution and exchange.' William and his fellow Christian Socialists would probably have broadly agreed with this objective but would have described it rather differently, defining the route to socialism as the establishment of co-operative partnerships between those engaged in the process of production and a fair distribution of the ensuing profits. Underpinning the ambitions of all who espoused 'socialism' in the nineteenth century, however, was a more fundamental issue, the need for a democratically elected government which represented the whole population rather than the interests of a select few. And in this they made common cause with the contemporary Chartist movement.

During the middle years of the nineteenth century, riots and demonstrations inspired by Chartism were a fairly regular feature of life in many British cities. Some clergy were undoubtedly in sympathy with the Chartists, not least in terms of Chartist criticism of the Church's wealth and its inactivity in the face of the problems of the poor. However, for many, the relationship with the Chartist movement was often an uneasy one. They denounced its more revolutionary tendencies, focussing

---

7. 'The Churches and Social Questions. Address by Canon Moore-Ede on the Christian Ideal of Society,' BNA, *Newcastle Evening Chronicle*, 13 September 1906.

instead on a Christian belief in peaceful reform, including the reform, rather than the rejection, of their own church. Specifically, they wished the Church of England to be transformed into a force for social change that better reflected what they considered to be the core of Christ's message. In 1848, the year before William was born, the Chartists delivered the third (and last) of their major petitions to Parliament and staged a people's rally on Kennington Common in South London. In the event, this rally of around twenty thousand was peaceful and in fact much smaller than anticipated (it was a wet day) but such was the government's fear of violence and even revolution that they had mustered eight thousand troops and special constables to defend London and had dispatched Queen Victoria to the Isle of Wight. These extreme precautions reflected the anxiety engendered by the wave of protests currently sweeping the country, variously focussing on poor wages, hunger and disease. Socialists were thus considered to be unequivocally 'radical'. They were unwelcome in many political circles and to some extent marginalised in the Church of England. French revolutionary horrors still hovered uneasily at the back of many middle-class minds and those who promulgated the principles of Christian Socialism and acted accordingly tended to arouse suspicion and apprehension.

In the late 1840s just as the Chartist movement appeared to be running out of steam, a group of men based in the East End of London, formed themselves into a group called the 'Social Christians', led by Frederick Denison Maurice, the man who thirty years later would provide the inspiration for the life and work of William Moore-Ede. Underlying the objectives of what later became the Christian Socialist movement was the belief that economic and social systems were inextricably linked. It aimed to demonstrate the feasibility of an alternative, more democratic approach to production and trade, in which the benefits were shared equally between those who contributed to it. To this end they established the Society for the Promotion of Working Men's Associations, a consortium of trades operating according to these co-operative principles. A number of such co-operatives were established by the Christian Socialists during the 1850s, largely in the London area.[8] Essentially these espoused similar principles to the Co-operative movement which had its formal establishment in the Lancashire town of Rochdale in 1844. William would be a dedicated supporter of 'Co-operation', throughout his life, teaching its principles and urging the development of new branches of the Society in every place he lived and worked. In the early 1860s the Christian Socialists also established the Working Men's College, with Maurice as its first Principal, providing accessible education for those excluded by class, religion or income from existing educational provision. The transformation of the economic system, they considered, depended on the educational transformation of society, another principle that William was to take enthusiastically to heart. Ten years later the Working Men's College would provide a blueprint for the Cambridge University Extension Scheme, to which William would become a major contributor, and which ultimately would lead to the foundation of several provincial universities. In parallel, the Christian Socialists also founded Queen's College, an early pioneer of girls' secondary education. By the 1870s this college had begun sending its students to the University of Cambridge to take advantage of the higher education offered by its two newly established women's colleges.[9]

During this period a number of initiatives of this type were springing up around the country spearheaded by those who had, by now, acquired the label 'radicals'. A distinctive feature of the specifically Anglican element of this more general movement, however, was the theological base on which it was founded. The writings of Frederick Denison Maurice, which no doubt owed much to his own early Unitarian roots, represented an important departure from contemporary Christian doctrine as propounded by the established church.[10] The current focus

---

8. By 1852 there were twelve associations, including tailors, builders, shoemakers, piano makers, printers and bakers.

9. Girton College was founded in 1869 by Emily Davies, the daughter of the Reverend John Davies, a predecessor of William as Rector of Gateshead. Newnham College was founded in 1871 by a group of reformers led by suffragist campaigner, Millicent Fawcett.

10. Maurice's parents were Unitarians. Although he embraced Anglicanism in 1831 he wrote in 1866 that 'my ends have been shaped for me, rough hew them how I would, and shape has been given to them by my father's function and this name 'Unitarian' more than by any other influences'.

on the salvation of individual souls, Maurice argued, implied the need to earn one's entry into heaven. It offered the prospect of eternal life with God for those leading a virtuous life, but everlasting punishment for unrepentant sinners. This, Maurice maintained, was a fallacious interpretation of the Christian message, encouraging the view that heavenly life after death represented a reward for individual avoidance of sin, essentially operating as a mechanism of social control directed at the poor. By contrast, he argued, God was already a part of each human being and eternal life referred to an on-going communion with this indwelling presence rather than a never-ending life in the hereafter. Hence the aim of the Christian life was not to adhere to a set of rules, supposedly contained within the Bible, but to demonstrate the divine presence within the world. For Maurice, this proposition led inevitably to the conclusion that Christians should strive, not for individual piety, but to improve society by working co-operatively together for the common good.[11] It was this theological stance that would distinguish the specifically 'Christian' form of socialism from the more general secularly based reform movements of the period and would lead Maurice to comment famously on 'the conflict we must engage in sooner or later with the unsocial Christians and the unchristian Socialists.'[12]

For the following twenty years Christian Socialism enjoyed modest growth, but it remained a minority group within the Anglican church, both in terms of the number of its adherents and its reforming activities. It encountered some vehement opposition from many within the church hierarchy who both disputed its theological basis and maintained firmly that engagement with 'political' matters had no place in religious practice. Moreover, they feared that it might actually encourage labour unrest. In 1853 Maurice himself was dismissed from his post as professor of theology at King's College, London, where his views were regarded

---

11. A fuller exposition of Maurice's views is contained in his *Theological Essays* (MacMillan & Co, Cambridge 1853). Reproduced by Scholar Select, no date; See also R. L. Steel *The Contribution of F. D. Maurice to the Christian Socialist Movement of 1848–1854*. (Bachelor of Divinity Thesis, University of Oregon, 1971). www.core.ac.uk

12. J. F. D. Maurice (ed), *The Life of F. D. Maurice, Chiefly Told in His Own Letters*, vol. ii (Macmillan, London, 1884). Quoted in Wilkinson, *Christian Socialism*.

as heretical and likely to bring Christian education at King's into disrepute.[13] In a higher education system dominated by the Church of England it was feared that such controversial ideas would provide ammunition for the college's influential rival, University College London (Godless Gower Street), which in 1826 had been established as a secular alternative to the existing universities with their strictly Anglican entry criteria.[14] For the next few years, therefore, Maurice devoted himself to the promotion of Christian Socialism and to the development of the Working Men's College in particular. In 1866, however, he took up the offer of an appointment as professor of moral philosophy at the University of Cambridge, explaining to his Christian Socialist colleague, John Ludlow, 'My business now, because I am a theologian, is not to build but to dig.'[15] Essentially, he considered his work was now to provide, through his teaching and writing, the theological foundations for the movement that he hoped others would take forward. One such enthusiast was William Moore-Ede who arrived in Cambridge in 1868. By the early 1870s Maurice would have been heartened by the fact that Christian Socialism was enjoying a considerable resurgence. A new form was emerging, inspired by a larger number of Anglican priests who embraced a broader, practical social agenda. An important feature was a stronger recognition of non-conformism as a positive contributor to religious and social practice and a consequent move towards ecumenical co-operation. It is to this second phase of Christian Socialism that William Moore-Ede belongs.

---

13. In later years Maurice gained new recognition by the Church of England and in 1933 a lecture series in his honour was established at Kings College. A bust of him stands in Westminster Abbey, although in 1872 his family declined the offer of his burial there and chose instead for him to be buried in Highgate Cemetery.

14. A term coined after Thomas Arnold, headmaster of Rugby School, referred to University College London as 'that Godless Institution in Gower Street'.

15. J. F. D. Maurice (ed), *The Life of F. D. Maurice*. Quoted in Bryant, *Possible Dreams*.

Chapter Three
FORMATIVE YEARS

If family tradition had anything to do with it, William Moore-Ede would have been a naval officer. Generations before him had served their country as part of the 'Senior Service' with varying degrees of heroism and distinction. His grandfather, John Ede, for example, had served with Lord Nelson at the Battle of St Vincent and his great uncle Denzil had reputedly been assassinated following the British defeat at the Battle of Leghorn. William's younger brother James would follow in these family footsteps, rising to the rank of commander in the Royal Navy and James's son, Ernest would become a naval lieutenant, sadly losing his life in the First World War. The Ede family emanated from the small Cornish village of St Germans on the Devonshire border a few miles from the major naval base at Plymouth. Meanwhile William's mother, Elizabeth Moore, came from a successful shipbuilding family also based in Plymouth. During his childhood William would spend a few years living at the house of his grandfather, Billy Moore, founder of the family firm, whose shipyard lay alongside Plymouth's historic harbour known as Sutton Pool.

When William was born, in the summer of 1849, his father, Edward Ede, already had two sons by a previous marriage, his first wife, Anna, having died in 1847. During this first marriage Edward had been a storekeeper in Plymouth's naval dockyard but in 1848, when he married for the second time, the couple moved to Deptford in London where Edward had been promoted to the position of head storekeeper at a much larger establishment, Her Majesty's Victualing Yard adjacent to the Royal Naval dockyard on the River Thames. This vast fortress of government buildings on the south bank of the river provided the supplies for naval ships as they came into the Port of London. William and his younger sister Elizabeth were born here within the confines of the dockyard where senior staff had the benefit of designated housing. Throughout his young life William would have been surrounded by stories of the sea, enthralled by the fortunes and misfortunes of ships and sailors and the heroic tales of naval battles, including of course those involving his own family. During his clerical career his sermons would be peppered with illustrative maritime references. 'To make anything of one's life,' he informed a municipal gathering in Putney in 1910, 'one needs an ideal, an aim or conviction one wants to realise. Without conviction we are like ships on the ocean without chart or compass, carried along in self-gratification, drifting towards a shipwreck.'[1]

Family life within the solid stone perimeter walls of the dockyard was relatively comfortable and secure but a short distance away lay the teeming slums of Deptford, Rotherhithe and Bermondsey. Here people lived in poverty and squalor with large families occupying single rooms in damp, multi-occupied buildings, lacking water supplies and basic sanitation. This was the setting for the scene in Charles Dickens's *Oliver Twist* where Bill Sikes drowned in the fetid waters of Folly Ditch on Jacob's Island. Here the River Thames filled many such ditches surrounding the houses. Dickens was familiar with this 'Venice of Drains' and wrote of the inhabitants 'hauling up their drinking water from the ditches . . . every repulsive lineament of poverty, every loathsome indication of filth, rot and garbage.'[2] The London into which William was born was thus a scene of desperate poverty. That summer one of the periodic epidemics of cholera raged through the city killing an estimated thirteen thousand of its inhabitants. The situation was graphically documented in London's *Morning Chronicle* by journalist Henry Mayhew who described how the sewer of Mill Lane on Jacob's

---

1. WME, sermon at the Church of St Mary the Virgin, Putney, on Mayoral Sunday. 7 January 1910. WCL. Scrapbooks.
2. Charles Dickens, *Oliver Twist* (Bentley, London, 1838).

Island was 'as solid as black marble.' Mayhew's series of articles entitled *London Labour and London Poor*,[3] published between 1851 and 1862 was to prove the catalyst for the birth of a new movement, initially referred to as the 'Social Christians' and later 'Christian Socialism'.[4] Writing in *Fraser's Magazine* in 1850, founder member John Ludlow urged the recognition of the 'essential communism of the church that should leaven the whole of society with a spirit of self-devoted industry.'[5] Interestingly, therefore, the dawn of this movement, which was to underpin so much of William's work in the future, took place during his own early years less than a mile from his home. Whether, as a small child, he was aware of the early beginnings of Christian Socialism in this part of London is doubtful. He may not have heard of the delivery of clean water by cart to the inhabitants of Jacob's Island, the attempts to establish a National Health League to campaign for a healthy environment, the development of co-operative workshops to counteract the injustices of sweated labour or the articles in the press which urged the reform of prisons and workhouses. In later years, however, when the name of Frederick Denison Maurice came into his life, he must have cast his mind back to the poverty and degradation that existed only a short distance from the majestic gatehouse of the dockyard, and the wretched lives of so many of the nearby inhabitants.

William's mother, Elizabeth, was a wealthy woman. The Moore family of Plymouth were not only highly successful shipbuilders but also owned large amounts of residential property in the town. When William was five years old his father was posted to another large naval dockyard, Haulbowline in Ireland, situated on an offshore island in Cork Harbour. Here William's brother James was born in 1854. William, however, did not go to Ireland with the rest of the family but was sent instead to live with the Moores in Plymouth. It was a separation that was probably motivated by educational concerns, for the Moore family

---

3. P. Quennell (ed), *Mayhew's London* (Spring Books, London, 1969).
4. Maurice preferred this term as he considered that the objective of the movement was to 'Christianize Socialism'.
5. J. M. Ludlow, *Fraser's Magazine*, January 1850.

seem to have taken over the responsibility, and presumably the cost, of William's upbringing and education at this stage of his life. Whatever the reason, it seems to have been the point when his ambitions began to diverge from the traditions of the Ede family. He first attended Plymouth Grammar School (or Dr Weymouth's school as he called it) and then went on to Marlborough College. There are no hints that he experienced any sense of rejection at being separated from his parents at such a young age. Years later he would describe his complete delight when, freed from the crowded constraints of London, he happily played cricket and flew kites on Plymouth Hoe. The Moore family lived at the Friary, an old medieval house next to their shipbuilding yard, and he loved to watch the unloading of the fishing boats as they crowded alongside the quay at Sutton Pool. From Marlborough he went to the University of Cambridge, by which point he had adopted the name William Moore-Ede. Perhaps the Moores entertained hopes that William would take over the family shipbuilding business since Elizabeth's two brothers remained unmarried, producing no prospective heirs to the family firm. However, the influences William encountered at Marlborough and at Cambridge appear to have steered him in an entirely different direction.

With its longstanding reputation as a centre of Christian education Marlborough had always been popular with the clergy as a place to send their sons and William would have met a strong Anglican influence there. Under the leadership of George Bradley, however, the school was undergoing considerable reform. Bradley had earlier been a master at Rugby School, working under its famous headmaster Dr Thomas Arnold, and he brought to Marlborough many of Arnold's pioneering methods. In particular he was keen to broaden the school curriculum, inspired like many new schools of the time by the education provided by the German Gymnasia, where the traditional focus on the classics and theology was gradually being replaced by a wider range of subjects such as science, mathematics and the humanities. By the time William arrived in Marlborough many of its pupils would be considering a career in the professions and various forms of public service.

In 1868 William went on to St John's College, Cambridge from where, in 1871, he emerged with a first-class Degree in the recently introduced Moral Sciences Tripos, and a prize for moral philosophy. Like Marlborough, late nineteenth-century Cambridge was engaged in aspects of educational reform. The new Moral Sciences Tripos encompassed not only philosophy, but also psychology, metaphysics, logic and scientific method. Importantly it also covered 'political economy' exploring different forms of industrial organisation, trade and exchange and the production and consumption of commodities. Students were taught by many of the prominent academics of the day, several of whom had distinctly socialist leanings. One of the most notable of these was a young lecturer called Alfred Marshall whose seminal work *Principles of Economics*, first published in 1890, would maintain a dominant influence over British economics teaching and research well into the twentieth century. Marshall famously described 'the revolting extremes of wealth and poverty that arise in societies where competition is the fundamental principle.'[6] William would echo this sentiment many times in future years. One contemporary student described Marshall's teaching as 'very human, the living application of theoretical knowledge to the economic and industrial problems of the day.'[7] He undoubtedly regarded practical knowledge as equal in value to his own theoretical considerations, frequently inviting labour leaders whom he described as 'comrades' to Cambridge to discuss their own first-hand experiences. Often students were invited to dinner at the Marshalls' home to meet these working men or were taken on visits to factories and mills. Many of these students subsequently recalled how, during these visits, their eyes had first been opened to the harsh working conditions experienced by so many. 'When I saw the mill girls slaving in those hot fluffy rooms, it struck me that no-one who had not lived the life could understand its peculiar hardships,' commented one

---

6. Alfred Marshall, *Principles of Political Economy* (Macmillan, London, 1890). Reproduced by Prometheus Books, 1997).

7. E. E. R. Mumford, *Through Rose-coloured Spectacles: The Story of a Life* (Edgar Backus, Leicester, 1952).

aspiring engineer who had primarily joined the tour with a view to examining the factory machinery.[8] William was similarly affected. It was Marshall's teaching, he said later, that first aroused his interest in social questions. Many years later he would dedicate a set of his own controversial Christian Socialist lectures, published under the title *The Attitude of the Church to Some of the Social Problems of Town Life* to his mentor Alfred Marshall.[9] There is little doubt that this young, charismatic teacher, fondly known as 'the walrus' by his students, provided one of the major sources of inspiration for William's own future work – and his appearance. The droopy moustache was born!

At St John's College students explored the ideas of influential philosophers such as Edmund Burke, Jeremy Bentham and John Stuart Mill as well as the works of Hegel and Weber and the early contemporary writings of Karl Marx and Frederik Engels. Prominent among the teachers there was Frederick Denison Maurice, professor of moral philosophy. Like Marshall, Maurice denounced the idea of a society based on competition as the defining feature of industrial relations. Co-operation was the watchword of socialism, he maintained, whereas competition was 'a lie . . . a hateful devilish theory put forth as the law of the universe'. 'The time has come to declare that it is a lie by word and deed,' he told his students. 'It must be fought with to the death.'[10] He too invited small groups of his students to his home for drinks and discussion, much of which centred on the human consequences of different forms of social organisation and of socialism in particular. Both Marshall and Maurice, it seemed, were keen to distance themselves from a particular interpretation of Darwin's theory that had grown up in the years since the publication of *On the Origin of Species*.[11] While Darwin himself never intended

8. E. Sharp, *Hertha Ayrton: A Memoir*. (Edward Arnold & Co, London, 1926).
9. William Moore-Ede (WME) *The Hulsean Lectures for 1895. The Attitude of the Church to Some of the Social Problems of Town Life*. (Cambridge University Press, Cambridge, 1896). Reproduced by Scholar Select.
10. J. F. D. Maurice (ed), *The Life of F. D. Maurice*. Quoted in Bryant, *Possible Dreams*.
11. C. Darwin, *On the Origin of Species by Means of Natural Selection* (John Murray, London, 1859).

his theory as a justification for competitive capitalism there was, it seems, no shortage of successful industrialists happy to espouse this view, arguing that competition was intrinsic to human nature. While both Maurice and Marshall rejected this idea, they differed widely in what they considered to be the source of an alternative view of social organisation. While Marshall focussed on the economic laws of supply and demand Maurice espoused socialist ideas within a strictly Christian context. 'Economics and politics', he argued, 'must have a ground beneath themselves. Society is not to be made by any arrangement of ours but is to be regenerated by finding the law and ground of its order and harmony, the only secret of its existence, in God.'[12] Several of the prominent protagonists of late nineteenth-century Christian Socialism would formulate their beliefs and their practical ideas during Maurice's theological 'at homes'. William's own friendship with Maurice would be relatively short, abruptly curtailed by Maurice's death in the spring of 1872 just as William was completing his final examinations. However, the influence of this contact would be profound. He regarded Maurice as 'the noblest saint, the deepest thinker, the profoundest theologian'[13] and 'one of the greatest churchmen of the nineteenth century, alike in life, vision and achievement.'[14]

It is clear that during his time at Cambridge William's thoughts began to move not only in the direction of Christian Socialism but also more specifically towards the priesthood as the means by which he might live out his emerging ideals. Unlike many of his fellow students he seemed to find no inherent contradiction between the thinking of Marshall and Maurice, but for him it was the Christian foundation that held the greatest attraction. There is no record either at Cambridge or elsewhere that he ever received any formal theological

12. op cit., J. F. D. Maurice (ed), *The Life of F. D. Maurice*.
13. WME's address at Worcester. Celebration of the Centenary of the Oxford Movement. BNA, *Evesham Standard and West Midlands Observer*, 15 July 1933.
14. From an article by WME in *Modern Churchman* (1933), quoted by Canon Graham Neville in *William Moore-Ede, Dean of Worcester 1908–1934* (Office of the Friends of Worcester Cathedral, 2008).

instruction. His name does not appear in the lists of those taking theological examinations, but his lack of formal qualifications may not have been particularly unusual or any great disadvantage in the early 1870s. His student days just preceded the introduction of the Theological Tripos at Cambridge which was first recorded in 1874. As a result, he seems to have been spared the 'rather slight' (and apparently optional) Theological Examination described in the preface to early editions of Crockfords. Towards the end of 1872, therefore, William left Cambridge and was enrolled as a deacon in the Church of England.

Chapter Four
ALSTON MOOR

The location of William's first clerical placement would have presented a certain amount of difficulty both for him and the church. He had none of the usual requirements, no familial connections with the Church of England, no money and no patrons to smooth his way. In the event it was his tenuous associations with the Navy that seems to have solved the problem. In the late autumn of 1872, therefore, he found himself *en route* to an obscure moorland town called Alston in Cumberland.[1] Situated high on Alston Moor, within a designated Area of Outstanding Natural Beauty, Alston is today both picturesque and ruggedly beautiful, an attractive destination for hikers and tourists. In the late nineteenth century, however, it was a major centre of lead mining, the principal industry of the area. Both its mineral rights and its church living were then the property of the Royal Hospital for Seamen at Greenwich in London.[2] This rather curious arrangement was the result of a transaction effected after the failed Jacobite Rebellion of 1715 when the Earl of Derwentwater, who then owned Alston Moor, had been required to forfeit both his lands and his head as punishment for his support of the rebel cause. His land, with its lucrative mineral deposits, was subsequently granted to the Greenwich Hospital to supplement their ongoing needs for funds. Traditionally, therefore, clergy with some kind of naval connections were selected to serve there.

1. Cumberland and Westmorland were amalgamated in 1974 to form the present county of Cumbria.
2. Sheltered housing for retired members of the Royal Navy, established in the seventeenth century.

Alston would have presented William with a hard test of his clerical convictions. The balmy and intellectually stimulating Cambridge summer of 1872 would have offered little preparation for the environment he encountered on Alston Moor. The *Penrith Observer* reported that the current winter was the worst Cumberland had suffered for many years. However, it wasn't just the months of blanketing snow and bone-numbing cold that would have would have threatened his resolve. On Alston Moor those earnest discussions in Frederick Denison Maurice's parlour took on a very practical reality. Here he would encounter for the first time the relentless grind of nineteenth century industry and of mining in particular. In the lead mines surrounding Alston men and boys laboured with picks and shovels to extract the ore from shafts (levels) dug into the hillside, working for hours in cold, damp conditions by the light of tallow candles. Pay was determined by the traditional tribute system, dependent on the amount of lead obtained and the bargain struck between the tribute man (gangmaster) and the mine owners. It was hard, dangerous work that fostered close relationships between the men and their families. This was a close-knit community with a well-defined social structure, bound together by the interrelated ties of employment and religion. The religion in question, however, was almost entirely non-conformist. The situation was neatly encapsulated in the words of a nineteenth century former miner from Alston, Chester Armstrong, who wrote about his early life in the town.

> The divisions of sect corresponded very closely to those cleavages of class which mark the social strata everywhere. The handful of adherents to the Church of England were those who held posts of authority outside it. Since the greatest majority of the people came within the lowest category of the scale they gravitated to Primitive Methodism. Wesleyan Methodism, though decidedly a dissenting body, was a little higher in the scale. It was represented by those whose level of prosperity was rather higher than the common level.[3]

3. C. Armstrong, *Pilgrimage from Nenthead: An Autobiography* (Methuen, London, 1938).

Methodist Chapel, Alston, pictured in 2019.

Methodism had first arrived in Alston in the mid eighteenth century with a first visit to the town by John Wesley in 1748. By 1872 there were numerous places of non-conformist worship dotted across the moor and in Alston itself there was large Methodist Church and Sunday School Hall, built just two years before William arrived, at a cost of £2,000. Today this striking building, a curious cross between Norman and Italianate, stands empty and forlorn, the result no doubt of an inability to find any useful purpose for it in twenty-first century Britain. Somewhat ironically, the remnants of its congregation now share a small stone building with St Wulstan's, home to the Roman Catholic faithful of the area. In the 1870s, however, the Methodist congregations in Alston ran into the hundreds on a typical Sunday.

The dominance of Methodism in the area would not have surprised William unduly for this was a situation widely replicated across nineteenth century industrial England. However, in other ways Alston was very different from most other industrial towns. In the middle of the eighteenth century the mineral rights of the area had been leased by the Greenwich Hospital to the Religious Society of Friends (the Quakers), owners of the London Lead Company. Nineteenth-century Quakers took their responsibilities towards their workers far more seriously than did most other industrialists of the period. The remote and challenging environment of Alston Moor, inhabited by a population that was almost completely dependent on them for employment, provided an ideal opportunity for the Friends to develop to the full their particular approach to industrial and social organisation. By the time William arrived in the early 1870s the company had instituted a comprehensive welfare system which was far in advance if its time and couldn't fail to impress a young enthusiastic Christian Socialist. Close to the mine the company had built the village of Nenthead to provide decent housing at affordable rents with a clean water supply and good sanitation. There were various recreational activities in the village such as a cricket club, a gardening society (many cottages had a small plot of land for the cultivation of vegetables), a town band, and also a library and reading room where educational lectures were provided. Heath care was provided by resident surgeons and medical assistants who adhered to a strict code of conduct, which included the instruction to 'attend in their own homes with all convenient speed all afflicted workers and their families.' This was funded by the 'Workman's Benefit Fund' which, for a modest weekly contribution, and adherence to strict rules of sobriety and good behaviour, provided injured or sick workers with payments for 'as long as they remained incapable of following their employment,' as well as a weekly pension on retirement at age sixty-five, funeral costs and financial provision for widows and children. From 1818 the company had also built a number of schools, where children received education at a cost of one shilling per quarter and had instituted compulsory education from age six to twelve for boys and six to fourteen for girls.[4] Subsequent employment in the company depended on the production of a certificate of satisfactory attendance together with a good behaviour report.[5]

Friends (Quaker) Meeting House, Alston, pictured in 2019.

This highly successful mix of paternalistic control and enlightened self-interest provided the company with a steady supply of sober, educated and industrious workers, while at the same time providing these workers with living and working conditions that were unequalled in Britain during the late eighteenth and nineteenth centuries. This was essentially a model industrial community of the type more famously

4. These requirements pre-dated by over forty years the provisions of the Mining Act of 1860 which raised the age at which boys could be employed underground from ten to twelve years.

5. A. Raistrick, *Two Centuries of Industrial Welfare: The London (Quaker) Lead Company 1692–1905* (Kelsall & Davis, UK, 1988).

initiated by textile manufacturer Robert Owen at New Lanark and later by Titus Salt at Saltaire. However, its application to the mining industry, renowned for its appalling working conditions and huge levels of morbidity and mortality as well as its exploitation of child labour, remained unique during the Victorian age.

Significantly the company was not prescriptive about the form of religion required from its workers. It had contributed the lion's share of the money needed for the construction of the Methodist chapel and for many of the other small schools in and around Alston. And it required that all children who were enrolled at one of their schools should 'attend a place of worship twice on the Sabbath day.' However, they were at pains to stress that their schools were not 'Church schools'. They prohibited the use of any 'Catechism peculiar to any religious denomination' and forbade that 'any peculiar tenets of any religious sect should be inculcated in the scholars.' An attempt by the Bishop of Durham in 1824 to claim these schools for the Church of England and insist that only church members could be employed as teachers had been firmly resisted by the Friends. Thus their requirement for worship was tempered with the proviso that church attendance should be 'at such a place of religious worship as his or her parents think proper.'[6]

A couple of years before William arrived in Alston the Friends had received a degree of official support for their approach to religious teaching in the form of the Forster Education Act of 1870 which required the introduction of a large number of non-denominational schools to supplement the nationwide shortage of educational provision.[7] Prior to this the education of working-class children had been largely provided by the Church of England, much of it in the National Schools run by local vicars and church members, who maintained a near monopoly

---

6. ibid.

7. The Elementary Education Act (Forster Act) of 1870 defined a framework for the education of all children between the ages of five and twelve in England and Wales. It established local education authorities and authorised public money to improve existing schools and build new ones.

on religious teaching.⁸ In these new non-denominational schools, however, which were administered by the local Board of Education and largely financed by a combination of central government funding and local rates, denominational teaching was abolished. Moreover, even in denominational schools, which in many rural areas remained the only form of educational provision, children could not be compelled to attend worship or to learn the catechism if their parents objected.⁹ All this would have given William significant pause for thought. He himself was required to teach in the remaining National School at nearby Leadgate where religious instruction was, of course, specifically based on the tenets of the Church of England. Here he also taught arithmetic and reading and acted as secretary to the Management Committee. In May 1873 he reported in the school log (no doubt with some satisfaction) that a school inspector had found that in the school 'the order is good, and the examination has been very creditably passed in Reading, Writing and Spelling.' On the other hand, the arithmetic was described as 'fair, but not quite so good as usual.'¹⁰ Regardless of William's talents or otherwise as an elementary school teacher, however, the new Act of 1870 and the on-going debate within the school system must have forced him to confront the issue of the role of religion in education and in wider terms the questions surrounding ecumenicalism and religious freedom. It was something that would surface several years later in Tyneside when, as chairman of the School Board, he faced the implications of developing non-denominational educational provision in Gateshead.

A traditional aversion to proselytising was a notable feature of the Friends. Another was an attachment to the virtue of simplicity. Thus

    8. National Schools were set up by the National Society (established in 1811) for 'Promoting the Education of the Poor in the Principles of the Established Church in England and Wales'. Its stated aim was that 'the National Religion should be made the foundation of National Education and should be the first and the chief thing taught to the poor, according to the excellent Liturgy and Catechism provided by our Church'.

    9. This was the 'Cowper-Temple conscience clause' introduced into the Bill to cater for dissenting or non-religious parents who found themselves in areas where the only school available was that provided by the Church of England.

    10. B. Edge, *History of Leadgate School* (Local Studies, Alston Library, Cumbria, 2009).

in Alston they built a small, stone Meeting Houses for worship that resembled a cottage rather than a church or chapel. With perhaps an intentional degree of symbolism this building was completely dwarfed by the imposing grandeur of the nearby Anglican church. For in 1870 the 'handful of adherents' to the Church of England described by Chester Armstrong had, like their non-conformist neighbours, been endowed with a handsome new building. The church in Alston, dedicated to St Augustine of Canterbury and containing some possessions of the hapless

St Augustine's Church, Alston, pictured in 2019.

earl (an antique clock and a medieval bell) had been completed just a year after the Methodist chapel. It was the third church to be built on the site, both of the previous buildings having been demolished. The precise motive for the decision, in 1869, to pull down the existing church and build a new one is unclear. It appears to have been initiated by the current incumbent, the Reverend William Cecil Baylee and a committee of local worthies who, within a year, managed to raise sufficient funds to construct the new building. The existing church, then a century old, may of course, like its predecessor, have been in a poor state of repair. However, another proffered explanation, that it was considered to be 'too small', seems entirely in keeping with the current over optimistic thinking of the Church of England. Given the recent completion of a handsome Methodist chapel it is hard to avoid a suspicion of religious rivalry as the driving force for this endeavour. If so, it was like so many other projects of the time, a spectacular misjudgement. Unsurprisingly the number of adherents to the Church of England on Alston Moor remained stubbornly low.

It was probably with mixed feelings that William considered the situation in Alston. Here he was an outsider, forced to concentrate his attentions on a small traditional congregation who represented the interests of the wealthier people in the town. Meanwhile he was largely a bystander in the lives of the larger non-conformist population. However, he would have learnt a great deal from the activities of the Friends and many of the projects in which he involved himself in later life had echoes of the community he encountered in and around the town. He would, in fact, spend only a few months in Alston but the effects of this first appointment would be profound, both professionally and personally. From the professional point of view he was faced not only with the obvious failure of his own church to engage spiritually with the industrial population but also with the successful approach of the Friends in terms of addressing the question of social conditions. One suspects that he had little in common with the long serving vicar of Alston who seems to have been a kindly yet entirely traditional man who was devoted to the established church. The Reverend Baylee was, of course, a former naval chaplain, in his case a veteran of the Crimean war. By all accounts he had been severely affected by the suffering he had witnessed during this period, keeping an inkwell on his desk modelled from the remains of a piece of a cannon ball as a daily reminder of the death and destruction wrought by war. His harrowing experiences had left him deeply committed to non-violent forms of conflict resolution, a significant departure from the conventional military script and perhaps, at least, one area of common understanding with his radically minded young curate. However, the Reverend Baylee was not a man given to anything resembling 'radicalism'. By his own admission he 'depreciated the idea of entering on controversial subjects.'[11] Yet for entirely unforeseen reasons he was to have a profound effect on William's life.

In November 1872, just prior to William's arrival in Alston, William Baylee and his wife Eleanor had suffered a personal tragedy. Already the mother of two young daughters Eleanor had given birth to their third child, Laetitia Lucy, at the end of October. Shortly afterwards, however, the tiny baby developed sickness and diarrhoea and sadly died at the age of only three weeks. On arrival in the parish, therefore, William was confronted with a couple in mourning for their lost child. But there was worse to come. Five months later at the end of April 1873, with the parish in the midst of Holy Week, William Baylee collapsed with a severe attack of endocarditis. He died just two weeks later. He was only fifty-two years old and until a few weeks before had seemed to be in perfect health. Now his young inexperienced curate found himself in the position of taking the funeral of the vicar of Alston, something he accomplished, according to the *Penrith Observer*, 'in a distinct and impressive manner.'[12]

William stayed on in Alston until the end of July when the Admiralty found another retired naval chaplain (military history enthusiast, the Reverend John Milner) to replace the Reverend Baylee. On William's departure he was described as 'a popular and much respected curate... his general demeanour and the interest he has taken in a proper discharge of the duties of his high calling, have won for him many friends, who will regret his departure.'[13] Clearly William had not ruffled any significant feathers amongst the faithful of St Augustine's. However, these plaudits, reported in the *Cumberland and Westmorland Advertiser*, make no mention of another development, for at some

11. 'Alston Cattle Show. The Dinner,' BNA, *Penrith Observer*, 15 October 1872.
12. 'Death of the Vicar of Alston,' BNA, *Penrith Observer*, 29 April 1873.
13. 'Local & District Intelligence, Clerical,' BNA, *Cumberland and Westmorland Advertiser*, 29 July 1873.

stage during this period Eleanor Baylee and her husband's young and handsome curate had, it seems, fallen in love. It was a surprising but perhaps understandable development between two young people who were both, in their different ways, in need of comfort. William, having found himself in a completely alien and friendless environment, must have struggled with his first assignment in this Anglican wilderness. He may well have been assailed by doubts about a calling that had seemed so inspiring within the portals of Cambridge but now perhaps appeared somewhat daunting. Eleanor meanwhile would have been in a state of shock and grief, her ordered life suddenly turned upside down and her future uncertain. As the daughter of Edward Cookson, perpetual curate of Kirkby Thore, a small rural parish in Cumberland, Eleanor had led a somewhat sheltered life prior to her arrival in Alston. She had been born in the vicarage in the North Yorkshire village of Sharow, moving to Kirkby Thore when she was seven years old. Like most middle-class Victorian girls, she had been educated at home, in her case by her father, sharing her schoolroom with a brother and sister and her two cousins Norman and George, sons of Edward's brother William, who ran a large industrial concern in Newcastle upon Tyne. Eleanor had been only twenty years old when she married William Baylee and now, at the age of twenty-eight, she was left a widow with two small children. He had been a kind but, to her at least, a relatively elderly husband. Twenty-five years her senior, he had followed a familiar pattern of those who pursued a naval career, many years at sea followed by a shore-based assignment and a late marriage.

Obviously, the formation of a romantic relationship between William and Eleanor so soon after her husband's death would have been seen as entirely inappropriate in Alston, not least, one suspects, by the couple themselves. Queen Victoria's own widowhood in 1851 had spawned some severe behavioural restrictions on the bereaved, especially if they belonged to the respectable middle-classes. Widows in particular were expected to spend at least two years discreetly veiled, enveloped in black (preferably bombazine) and eschewing all social engagements. Remarriage during this period was of course unthinkable.

William's abrupt departure from Alston in July that year may have been provoked by a desire to put a respectable distance between himself and Eleanor. Shortly after John Milner's arrival in Alston he moved to South Shields on the North East coast, a well-trodden path for curates in the area. And later that year he reaffirmed his commitment to his calling and was ordained by the Bishop of Durham. It is not known where Eleanor spent the next few months, but it is perhaps of note that her own family roots lay primarily in the North East, where her uncle William Cookson and his two sons (her former classmates) now presided over a vast business empire stretching along the banks of the River Tyne. William's potential relationship with Eleanor, it seems, connected him to a family of wealthy influential industrialists engaged in various types of manufacturing on a massive scale. These industries were of course run on somewhat different lines to the model he had encountered in Alston.

The town where William spent his second curacy occupied a stretch of coastline at the mouth of the River Tyne. South Shields, complemented by its counterpart North Shields on the opposite bank of the river, was a flourishing area, its mines, docks and shipbuilding industries providing work for many thousands of men, who flocked to Tyneside with their families. By the late 1860s the population, which at the beginning of the century had numbered around twelve thousand, had grown to approximately seventy-five thousand. During this boom period a number of impressive public buildings were constructed including the internationally renowned Marine Training School which catered for the scores of merchant navy cadets who could be seen striding confidently along the main thoroughfare of Ocean Road. Alongside this public grandeur, however, the industrial success of North and South Shields had generated the usual problems of inadequate housing and sanitation, and periodic epidemics of cholera amongst the poor. And once more William was confronted with the working conditions of miners, this time coal miners. The Newcastle and Durham coalfields dominated the coal industry producing nearly 30 per cent of the nation's coal and over two thirds of Britain's coal exports. There were several collieries in the immediate vicinity of South Shields, some with tunnels stretching far out under the sea. One bore the name of his own parish, St Hilda's, where the mine lay immediately adjacent to the old church and where the graveyard was filled with the remains of those men and boys who over the years had been crushed, asphyxiated or blown up in numerous mining accidents. St Hilda's colliery's worst disaster had occurred in 1839 when fifty-one men and boys (the youngest aged nine) were killed in a major explosion and fire.

Clearly, in South Shields the miners experienced similar dangers and discomforts to those in Alston but enjoyed none of the benefits provided by the Friends. The result was a very different workforce, militant and strike prone, raging against low wages, the imposition of a yearly bond, truck shops and indiscriminate fines by employers.[14] This was a volatile town riven by divisions, not only between employers and workers but also between different groups of workers who fiercely defended alternative visions of the path to reform. Since the 1830s there had been repeated bitter strikes in the various collieries of Northumberland and Durham and steadily worsening relations between the miners and mine owners. Moreover, during the 1860s there had been a series of appalling pit disasters, in which more than three hundred men and boys had lost their lives. From this turmoil there had emerged a miners' union, the Northumberland Miners' Association (NMA), which, under the leadership of Secretary Thomas Burt, had begun to establish the beginnings of meaningful negotiations between miners and owners. However, in the early 1870s, the Association was strongly supported by the Liberal Party, whose members were already active in the existing trade councils, dedicated like Burt himself to conciliation and arbitration and strongly averse

14. The bond system required miners to sign an undertaking that they would work continuously for one colliery for one year. They were subject to various conditions, for example a prohibition on union membership, and fines for various 'offences'. They were liable to arrest and imprisonment if they broke the bond. The colliery owners gave no undertaking to provide continuous work but gave workers an initial sum of $2s.6d$ (12.5 pence in modern currency) as an inducement to sign. Truck was the practice of payment in goods rather than money. Some employers ran Truck Shops, often stocked with inferior goods, from which the workers were required to buy their provisions with tickets issued in lieu of wages.

to strike action, except as a last resort. Many of the more militant miners, hardened by generations of maltreatment, saw the NMA under Thomas Burt's leadership as ineffectual and little more than a tool of the mine owners. Their misgivings had recently been reinforced by the outcome of a lengthy and acrimonious strike at Cramlington Pit, a few miles north of Newcastle upon Tyne. A dispute over pay, during which the NMA's offer of mediation and had been resolutely refused by the management, had ultimately resulted in the eviction of forty miners and their families from their cottages, the jailing of six miners accused of public disturbance and the importation by the mine owners of replacement workers from other districts.

Many miners were deeply suspicious of the support provided by local Liberals who, following the establishment of the NMA, had launched a successful campaign to extend the Parliamentary franchise to those miners who occupied tied cottages at the mines where they worked.[15] This had generated large numbers of new votes for the Liberal Party on the back of which, in 1874, they secured the election of Thomas Burt to Parliament as the Liberal member for Morpeth. Burt, the recipient of William's letter about lead poisoning in 1882, would ultimately, emerge as a long-term champion of the rights of miners and of other industrial workers. At the time of his election to Parliament, however, he was a controversial figure in mining circles, admired and mistrusted in equal measure.

When William arrived in South Shields in the late summer of 1873, therefore, he would have encountered a divided and discontented population, embroiled in political argument and simmering on the edge of violent unrest. His time there, like that in Alston, would be a matter of months but the experience would be entirely different and equally thought provoking. The situation in Alston had been relatively settled but strictly controlled, the area suffused by a form of benign paternalism which mitigated the harsher effects of industrialisation

15. They argued that miners were not servants of the mine owners, as previously defined, but occupiers paying rates and taxes for the Poor Law – the contemporary criterion for enfranchisement.

but, in other ways, rendered the working population powerless and dependent. Here, however, there was raw politics, freely expressed anger, militancy and competition for power and control. If the socialist lessons of Cambridge had taken on one reality in Alston, they seemed to have taken on an entirely different one here. The agitation of the 1870s and '80s would ultimately result in the establishment, in the 1890s, of the Independent Labour Party in the North East of England with a consequent shift in the political landscape. By that stage William, himself, would be a central figure in the wider community known as Tyneside and forced to confront the relevance of his Christian faith and his pacifist attitudes in this rough, tough, irreligious area. Yet despite its obvious challenges Tyneside seemed to have gained a firm hold on his affections and in a few short years he would return there, first to Newcastle and then to Gateshead and finally to Whitburn, where the local pit at Marsden was widely regarded as one of the most militant of them all. Before then, however, another venture and another area was to occupy the major share of his attention, for in the spring of 1874 he left South Shields and took up residence in the small market town of Newark, near Nottingham.

Chapter Five
A PERIPATETIC UNIVERSITY

William's move to Nottinghamshire was prompted by a letter he received entitled 'A Letter on University Extension' which had been sent out to all members of the University of Cambridge. It described in detail a proposed educational scheme which aimed to provide lecture courses for working people 'rendering our Universities more accessible to all classes.' It urged 'the desirability of members of the university considering the subject both in their corporate and their individual capacity.'[1] This was essentially a recruitment drive, enlisting the support and participation of potential lecturing staff. Aware that the scheme had been inspired by his mentor, Frederick Maurice, William was immediately enthused by this proposition. Under the influence of his socialist-leaning tutors at Cambridge he was convinced that a further expansion of education was an essential basis on which to build a democratic society, providing an important route out of poverty and establishing equality of opportunity for the population. In the 1870s the lack of such opportunities for all but the wealthy was very much on the social and political agenda, but education of the masses, particularly when this extended beyond the traditional 'three Rs', was a controversial issue.

When William began his own formal education at Plymouth Grammar School in the late 1850s approximately seventy thousand other English children of about the same age (children over the age of nine) would already have begun working six days a week as 'half-

---

1. E. Welch, *The Peripatetic University: Cambridge Local Lectures 1873–1973* (Cambridge University Press, Cambridge, 1973).

timers' in mills and factories up and down the land. The term 'half-timer' was a somewhat misleading description of the lives of these children. The Factory Act of 1833 had prohibited the employment of children under the age of nine in textile mills and had introduced the requirement for two hours of schooling each day for those aged nine to thirteen. Fulfilment of this requirement entitled them to the doubtful privilege of spending up to nine more hours of the day at work. By 1847 subsequent legislation had reduced the permitted working hours of these children from nine to six and a half per day. At the age of thirteen, however, when William would have started at Marlborough, children were allowed to commence 'full-time employment' (no more than ten hours per day until they were eighteen years old).

These educational arrangements, imperfect as they were, had been instituted in large part as a result of pressure from social reformers who perceived that the most effective way to reduce child labour was to introduce a legal requirement that children should attend school. Parents, however, were not universally supportive of the idea that their children should receive an education, for many were anxious for them to begin working as soon as possible in order to contribute to the family income. School attendance was not compulsory until the School Attendance Act of 1880 and even then only applied to children between the ages of five and ten.[2] Thus both parents and employers were inclined to flout the law on working hours. Meanwhile many in the middle-classes considered that schooling for the masses was at best unnecessary and at worst liable to sow seeds of subversion. Unsurprisingly, therefore, the results of these first attempts at universal education were somewhat unpredictable, especially as they were often delivered by untrained teachers of questionable competence presiding over large groups of reluctant, unruly children. Notwithstanding the good intentions of such a policy the practical infrastructure to deliver it was, in many places, somewhat lacking and the education received

---

2. The Elementary Education Act (1880) introduced compulsory education between the ages of five and ten years. Subsequent Acts gradually raised the school leaving age until it reached fourteen years in 1900.

by many working-class children was of doubtful quality. Moreover, few people received any education at all after the age of fourteen.

By the middle years of the nineteenth century there had been a number of initiatives to improve the education and, by implication, the life chances of the poor. There was a growing thirst for knowledge amongst all classes, eager to learn about the exciting new scientific and technological developments of the day. In the industrial North and Midlands the Mechanics Institutes, established in the 1820s and '30s, were perhaps the most prominent and widespread examples of these initiatives, intended as working class equivalents to the Literary and Philosophical Societies that proliferated amongst the middle-classes. Considerable numbers of impressive buildings were constructed across the industrial landscape, the words 'Mechanics Institute' carved with a confident sense of permanence into the stonework of their invariably classical facades. Many remain today in various states of decay, adding to the general air of dilapidation that pervades so many formerly proud industrial towns of the past. For after an initial period of enthusiasm student numbers began to decline, primarily it seems because of a mismatch between the type of education on offer and the expectations of the recipients. In many places there developed an on-going tension, often underpinned by differing political allegiances, between those who considered that the Institutes should be places of technical and practical knowledge and those who favoured a more philosophical approach which emphasised liberal intellectual thought. Added to this, the annual subscription demanded by the Institutes was often beyond the resources of the average working man. By the 1870s many working-class supporters had withdrawn from these establishments and increasingly Mechanics Institutes had become the haunt of middle-class ladies who sought artistic, musical or literary pursuits rather than training in science or engineering. Some buildings were turned into concert halls or provided a base for the ever-popular circulating libraries, purveyors of romantic and sensational fiction targeted, it seemed, at a largely female audience.[3] Derby, for example, a place that in 1839 had proudly staged its own version of the Great Exhibition, was by 1870 described witheringly by one critic as 'a town that contained a Mechanics Institute without a mechanic and a lecture hall without lecturers.'[4]

Into this widening void in the late 1860s stepped a man called James Stuart, fellow of Trinity College, Cambridge. Stuart was convinced that there were 'vast masses who desire education ... our countrymen and countrywomen who are eager for education and cannot get it.'[5] He was unimpressed by the offerings of the Mechanics Institutes. 'When these people cry for bread, a stone should not be given to them, as is all too frequently the case with these popular lectures which are got up by the Mechanics Institutes and the like.'[6] He was keen that philosophical and cultural education should continue but was also conscious of the importance, in an increasingly industrial age, of advanced scientific education. In the 1850s he had supported Maurice in the establishment of the London Working Men's College in London's Red Lion Square and the Working Women's College in Queens Square. A few similar colleges had been established in various towns throughout the country, with the aim of providing a wide range of classes scheduled at convenient times for working men and women.

In the early 1870s this scheme provided Stuart with the blueprint for one of his most cherished ambitions, 'to establish a sort of peripatetic university, the professors of which would circulate among the big towns, and thus give a wider opportunity for receiving such teaching.'[7] From 1867 he began to give a series of hugely popular lectures in the Midlands and the North of England to working class men and women. In the process he established a network of supportive contacts amongst

---

3. Some institutes did survive, notably the London Mechanics Institute, later Birkbeck College, part of the University of London, which continues to specialise in evening and part-time classes.
4. op cit., *The Peripatetic University*.
5. ibid
6. ibid
7. ibid

sympathetic Anglican clergymen and non-conformist ministers, as well as organisations such as the Co-operative Society and its sister society the Women's Co-operative Guild. Public meetings were held in a number of provincial towns, evincing widespread enthusiasm for the extension of the scheme. The ambition was to instigate a series of lectures and examinations in large towns, under the auspices of the University of Cambridge. The university was soon in receipt of a number of petitions from prominent citizens and influential organisations in places such as Leeds, Rochdale, Crewe, Derby, Leicester and Nottingham. The general objective, described by one strong supporter, the Reverend John Brown Paton, a congregational minister in Nottingham, ran as follows:

> ... to appoint lecturers of approved eminence and skill, who may conduct evening classes for working men in our large towns ... so as to spread the advantages of university education throughout the country, and to all classes.[8]

In time this would prove to be a relatively modest objective, given what was eventually achieved, for what became known as the Cambridge University Extension Scheme would ultimately lead to the establishment of a number of provincial universities, including Nottingham.

The senate of the University of Cambridge was broadly sympathetic to the idea and early in 1873 appointed professors Lightfoot, Westcott, and Sidgwick, together with James Stuart himself, to explore the feasibility of the project. They proceeded to conduct some exhaustive interrogations of the petitioners, sending out detailed questionnaires aimed at establishing who they considered would benefit from the lectures, the subjects preferred and the timing and cost of such a programme in their locality. Many towns held public meetings, chaired by the Mayor, to formulate their responses to these questions. These

8. ibid.

replies indicated a very high level of support for the scheme, even if this enthusiasm was perhaps driven more by an emphasis on the moral rather than the intellectual improvement of the population, which hopefully might ensue. In terms of the question about 'who might benefit' for example, the response from Nottingham was a typical one.

> The young men and women of the working classes, many of whom now spend their evenings in walking about the streets, or at places of amusement, theatres, music halls and dancing rooms.
>
> The elder men of the working classes; many of whom now spend a great part of their leisure time in public houses.
>
> Young men, sons of manufacturers and professional men, who have been taken from school early and put into business but have no occupation for their leisure hours and are consequently liable to the temptations of billiard rooms, theatres, etc.[9]

James Stuart's plan was to divide towns into circuits, each with their full-time lecturer and organiser. Courses of twelve lectures would be delivered in each of the standard university terms of Michaelmas, Lent and Summer, followed by an optional written examination. Every session consisted of an hour's lecture followed by a 'class' that was essentially a discussion period in which students could address their questions to the lecturer. Reflecting the assumptions of the day each course was advertised with a suggestion as to which groups might find it interesting or useful. For example, in the Michaelmas term of the first year there was to be a course on political economy that was 'intended specially, though not exclusively, for the working classes.' There was also to be a course on 'English Literature', delivered 'at a time which is expected may generally be found most convenient for the ladies' and a third course entitled 'Force and Motion' was intended 'mainly for young men engaged in commercial and professional

9. ibid.

pursuits.'[10] Despite this entirely conventional steer, however, all courses were open to anyone who could find the necessary fee, or the necessary time.

The economics of the enterprise seem rather shaky, especially in the early days when its popularity in terms of numbers of attendees could not be guaranteed. Each circuit was required to pay the university £375 per term for the supply of teachers and examinations and an additional sum to cover lecturers' travelling expenses. Lecturers' fees recorded in 1875 were £10 per lecture with a further £10 for expenses. Added to this was the cost of the hire of the room, together with printing and stationery expenses. Attendees, meanwhile, rarely seem to have been required to pay more than a few pence for an entry 'ticket' to a single lecture, reflecting the ethos that the scheme was primarily aimed at working people. As with so many Victorian enterprises, however, local committees were set up and subscriptions sought from benefactors. In Leeds for example £600 was raised to help fund the scheme and most circuits seem to have benefited from donations of one sort or another. At the inaugural meeting of the scheme in Sheffield £1064 was raised immediately to help cover the expenses of the lecturers for three years. And in Nottingham the circuit was particularly blessed when it unexpectedly received an anonymous donation of £10,000, presented to the Corporation for the building and maintenance of a permanent home for the scheme.[11] Ultimately this would provide the basis for the development of the University of Nottingham. Most contributions were, of course, more modest but they enabled schemes to get off the ground and supported them in the early days.

The first lecture circuit to be established comprised the towns of Nottingham, Derby and Leicester, carefully chosen by James Stuart because of the growing prosperity of each town, which had stimulated the demand for further education. In Derby this related to the establishment of the Midland Railway headquarters while Leicester

10. ibid.
11. The identity of the donor has never been confirmed but is widely thought to be William Henry Haymen, a Nottingham lace manufacturer.

was benefiting from the growth of the boot and shoe industry which was now rapidly replacing knitwear as the major source of employment in the area. Meanwhile in Nottingham, new machinery for making hosiery and lace had considerably enhanced the scale of this well-established industry. More practically, however, these towns were well situated in relation to one another geographically, less than twenty miles apart and linked by the Midland Railway Company's main lines. The inaugural lectures took place on the evening of 8 October 1873. William, who joined the circuit early in 1874, later explained the significance of this particular start date in the East Midlands. It was, he said, 'useless to begin lectures until the Nottingham Goose Fair and the Leicester Races were over.'[12] His own lectures, predictably on his favourite subject, Political Economy, began in January 1874. Of all the subjects on offer this one, dealing as it did with the organisation of production and trade and the relationships between employers and employed, held the most potential for controversy, and even accusations of subversive incitement. Unsurprisingly William favoured an approach that effectively followed the Cambridge curriculum, which he himself had so recently completed. To this end he began with a course on Logic to teach students the first principles of reasoning and to instruct them in the nature of proof. This was followed by a course on Constitutional and Social History which explored economic development throughout history, both in the British Isles and overseas, before embarking on more recent developments in economic theory. Essentially, he taught Marshall's approach to economics, explaining the mechanism of market regulation in terms of the laws of supply and demand and the principles underlying a rational basis of consumer choice. He also promulgated the value of cooperation as opposed to competition in industrial relations and the fair division of industrial profit between employers and workers, much like the practices of the Co-operative Society. It was an approach that combined Marshall's secular economics with Maurice's Christian view of a just society.

---

12. op cit., *The Peripatetic University*.

On both counts it seems to have represented something of a threat to many contemporary industrialists. When for example the Extension Scheme was introduced into Newcastle upon Tyne a proposal was made that it might amalgamate with the existing Literary and Philosophical Society. This raised a degree of consternation among the predominantly entrepreneurial membership of the 'Lit and Phil.' In truth it was probably the idea of rubbing shoulders with the working classes that most worried its members, but the expressed concern was a suspicion that the amalgamation represented a 'radical dodge', an attempt to use the lecture course to promulgate socialist ideas amongst the population.[13]

Meanwhile, whatever took place during the months that followed William's departure from Alston, his relationship with Eleanor was by no means extinguished by the distance between them. Absence, it seems, had most certainly made the heart grow fonder, for on the 14 May 1874 the two were married, many miles away from the North of England in the parish church of Dawlish in Devon. This marriage, little more than twelve months after William Baylee's funeral, was a bold move for William and Eleanor and speaks of a love affair that engendered a reckless disregard for social convention. This may explain why the couple travelled to Dawlish to marry, rejecting what might have seemed the more obvious venues of Alston itself or Kirkby Thore, where Eleanor's father, the Reverend Edward Cookson, still occupied the living. It is hard to imagine that the marriage evoked anything other than family disapproval, at least on Eleanor's side. While the marriage certificate records that William was a resident of Plymouth where his extended family lived, Eleanor, rather oddly, is recorded as a resident of Dawlish, a place to which neither she nor William had any obvious connection. One suspects that her time in Dawlish may have represented simply the acquisition of a qualifying connection to the parish. A brief factual announcement of the marriage appeared subsequently in the *Exeter and Plymouth Gazette* but there was no

---

13. R. Spence-Watson, *The History of the Literary and Philosophical Society of Newcastle-Upon-Tyne, 1793–1896* (Walter Scott Ltd, London, 1897).

mention of it in any newspaper that might be read by the inhabitants of Alston, South Shields or indeed Kirkby Thore. Witnesses to the marriage were William's sister Elizabeth and her fiancé, Thomas Lawrence, the future parents of William's nephew Arthur who would marry the daughter of James Eadie-Reid. After the wedding the newly married couple returned immediately to William's house in Newark, where their first child William Edward would be born eleven months later.

Chapter Six
A REAL SHEFFIELD BLADE

William seems to have been a very popular lecturer with above average attendances and he was soon lecturing regularly on an additional circuit comprising Bradford, Halifax and Keighley. By the end of 1874 he also seems to have assumed the position of James Stuart's righthand man for, as well as lecturing and organising courses and examinations, he travelled endlessly around the country to respond to requests for information from various interested towns and cities. He conducted public meetings, placed adverts in local newspapers and negotiated with influential townspeople, potential sponsors and owners of useful venues. Even in Newark, a relatively obscure market town, he persuaded a group of local vicars gathered in the Town Hall to support the development of a lecture course that began in October that year. In December 1874 James Stuart was asked by the Syndicate to prepare a report on the progress of the scheme in the Midlands, a task he delegated to William who tackled it with his usual enthusiasm. He showed that thirty-one courses had been delivered between January and April that year, rising to fifty-six between October and December. During the same periods the number of students entering examinations had risen from 744 to 980 and of these the number studying Political Economy, William's major subject, had risen from 113 to 177.[1] Importantly he also took the opportunity to record some far-sighted recommendations about potential future developments of the scheme. His proposal of long-term courses which ultimately

---

1. op cit., *The Peripatetic University*.

mimicked those undertaken by undergraduates at Cambridge, together with the notion that successful students might be awarded the Degree of AC (Associate of the University of Cambridge), lay some distance in the future. As things turned out, however, these were not entirely fanciful ideas, and they certainly underlined the extent of his own ambitions for working class education.

Late in 1874 James Stuart received a petition from the town councillors of Sheffield who wished to develop an Extension course in the town. Early in January 1875, therefore, William took the train to Sheffield where, that evening, he was introduced to an assemblage of local dignitaries gathered in the splendour of the Cutlers Hall. The presence of such a large gathering prepared to leave their firesides on what was a miserably cold night testifies to their undoubted enthusiasm for the scheme. Opinion here was already firmly on the side of University Extension. The Education Act five years earlier, which had established non-denominational primary education for all of Sheffield's children, had been greeted with almost universal support in this overwhelmingly non-conformist town. As William, himself, often remarked the Act had vastly increased the level of literacy in the population, and the effects of this would soon be seen in the desire of people for knowledge and information. And now a new level of education had appeared on the horizon. The local Liberal MP, Anthony Mundella, a fervent supporter of the 1870 Act, saw the Extension Scheme as an advancement of his hope that one day there would indeed be 'a ladder from the gutter to the university.'[2] The Mayor, Mr Mark Firth, concurred, suggesting that 'where boys showed themselves apt, and were desirous to improve themselves, and wished to extend their education further, they could go up to the University of Cambridge to receive a Degree themselves.' He dared venture to say that gentlemen would be found in Sheffield who would render the necessary financial assistance.[3] Mark Firth was well-placed

---

2. 'University Education in Sheffield,' BNA, *Sheffield and Rotherham Independent*, 19 January 1875.

3. ibid.

to make these sorts of promises. A former master cutler, he was a wealthy self-made industrialist, the owner of Sheffield's largest steel rolling mill. A Methodist and a Liberal, he had already established himself as a major benefactor of the town. That year alone he had presented a thirty-six-acre estate, Firth Park, to the people for their recreation and enjoyment. At the meeting in 1875 he took careful note as the Reverend Francis Morse, vicar of Nottingham, discussed the finances of the scheme and recounted the story of Nottingham's £10,000 donation. With, no doubt, one eye on the Mayor, the Reverend Morse fervently expressed his confidence that Sheffield 'was not going to be beaten by a trumpery town like Nottingham.'[4] Meanwhile Alderman Allott, rising to second the resolution to adopt the scheme, warmed to the same theme. He would, he declared 'be very much surprised if the metal of Sheffield men allowed itself to be eclipsed by the lace manufacturers of Nottingham.'[5] His confidence was well founded. A few years later, in 1879, Mark Firth would fund the establishment of Firth College, the forerunner of the University of Sheffield, with an endowment of £25,000. It was a development that would have far reaching consequences both for William and also for the Extension movement itself. For the moment, however, things looked extremely promising.

As ever, the extension plans were about moral as well as physical improvement. 'Nothing tends to elevate the character more than a sound education' declared the Mayor to loud cheers from the audience. 'In future generations we might hope to see improved morals and an improved state of living amongst the populations of large towns.' And not only would Sheffield set an example to other large towns, he declared. He hoped that the people of Sheffield would 'show the world that we can appreciate the improvement of the intellect and the education of the people as well as make money.'[6] This heady combination of ambitious hopes, fierce determination and civic pride was to prove the making

4. ibid.
5. ibid.
6. ibid.

of the scheme in Sheffield. This was a busy industrous town, proud of its reputation as a centre of high- quality cutlery making. It had long been a place that relied on and respected the quality and craftsmanship of its workers. Unlike many other industrial areas where the owners of mines, mills and factories presided over large and often powerless workforces, and made substantial fortunes in the process, the skilled artisans of Sheffield were organised into small scale production units, gathered together under a 'master' where the individually skilled workers were interdependent but essentially self-employed. In the 1850s and 1860s some notorious outrages, known as 'rattening' had occurred in the town when attempts had been made to intimidate workers into leaving masters and join the fledgling but currently illegal unions.[7] Action began with repeated sabotage and confiscation of the tools of workmen who refused to comply with union demands. Subsequently it escalated into violence and even, ultimately, into murder. In 1867, however, the perpetrators had been brought to justice and for the moment at least this well-organised industrial structure, built up over generations had prevailed. Resisting the contemporary pressures of industrialisation, the highly skilled artisans of Sheffield had elected to maintain their place as makers of superior tableware rather than succumbing to the temptations of lower quality mass production.

William was not the only person to arrive in Sheffield that year with a view to developing the potential of its workers. In the summer of 1875 John Ruskin, a former lecturer at Maurice's Working Men's College and now a renowned art critic and patron of the Arts and Crafts movement, would choose Sheffield as the place to set up his first People's Museum containing paintings, drawings, architectural models, as well as rocks and minerals derived from the natural world. Ruskin believed passionately that people should reconnect with the beauty of the world in the face of rapid industrialisation and the despoiling of the landscape. Sheffield, he considered, was an ideal

---

[7]. The origin of the term 'rattening' is thought to relate to the habit of rats, entering a building and destroying the belongings of the inhabitants.
Unions did not become formally legal entities until the Trade Union Act of 1871.

place to further his cherished project, the formation of the 'Guild of St George', an organisation which aimed to develop cultural communities that promoted sustainable agriculture and art and craftsmanship rather than mass production. Essentially, he wanted to educate and inspire working people in order to broaden their cultural horizons and ultimately to bring an end to industrial capitalism.[8] Ruskin considered the skill of the metal workers of Sheffield to be 'the best in the world'.[9] As William detailed the structure and benefits of the Extension Scheme, he was greeted with more loud cheers as he too tapped into this strong vein of civic pride. The education on offer, he said was 'like a real Sheffield blade, the genuine article.'[10]

Following this highly successful meeting it was immediately decided that William should relocate to Sheffield to develop the scheme fully, and in the spring of 1876 he and Eleanor, with Eleanor's two daughters, Eleanor and Mary, and baby William, set up home in the Highfield district of the town. Two more children would follow in quick succession, another son Alfred and a daughter Laetitia, poignantly named after Eleanor's lost child in Alston. Unlike her tragic half-sister this Laetitia remained strong and healthy. She would grow up to become a doctor, graduating from London Medical School in 1895 during the early days of women's entry into the medical profession. Meanwhile, as his family grew, William needed to maintain some regular employment to supplement the fees he received from his teaching activities. Officially, therefore, he acquired an appointment as a curate, first at All Saints Church, Ecclesall, a suburban area on the edge of the town and subsequently at the more central St Paul's.[11]

Once more, of course, he found himself to be part of a minority institution, largely divorced from the overwhelmingly non-conformist

8. The Guild of St George still exists today in the form of rural communities which aspire to live according to the values which Ruskin inspired.
9. The Museum remains today, relocated from its original cottage site in Walkley, Sheffield, to the Millenium Gallery of the Museum of Sheffield.
10. op cit., *Sheffield and Rotherham Independent*, 19 January 1875.
11. St Paul's Church was demolished in 1937. The site is now a public space called the Peace Gardens.

setting within which his church operated. Again, the prominent clerics of the area were more strongly associated with the wealthier members of society. The vicar of Ecclesall, the Reverend Edward Newman, and the vicar of St Paul's, the Reverend Thomas Sale, were among a number of Church of England clergymen in the area who belonged to an exclusive club, the politically and economically powerful Sheffield Club. This longstanding organisation, similar in structure to the London clubs

> THIS DAY.
>
> UNIVERSITY EXTENSION,
> SHEFFIELD.
> OPENING LECTURE ON HISTORY—THE ENGLISH REVOLUTION,
> By Rev. W. MOORE EDE, M.A.,
> At Twelve o'clock at Noon, in the CUTLERS' HALL.
>
> OPENING LECTURE ON LITERATURE—
> "The Influence of the Renaissance on English Poetry and Prose,"
> By R. G. MOULTON, Esq., B.A.,
> At Half past Seven o'clock, in the OLD BANQUETING ROOM of the CUTLERS' COMPANY.
> Admission Free to First Lecture.

Announcement of the first session of the University Extension Scheme in Sheffield. *Sheffield Independent*, 27 September 1876.

of the age, comprised a social elite of local landowners, the majority of larger employers and the successful professional men of Sheffield. William's aspirations, however, leaned in a different direction and he put much of his energy into the promotion and development of the Extension Scheme. During 1876 lecture courses were established in history, literary analysis (poetry and prose), geography and geology. Often these were supplemented by excursions. In July that year, for example, eighty students (both men and women) set off in waggonettes for a three hour drive to Castleton from where, under the guidance of a Mr Rooke Pennington and Mr J. J. Teall, fellows of the Geological Society, they studied the rocks in Side Gate stone quarry. Mr Teall, it was reported, 'interpreted the mysteries of the earth in a very able and lucid manner.'[12] William, who began his own course on Political Economy in October 1876 soon had a regular attendance of about 450 students at his lectures, sixty-three of whom presented themselves for the examination set by the University of Cambridge. Of these fifty-eight passed, with twenty graded as first class, and thirty-eight as second class. The Executive Committee appointed to assess the scheme at the end of its first term professed themselves delighted with its popularity and success.[13]

William's impressive administrative skills were not lost on the vicar of St Paul's who in 1878 put him to work as an organiser when Sheffield was chosen as the venue for the Annual Church Congress held in October that year. This large gathering, now in its tenth year, provided a forum for clergy and laymen at all levels in the Church of England to discuss matters of current interest and opinion. William set about the task with his usual energy and enthusiasm. Mindful of the reputation of the town, and in particular its recent patronage by John Ruskin, he proposed an Ecclesiastical Art Exhibition to accompany the usual programme of speakers. These additional delights were a considerable draw and the meeting was very well attended. The Congress, however, had often been a scene of controversy over matters of doctrine and practice and that year was no exception. The battle over the supposed infiltration by 'Romish doctrine' into Protestant worship, described by the Dean of Carlisle as 'the secret and subtle advances of this semi-Popish phalanx within our Church' was still raging.[14] The issue had supposedly been dealt with the previous year

---

12. 'Cambridge University Extension Scheme. Geological Excursion to Castleton,' BNA, *Sheffield Independent*, 27 July 1876.

13. 'University Extension Committee,' BNA, *Sheffield Daily Telegraph*, 7 August 1875.

14. *Church Times*, 4 October 1878. Francis Close, Dean of Carlisle, was a vociferous opponent of the Anglo-Catholic movement.

by the Public Worship Regulation Act which had caused Thomas Burt so much annoyance but this, apparently, had done nothing to dampen the ardour with which Catholic leaning clergy pursued their cause. At the Church Congress in Sheffield members of the Anglo-Catholic English Church Union (ECU) who, according to a 'special correspondent' of the *Church Times* 'happened to be present in the town' held a separate fringe meeting in which they rallied supporters to challenge the judgement. The special correspondent, presumably a supporter of the ECU, took the opportunity to launch a denigrating attack on the Congress, ranging from the 'miserable moral and social state of the town itself' to the poor quality of the organisation and speakers. The opening procession was he considered 'wretchedly arranged. Evangelicals never know *how* to come into church and choirboys look better in *clean* surpluses,' the music was 'far too elaborate' and 'not only beyond the congregation but often rather above the reach of the choristers themselves.' He reserved his most scathing comments, however, for the Archbishop of York, whose whole tone he found to be 'nasty' in the pursuit of his 'narrow and persecuting policies'.[15] In his opening address the Archbishop had made it clear that he supported whole-heartedly the suppression of 'Romish tendencies' and that as far as he was concerned the matter was now closed.

William would have known that the waspish remarks in the *Church Times* had their origin in the liturgical disputes that continued to plague the Church of England but, having worked very hard to make a success of the Congress, he must have read the report with dismay. Over forty years later, in 1922, when the Congress was once more held in Sheffield, he took the opportunity to put the record straight, at least in relation to the processional arrangements. Interviewed by a local reporter about his memories of that earlier Sheffield Congress he described how the clergy and the choirboys robed at the Church Institute in nearby St James's street and went in procession to what was then the parish church. 'Unfortunately, it began to rain just as the procession was about to start,'

---

15. ibid. *Church Times*. Archbishop of York, William Thomson, in office 1862–90.

he said, 'and I'm afraid we did not present a very dignified spectacle, as the Bishops and others scuttled across the churchyard holding umbrellas with one hand and lifting up their clerical robes with the other.'[16] As regards the liturgical disputes, of course, the matter was far from closed, however much the Archbishop of York asserted that it was. It would rumble on over successive decades of William's career, as would his own personal antipathy towards the ECU. His close links to the Methodist church, his strongly ecumenical views as well as his support for the introduction of women clergy, meant that he would always be unsympathetic towards the extreme end of the Anglo-Catholic movement, at least in the form it presented itself in the late Victorian period. In 1932 he wrote to *The Times* complaining about the ECU's vehement opposition to 'the very small steps the Bishops propose to take in the direction of inter communion.' He said:

> Personally, I cannot understand how anyone who has endeavoured to understand the mind and spirit of Jesus Christ by a study of the Gospels can think Christ approves of the erection of fences for the purpose of keeping off any disciple of His, who desires to approach His Table or His Altar.[17]

More generally William had little time for the niceties of ceremonial ritual and often ridiculed pomposity and self-importance amongst the clergy. When questioned about the role of the laity in Gateshead in 1898 he said he considered that it was always necessary to adapt the ritual of the Church to new needs and that in every parish the laity should have a legal voice in the arrangement of church services. 'One should remember,' he said, 'that all these questions of ritual are only of secondary importance – they are not religion. The real worth of the Church is to render life holier.'[18] In 1927 he repeated this view.

---

16. 'Dean of Worcester on Last Sheffield Congress,' BNA, *Sheffield Daily Telegraph*, 13 October 1922.

17. WME, letter to *The Times*, January 1932. Reproduced by BNA, *Bury Free Press*, 16 January 1932.

18. WME, 'Sunday afternoon lecture. St Columba's Church, Gateshead,' BNA, *Newcastle Journal*, 17 October 1898.

There is a great danger, unintentionally it may be, in thinking there is a magical efficacy in the reception of bread and wine at the Communion service. There are people who seem to think that attendance at Holy Communion is religion, and it is to be regretted that we clergy are so often apt to estimate the spiritual life of our parishes by the number of communicants.[19]

Meanwhile, the preoccupation of the Anglican church with the onward march of non-conformism was to prove unexpectedly beneficial to clerics of a Christian Socialist persuasion. The construction of new buildings in industrial areas had brought into sharp focus an uncomfortable truth, that traditional clergy with their largely aristocratic origins were ill-equipped to engage with the typical working man or woman. Suddenly, clergy of rather more 'working-class' origins were increasingly sought after for placement in the new industrial parishes. It is perhaps a measure of the exalted pedigree of the existing church hierarchy that William, himself a product of Marlborough and Cambridge, was considered to be one such 'working-class' candidate. However, with his growing reputation as someone who could communicate effectively with ordinary working people, it would not be long before he came to the attention of the Bishops, particularly those who were themselves of a Christian Socialist persuasion. Coincident with this, events that occurred in Sheffield in 1879 led William himself to consider whether he wouldn't, after all, be better devoting himself to more conventional ministry. His experience in this respect, largely that of a part-time curate, was still rather limited. Instead, he had directed his energies tirelessly towards the Extension Scheme. In Sheffield this was flourishing with a total of 3566 lecture tickets sold in three years, and he was central to this success. The problem, however, was that the very support that had enabled the scheme's inception, the benefaction of Mark Firth, now threatened its existence, at least in the form which William had created.

19. WME, 'Sermon Sunday evening service in Worcester Cathedral,' BNA, *Belfast Newsletter*, 25 October 1927.

Chapter Seven
THE MUNIFICENCE OF MR FIRTH

In 1879 the organising committee in Sheffield were delighted when the donation they had always hoped for arrived. That year Mark Firth announced that he had bought a large building on the corner of West Street and Church Street. He said,

> [I am] desirous of aiding to carry out in my native town of Sheffield a system of higher education in connection with the English Universities, for the promotion of moral, social and intellectual elevation of the townsmen and desirous of providing at my sole expense, a building containing a lecture hall, class rooms and other rooms with fixtures and furniture.[1]

The building, which would be the forerunner of the University of Sheffield, was opened that year by Prince Leopold, the youngest child of Queen Victoria.[2] Mark Firth's benevolence was greeted with delight by almost everyone but, much to many people's surprise, William was unenthusiastic. It was the first sign of his strong adherence to the virtue of self-help, something that would surface repeatedly in later years. Self-help, he considered, fostered independence, self-respect and a freedom from obligation towards others, something that operated both at an individual and an organisational level. Many years later a miner called Jack Lawson came to see William to ask for some financial help with the costs of pursuing a university course. Jack had been offered a place at Ruskin College, Oxford, following his exceptional

---

1. 'The Firth College,' BNA, *Sheffield and Rotherham Independent*, 21 May 1879.
2. Church Street was renamed Leopold Street in honour of the occasion.

results in an Extension course. He was given five pounds by William on the understanding that he himself collected the other six which was needed. Jack, who went on to become an MP, a government minister and finally a Baronet, was grateful all his life, not only for the five pounds but also for the motivation to provide the other six.[3] During a similar period, when William was involved in a scheme to build houses for retired miners, he rejected the idea of approaching the mine owners for financial help. Rather he felt the money should be raised from a fund set up and run by the miners themselves. It was a highly unpopular stance among many but one that he steadfastly refused to change. Perhaps it was a principle that emerged from his thoughts in South Shields when he compared the situation in that tumultuous town with the calm passivity of Alston. While he had been willing to countenance some modest donations to get the Extension Scheme off the ground, he considered that, ultimately, it should be run by the people, for the people and, thus remaining under the people's control. He was deeply suspicious of large donations from wealthy individuals, particularly manufacturers, who might then consider themselves entitled to control the type of education on offer and, moreover, use the skills gained by the students for the furtherance of their own enterprise. He had observed this in Alston where the Friends had sent promising workers to study chemistry at Newcastle College of Science, placing them under a lifelong obligation to use their skills for the enhancement of the company. William's commitment by contrast, was to a liberal educational tradition, fostering an ability to think logically and philosophically and focussing on the exploration of ideas rather than the acquisition of specific technical skills, which might be subverted by wealthy donors to feed their own industrial ambitions.

In short, William wished his students to experience the type of education received by the middle and upper classes at Cambridge, something which he considered was denied to ordinary working people, thus stifling any prospect of a more democratic and just society.

3. J. Lawson, *A Man's Life* (Hodder & Stoughton, London, 1932).

Thinking back to the ethos of the Working Men's College in the early days of Christian Socialism he would have been in agreement with Maurice's conviction that ultimately the transformation of the nation's economic system depended on the educational transformation of society. William would never depart from this position. Over thirty years later, as Dean of Worcester, he was invited to deliver the address at Birmingham Cathedral when staff and students of the University of Birmingham gathered to celebrate University Sunday. The message he gave that day reflected the same sentiments he had expressed in Sheffield. Was the idea of a university simply an instrument to send out men better equipped in manufacturing and commerce and more efficient at making money, he asked his audience.

> The training in the university will doubtless have that effect, and the men who founded it, or their sons, will get their money back and the university will prove for Birmingham a profitable, wealth producing investment. But the university must be more than a science college. It must aim to train the future citizens of Birmingham not only in science but also in culture, in knowledge of the history of the world and of the great philosophical problems lying at the back of all knowledge. In a busy commercial centre like Birmingham, where men are so much absorbed in material things and in the pursuit of gain, it needs a university to uphold in its midst the ideals of knowledge and culture.[4]

William considered that in some of the new universities which had emerged in the provinces since the early days of the Extension Movement the ethos and culture of places like Oxford and Cambridge, which he had hoped to transmit to the people, had in fact been lost to them.

In 1880 there was another development which added to William's disquiet. That year it was also proposed that Firth College should become part of the Victoria University, an organisation that had ambitions to become a single university comprised of colleges situated in the large

---

4. 'University Sunday. Dean of Worcester Suggests Ideals to Birmingham,' BNA, *Birmingham Daily Gazette*, 7 October 1912.

cities of Northern England.⁵ A move such as this would effectively sever Sheffield's links with Cambridge and, William thought, change the essential nature of the scheme as a means of education for the working classes. The plan was to offer residential as well as evening classes and to admit wealthier students, presumably as a means of securing the organisation's on-going finances. The scheme would, he considered, soon depart from its original mission, with ordinary working people becoming sidelined as somewhat 'second-class' in favour of residential students from wealthier middle-class backgrounds. Essentially it would increasingly mirror the traditional educational route provided for the wealthy by Oxford and Cambridge and thus become inaccessible to 'all classes of men and women.'

William was fiercely protective of his working-class students and in October that year he sent a sad letter to the organiser of their thriving alumni society, of whom he was the founding president, explaining that he had decided to resign and to end his association with further education in Sheffield. On receipt of the letter the society initially refused to accept his resignation but failed to persuade him to change his mind. He was determined to have no connection with Firth College, he said, 'while it is in the hands of the present governing body rather than remaining under the influences and traditions of Cambridge.'⁶ James Stuart, on hearing the news, was also saddened. He was, he said, 'exceedingly sorry that Firth College has lost the services of Mr Ede. He has throughout been my right hand in the University Extension Scheme in the North of England.'⁷ But he could not agree with William, for he considered that the best chance of continuing and expanding the work they had begun was to take advantage of the generosity of Mark Firth and to proceed under the auspices of Firth

---

5. Victoria College initially comprised Liverpool College, Leeds College and Manchester's Owen College, the forerunners of the Universities of Liverpool, Leeds and Manchester.

6. WME, 'Letter to the Students' Association, Sheffield Extension Scheme,' BNA, *Sheffield Independent*, 12 November 1879.

7. 'Letter to Students' Association from James Stuart,' BNA, *Sheffield Independent*, 12 November 1879.

College. And later that year, as William had feared, negotiations began for the college to became part of Victoria University.

Effectively Mark Firth's intervention spelled the end of the Cambridge Extension Scheme in Sheffield but what replaced it turned out to be much more to William's taste than he had anticipated. Ultimately, Victoria University would divide into its component parts to form a series of 'red brick' universities in the North of England, but Firth College would not be part of these developments. Rather it

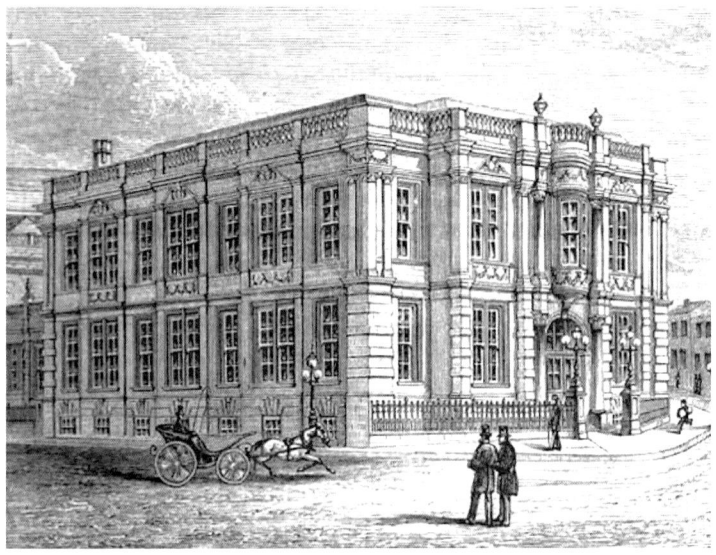

A drawing of Firth College, Sheffield, opened in October 1879. (Courtesy of www.picturesheffield.com)

would follow a very different path combining with Sheffield School of Medicine and Sheffield Technical School to form the University of Sheffield. This last development, it must be said, was hugely supported by the local population of steelworkers, coalminers and factory workers who between them raised over £50,000 to support the establishment of the university. Posters which encouraged them to donate appealed to the same sense of civic pride that had persuaded them to support the development of the Extension College a few years earlier, emphasising that Sheffield was 'the only large town in England without a university and could not afford to remain in this position.'

The university, it said, 'will bring the highest education within the reach of the child of every working man.'[8] William, however, maintained deep suspicions that industrialists would always promote technical education in order to benefit their own industrial enterprise rather than risk opening the minds of their workers to progressive and possibly radical ideas. But he had misjudged Mark Firth, who turned out to be the driving force of liberal education in Sheffield. Unlike several other provincial universities founded during this period Sheffield continued to cultivate strong links with the older established institutions, notably Oxford and Cambridge, and to appoint professionals and academics rather than industrialists to its teaching staff and governing bodies.

William, however, saw the developments in Sheffield as the beginning of the end of his own particular dream for the city and it precipitated a serious falling out with his colleagues there. It was a very difficult year for him, both professionally and personally, for in July 1879 Eleanor gave birth prematurely to a stillborn daughter. This child would have been their fourth, a sister for Laetitia who had just celebrated her second birthday. At the beginning of 1880, therefore, amidst acute family sadness and professional disappointment he decided to seek a post elsewhere. It was clearly a decision he took with a heavy heart for he and Eleanor and their growing family had been very happy in Sheffield. They had made many friends and been involved in numerous aspects of life in the town. As well as his usual parish duties as a curate at both St Paul's and Ecclesall, William was founder and chairman of the board of directors of the Sheffield Café Company which built the innovative Highfield Cocoa and Coffee House, a temperance establishment which opened in 1877. This newly fashionable and highly successful alternative to the Public House was a project close to his heart and the Cafe Company in Sheffield was a pioneer in the

---

8. Text from the poster which helped to raise funds for the university, which opened in 1905.

field. Always in pursuit of equality of educational opportunities, he was also the directing mind behind the establishment of Sheffield Girls' High School in 1878 and was a prominent member of the Highfield Free Public Library and Museum Committee established in 1876. Announcing his departure to a packed congregation a few weeks before he left Sheffield his sorrow at leaving the town was palpable.

> Having been so long amongst you and having entered into the life and work of this great and busy town it is a wrench to bid adieu, to part from many who have endeared themselves by all the ties and bonds of friendship, and to abandon different kinds of work which have absorbed my time, care and attention and leave to others social and philanthropic institutions with which I have been so closely connected, while I pass on, as it were, to begin life all over again, make new friends, and find new interests. In this world of change it has come my lot to say good-bye. May the God and Father of us all give us each the strength to do our duty in that state of life to which it shall please Him to call us.[9]

This whole chain of events revealed some important aspects of William's personality. His principles and his beliefs, once formed, appeared to be unshakeable, even when adherence to them involved great personal cost. This applied equally to his social convictions and his religious commitment. Some would characterise this as commendable determination, and certainly in future years it would often prove to be an important element in the achievement of other projects close to his heart. Others, however, would see it as stubborn, even rigid, an inability to moderate his views to accommodate changing circumstances. In Sheffield he was determined to see the financial intervention of Mark Firth as a corrupting influence which would take education in a direction that he could not support. In March that year he resigned from all his various activities in the town, including his two curacies. He had, in fact, been offered the post of vicar of St Jude's Church

---

9. WME, 'Farewell Sermon in the Albert Hall, Sheffield,' BNA, *Sheffield Daily Telegraph*, 3 May 1880. (The church was currently closed for renovations.)

which had recently become vacant, an obvious promotion that would have allowed him to stay in Sheffield. His swift rejection of this offer may, in part, have related to the religious leanings of the congregation and the nature of the worship at St Jude's. The previous vicar had been much lauded in the *Church Times* during the Church Congress as the only representative of the Anglo-Catholic wing of the church currently serving in Sheffield. Equally importantly, however, William's work on the establishment of the Extension Scheme was central to his sense of educational vocation and without it he would have felt bereft of any useful purpose in the town. Later that month, therefore, he accepted the post of professor of modern history at the Newcastle College of Physical Science. This college, established ten years earlier with the financial help of the University of Durham, was currently expanding and, for the moment at least, was much in tune with William's views on working class education. Those involved in its development were keen that it should not become 'a mere mining and engineering school, enabling engineers and coal-viewers to educate their pupils with less labour and cost.' The public, they argued, were entitled to 'Science for its own sake – Science with less direct reference to considerations of pounds, shillings and pence.' Ultimately, they hoped that their teaching would expand 'to include all the higher branches of liberal education.'[10] The establishment in 1880 of a chair in modern history was clearly a move in this direction.

On 26 August at a subdued and sparsely attended little ceremony (there were several letters of apology for non-attendance) William was presented with an illuminated framed manuscript from 'the inhabitants of Sheffield' and a cheque for £100 'in appreciation of all the beneficial services rendered by you to the town.'[11] The ceremony was held, not in a municipal building, but at the residence of a friend of William where he was currently staying, for he had already given up his house in Sheffield. The little speech that accompanied the

10. 'The Newcastle-Upon-Tyne College of Physical Science,' *Nature*, 20 July 1871.
11. 'Presentation of the Town's Testimonial to the Reverend Moore-Ede,' BNA, *Sheffield Daily Telegraph*, 28 August 1880.

presentation noted that the town had made great strides in the pursuit of higher education during the previous few years owing to William's 'learned and judicious labours as one of the lecturers in connection with what is commonly termed the Cambridge University Extension movement.' It was graciously conceded that 'the scheme with which the Reverend gentleman was connected has not been a failure, although it has now ceased to exist as a University Extension movement.'[12] It was a rather lukewarm appreciation of someone who, by all accounts, had been central to the initiation and organisation of a highly successful scheme in Sheffield, introducing hundreds of working-class people to their first experience of higher education. A final comment that Sheffield now had a college of its own 'due to the great munificence of Mr Mark Firth' must have been difficult for William to hear.[13] The following day, just prior to his departure, a group of his students met with him in the Town Hall and presented him with 'a handsome marble carriage clock, a suite of matching ornaments and a number of volumes of history.' In a sad little acceptance speech, he told them that he felt there was no choice but to leave the town. He described feeling 'very great pain when he found it incumbent on him to sever the tie which bound him to Sheffield.' He had hoped, he said, 'that it would be my fate to live and work and die amongst the people of Sheffield, but it was ordered otherwise.' It was 'a great wrench' he said, when he 'found it necessary to move.'[14]

12. ibid.
13. ibid.
14. WME, 'Acceptance speech, Council Hall, Sheffield,' BNA, *Sheffield Daily Telegraph*, 27 August 1880.

Chapter Eight
RETURN TO TYNESIDE

The city of Newcastle lies on the northern bank of the River Tyne, a few miles inland from the North Sea. Here lay the bustling quaysides that played host to the keels, the boats which transported the coal on which the nineteenth-century city was based, from the riverbanks to John Masefield's 'dirty British coasters' that could be seen 'butting through the Channel in the mad March days'.[1] The keelmen and their families were a close-knit community, highly skilled, both in terms of their ability to navigate the treacherous shallow waters of the Tyne and to load their cargo on to waiting ships. They were just some of the working men who defined the atmosphere of this highly industrialised area. In 1895 the writer Robert Wood Johnson described how,

> Everywhere from the dancing waters of the harbour to the ebbing flow of the throbbing city are industry, resource and expansion, shipyards, engine shops, dry docks, chemical works, forges, electric lighting, laboratories, warehouses, merchants' offices, steamships, railway trains, without end, without number . . . there is not its like in any thirteen miles of river the world over.[2]

Newcastle was undoubtedly a hive of industry but, unlike its counterpart, Gateshead, on the opposite bank of the river, it also maintained a major commercial and financial heart and a strong

1. John Masefield, 'Cargoes' from *Ballads* (1903)
2. R. W. Johnson, *The Making of the Tyne, A Record of Fifty Years' Progress* (W. Scott, London, 1895).

artistic and scholarly heritage. This had developed in the eighteenth century with the early establishment of a Literary and Philosophical Society, public subscription concerts, theatres and architectural innovations in the development of its building and streets. The foundation of the Newcastle College of Science represented the continuation of this tradition.

In 1880 William concluded his speech to his students in Sheffield by reference to his hope that 'a useful and extensive sphere of work will be opened out to me in the more northern centre of industry, Newcastle on Tyne.'[3] As in Sheffield he also had a clerical appointment, this time as Chaplain of the Church of St Thomas the Martyr in the centre of the town. If he had to leave Sheffield he was pleased to return to Tyneside and so, perhaps, was Eleanor who had family roots there. In fact, his short period in Newcastle would be a precursor to a more permanent appointment as Rector of Gateshead less than a year later. All this, no doubt, was arranged by the Reverend J. B. Lightfoot, currently the Bishop of Durham, who had been a prominent figure in the establishment of the Extension Scheme and would have known William well.[4] Later that month William and Eleanor, who was now expecting another baby, arrived with the children in Jesmond Village on the northern outskirts of the town. Jesmond Vale House, where the family spent the next few months, was situated on the edge of a local beauty spot, Jesmond Dene. Today the site of their home is occupied by a high-rise block of flats which bears the same name as the house where William and Eleanor lived. The occupants of this twentieth century tower block live a somewhat different life to those who inhabited the detached Victorian villa it replaced, but they do enjoy the same lovely surroundings that William's family experienced in 1880. Jesmond Dene was part of the land of local industrialist William Armstrong who had commissioned the architect John Dobson to landscape the area such that it was transformed from an unkempt wilderness of tangled woodland into a fairyland of valleys, streams and waterfalls.

3. op cit., *Sheffield Daily Telegraph*, 27 August 1880.
4. Bishop of Durham, J. B. Lightfoot, in office 1879–89.

That year Armstrong opened his creation to the public on two days a week for a small fee. Later, in 1883, he gave the whole of Jesmond Dene to the Corporation of Newcastle for public recreation, much in the way that Mark Firth had donated Firth Park to the people of Sheffield. It remains today a beautiful area, situated surprisingly close to the centre of a large and busy city. William and Eleanor must have enjoyed their few short months there. Eleanor gave birth to a son, Stuart, in September 1880, shortly after their arrival.

As professor at the College of Science William immediately returned to his major passion and began to promote the Durham University Extension Scheme. Although this scheme was already in existence in fledgling form in Newcastle, Durham and Sunderland, William's arrival in the area undoubtedly gave it a new impetus and widened its appeal to include new groups of students spread across a larger geographical area. Prominent among these new recruits were the coal miners whose enthusiasm must have been a balm to William's wounded soul. Here among the scattered mining villages of Northumberland he found a great hunger for education, undaunted by the long distances people would need to travel to take part. On a Saturday in the middle of August, accompanied by a prominent supporter Lord Grey (Albert Grey MP), he convened a meeting at the school hall in the largest mining village of Seaton Delaval, the colliery where Thomas Burt had worked as a coal hewer some twenty years earlier. By early afternoon, delegates had arrived from villages all over the Northumberland mining district to hear an address by William, who was greeted with loud applause. The meeting that followed was business-like and efficient. It was agreed that courses would be run in four centres around the area, at Backworth, Choppington, Blyth and Seaton Delaval itself, that a fee should be charged ('no-one should expect to be helped who would not help himself'). This would be set at one shilling per course, rising to one shilling and sixpence after September, which would in effect amount to only one penny per lecture ('a sum no-one could complain of'). The first subject, it was universally agreed, was to be William's own of political economy. He considered this to be 'the most important to those who earned their living by their labour.' Mindful of the suspicions of industrialists, however, he added 'or who had invested capital in any industry'. The subject was, he said 'important where huge trade organisations existed on every side, and where the whole trade of a district is sometimes paralysed by the prevalence of erroneous ideas.'[5] His experiences in South Shields were still very fresh in his mind and he was keen to emphasise the advantages to all involved in the mining industry of the particular type of education proposed. Several of the coal owners had already promised to support the scheme by agreeing to cover any deficit between the cost and the revenue recovered from the students. William was willing to accept this level of support, but it was important that the employers perceived the education of miners as an advantage not a threat, and that they were fully aware that this was not technical education as proposed by the Mechanics Institutes. Political economy did not teach abject submission on the part of anyone, he said. 'The workman who understands the science of political economy is the most likely to steer the course that will be most beneficial to himself and the community.'[6]

In terms of potential students, it wasn't only the miners that interested William. That September he was asked to present the prizes to those who had completed arts and sciences courses at the local Mechanics Institute in the nearby town of Jarrow, and he used the occasion to promote the idea of introducing Extension lectures. As an enthusiastic student of history, William would have been especially drawn to Jarrow, where the monastic scholar and saint the Venerable Bede had lived during the eighth century.[7] Moreover his own family roots would have sparked a particular interest in the area, for Jarrow was a ship building town, dominated by the firm of Palmer Brothers who, by the end of the nineteenth century, employed upwards of ten thousand men and boys. The large iron and steel ships built by

---

5. WME, 'Address to the Miners, Seaton Delaval,' BNA, *Morpeth Herald*, 14 August 1880.
6. ibid.
7. Bede reputedly wrote *The Ecclesiastical History of the English People* in the monastery at Jarrow in 731.

Palmers were of course a far cry from the wooden vessels of Sutton Pool but William's fascination with ships and the sea always inspired him. Moreover, he was convinced that this large skilled workforce would be keen to avail themselves of an Extension Scheme. By the following January he had established a series of weekly evening history lectures in Jarrow on the subject of the English Civil War. Following the usual format of the Extension Scheme each lecture would last an hour, followed by a further hour of questions and discussion. The same month he introduced a similar series in Walker, an industrial village on the eastern edge of Newcastle. Walker, described by the contemporary *Gazetteer of England and Wales* as 'presenting a blackened and disagreeable appearance'[8] was a centre for alkali manufacture and the shipment of coal but was also home to the iron founding and ship building firm of Armstrong-Mitchell, a major employer.[9]

The success of the scheme in the wider Northumbrian area was immediate and impressive. By the end of January 1881, lectures were underway at thirteen centres including South Shields, Darlington, Middlesbrough, Stockton, and Hartlepool, and over four thousand students were enrolled. In Sunderland, where lectures were held in the newly opened Subscription Library, the average attendance at William's lectures was reportedly about one hundred.[10] As the scheme progressed a number of people took to the printed media to express their surprise and admiration at the attitudes and achievements of these 'working men'. Quoted in the journal *Science,* for example, one lecturer, a Mr Roberts, who took part in the scheme for two weeks in 1887 wrote:

> I wish I could adequately describe the impression this fortnight's work made upon me. The sturdy intelligence of the pitmen, their determined earnestness, the appreciative and responsive way in which they listened, the

8. J. M. Wilson, *Imperial Gazetteer of England and Wales 1870-72* (A. Fullarton & Co. London.)
9. Later the armaments firm of Armstrong-Whitworth.
10. 'The University Lectures,' BNA, *Shields Daily Gazette,* 26 January 1881.

downright straightforwardness of their speech – all these it is impossible to fully express. The northern population is eager for knowledge and travels long distances to seek it in all kinds of weather, over the roughest roads.'[11]

Many of the students took part in examinations at the end of the course which were marked independently by examiners based at Cambridge. Successful applicants were awarded certificates from the University of Cambridge (first or second class). A typical and encouraging assessment of the students' work by Mr Oscar Browning, eminent historian and fellow of King's College, Cambridge, ran as follows: 'the work at Seaton Delaval is rather rough in form but is intelligent and interesting. The pupils seem to have done something more than merely follow the lecturers and study the syllabus. There are signs of independent and individual thought and expression.' Other examiners wrote comments such as 'the weekly papers have been generally well and carefully prepared and have shewn [sic] in some cases evidence of considerable reading.' 'The work has reached a high, in some cases a very high standard' and 'several of the papers shewed [sic] that the men had been trying experiments for themselves.'[12]

Just as in Sheffield a Students Association was established, this one beginning with over one hundred members, rising to over four hundred by 1883. Its committee of 'six ladies and six gentlemen' was established to assist with the organisation and promotion of further study, supplementary lectures and excursions during the summer recess. These excursions were a huge success, their description in the local newspapers undoubtedly serving to promote University Extension to large numbers of prospective students. Moreover, they were significant fundraisers for the scheme. One such excursion took place on a sunny Sunday in July 1881 when Lord Grey, now vice president of the Association, organised a visit by train to his home Howick Hall. Here the ninety-three participants were provided with 'a bountiful lunch' and

11. 'The University Extension Movement at Cambridge.' *Science Supplement*, vol. 9., no. 207, 21 January 1887.

12. op cit., *The Peripatetic University*.

a tour of the hall and gardens. This was followed by a walk along the coast to Dunstanburgh Castle, where 'amidst the ruins Mr Creighton (the local vicar of Embleton) delivered an instructive lecture on its past history and associations.' The party then proceeded to Embleton Vicarage for tea, were entertained with an organ recital in the church and finally took part in evensong.[13] Having absorbed these details readers of the *Newcastle Courant* would then have been informed of the next planned excursion, to the Roman Wall. Other events were closer to home. In April 1886 fourteen hundred people visited the Tynemouth Aquarium (the only large building in the area) for a 'conversazione', the *de rigueur* happening for any reputable scientific association of the period. Here attendees enjoyed a series of lectures by 'scientific and literary gentlemen living in the neighbourhood.' There were sessions on 'photography familiarly explained', 'light and heat waves', 'the sun' and, from William himself, 'the mind and how to use it', all illustrated by the ubiquitous magic lantern slides, while microscopes and other scientific instruments were available for exhibition and demonstration.[14] The whole day was concluded by a concert provided by the brass band of the training ship *Wellesley* where the boys had been 'expertly tutored' by military bandsman J. H. Amers.[15]

By the mid 1880s the University Extension scheme was a thriving successful organisation with an ever-expanding reach into the corners of the North East. The editor of the *Sunderland Daily News,* in an article entitled 'Trimming of Lamps for Winter' described it as 'carrying on a winter campaign against *ennui,*' adding that 'with a dozen centres of high-class teaching in Durham and Northumberland, and lectures by gentlemen of our great universities, at one penny each, the good time has certainly come for the dark places of the population.'[16] In 1882 it had been agreed that the scheme which had hitherto been experimental and temporary should be made permanent, and more firmly linked to

---

13. 'Tyneside Students' Association,' BNA, *Newcastle Courant*, 15 July 1881.
14. 'Conversazione at Tynemouth Aquarium,' BNA, *Shields Daily Gazette*, 2 April 1886.
15. This was a boys' reform school.
16. 'Trimming of Lamps for the Winter'. BNA, *Shields Daily News*, 19 August 1880.

the University of Durham. From henceforward it would be known as the Cambridge and Durham University Extension Scheme with specific centres designated as 'affiliated' to the University of Cambridge. William, himself, had first suggested this idea in his report of 1875. It brought the scheme into more direct official connection with Cambridge and gave the courses on offer an improved academic status. Lecture series which had previously taken place over one year could now be extended over a three-year period, following the pattern of a traditional undergraduate course. Moreover, students who successfully completed these three years could now claim the title of 'Associate of the University of Cambridge'.

It remained the case that the most enthusiastic supporters of the scheme were the miners. The rapid expansion in the Northumbrian coalfields soon went well beyond the original four centres, encompassing smaller places such as Bedlington, Cramlington and Newbrough where village halls and schoolrooms were brought into play. Finance, however, was an ongoing problem which occupied much of the business of official meetings as committees debated endlessly whether trade organisations should fund the shortfall when student pennies failed to meet the expenses of Cambridge lecturers. Should donations from rich benefactors be sought, or perhaps a grant from the State? William favoured the former as long as donations were not too large and simply supplemented other funds provided by trade unions, co-operative societies and the miners themselves. For example, in 1884 Mary Gladstone (daughter of William Gladstone, the current Prime Minister) offered an annual prize of £10 to be awarded to the best student among the miners, to cover the expenses of a month spent at the University of Cambridge. In subsequent years similar prizes would be offered by other eminent individuals. However, as far as the day to day running of the scheme was concerned William considered that self-help was key. To loud applause in Seaton Delaval in 1883 he declared that those who had come forward to help the miners did so because they found the miners were willing to help themselves. It is perhaps an interesting reflection on his thinking during this period, and on the shifting nature of terms such as 'socialism' and 'liberalism', that he also added that he hoped the day would never come when the

State would supply them with higher education, because if it did so he was certain it would render that higher education a very dull and lifeless thing. For it would lose the spirit of individuality and variety it now possessed.[17] William had grown up during the rise of classical liberalism with its emphasis on individual liberties and its embrace of a fully laissez-faire approach to industry and trade. During the 1880s, however, there had been a shift towards a form of 'social liberalism', a recognition of the need for a degree of state intervention to protect the rights of the poor. It was a development that, in the early twentieth century, would lead to the birth of the welfare state under the Liberal government of Herbert Asquith. William himself, with his emphasis on individual independence and rejection of state support for higher education, seems to have experienced a degree of ambivalence as he moved through these changes. While condemning competitive individualism which he considered disadvantaged many in society, he often appears to have championed the rights of 'the individual' above those of society as a whole. For William, however, 'socialism' represented the realisation of a 'brotherhood of man', a society which worked co-operatively rather than competitively to improve the lot of the majority. As such, therefore, his position might better be described as one of 'social liberalism', rather than 'socialist'. In the years that followed he would embrace more fully the need for state intervention to address the social ills that beset Victorian and Edwardian Britain, but his earlier liberalism would always linger, tempering any tendency to embrace fully the doctrines of socialism as they developed in the twentieth century.

---

17. WME, address at the Conference to Promote University Extension in Northumberland. Seaton Delaval. BNA, *Shields Daily Gazette*, 17 September 1883.

Chapter Nine
TEACHING AND TEMPERANCE

In the summer of 1881 the current Rector of Gateshead, the Venerable Archdeacon Edward Prest, accepted the offer of a move to Ryton, a small village a few miles outside Newcastle.[1] This was almost certainly a sinecure for the Archdeacon, an elderly man in very poor health who was desperately in need of a quieter life than that on offer in a busy industrial town. It also cleared the way for Bishop J. B. Lightfoot's preference for recommending a young and enthusiastic Christian Socialist, whom he had known since the early days of the Extension Scheme, to the newly vacant position at Gateshead. William had by now spent several years as a curate in a number of industrial areas and it was clear that this was the type of environment to which he was most strongly drawn. Gateshead, situated on the south bank of the River Tyne directly opposite Newcastle, was a town with which he was already well-acquainted. These two densely populated areas have long been inextricably linked, both physically by several bridges and socially by strong cultural ties born of a shared industrial heritage which reached its zenith during the nineteenth century. Tyneside as a whole was built on the products of the nearby coalfields which both nourished the wealth of its mine owners and fuelled its major industries such as engineering, ship building and chemical production, as well as the vast numbers of smaller workshops scattered around the area. In Dunstan, the place where William's name is remembered in two of its streets, Gateshead had developed an alternative to the keelmen of

---

1. Archdeacon Edward Prest, Rector of Gateshead, in office 1861–81.

Newcastle. Here coal travelled from the mines along railway tracks that extended out into the river on specially built wooden jetties known as 'staiths', enabling the products of nearby collieries and coke works to be dropped directly into the holds of waiting ships.[2]

All this activity attracted huge numbers of workers to the area and by the census of 1901 Gateshead's recorded population, which had stood around fifteen thousand in 1831, had grown to over one hundred thousand. By the early 1880s, when William set up home in the Rectory, Gateshead had turned into the archetypal overcrowded industrial town, encapsulating all the worst features of such a place. Rising in tiers above the quayside with its slums and grimy warehouses, were seemingly endless rows of substandard terraced houses, covering what had formerly been the lush green country estates of wealthy landowners. These crowded living conditions were breeding grounds for epidemics of measles, whooping cough, scarlet fever and diphtheria which periodically visited the town. Wages were low, working hours were long and accidents were frequent. With some justification Gateshead has been described during the nineteenth century as 'a dirty lane leading to Newcastle' and a 'huge dingy dormitory', reflecting perhaps the more salubrious nature of Gateshead's wealthier neighbour across the river.[3] Meanwhile, standing in a prominent position on the banks of the Tyne overlooking this scene was Gateshead's thirteenth-century parish church of St Mary the Virgin. Until 1825, it had been the only church in the town such that it continued to be referred to as the 'mother church' by the inhabitants.

On 25 July 1881, therefore, Bishop Lightfoot officiated at William's induction as Rector of Gateshead, an appointment that would last twenty years. Inevitably William's new responsibilities as Rector meant that he could spend less time directly concerned with teaching on behalf of the University Extension Scheme, especially as he also continued with his formal teaching appointment at Newcastle College

---

2. Dunston's staiths have now acquired the status of a tourist attraction.

3. I. C. Carlton, *A Short History of Gateshead* (Gateshead Corporation, 1974). https://www.genuki.org.uk/big/eng/DUR/GatesheadHistory

of Science. However, in a sense, the scheme had progressively less need of him in the years that followed. The organising committee, on which he remained an active member, was by now well-established and there was a large group of willing and able lecturers to draw on, together with a network of centres prepared to host the various sessions. During the next twenty years, the number of centres and the variety of courses multiplied to incorporate many of the subjects where new knowledge was expanding the horizons of science and technology. Soon there were courses available on physical geography, electricity and magnetism, chemistry, astronomy and geology to complement the more traditional subjects of history, literature and William's own speciality of political economy.

William may have retreated somewhat from the day to day teaching of the Extension Scheme but it is clear that education, and particularly adult education of working people, continued to be a major focus of his life. During the 1890s, he addressed this with something akin to missionary zeal, developing a host of other activities across Tyneside. Prominent amongst these was the development of a programme of 'Sunday Afternoon Lectures for Men' which began in the summer of 1892 at St Columba's, a newly opened church in the parish. These extremely popular lectures ran successfully for nearly ten years, covering a wide range of subjects designed to widen the social, political and literary horizons of the listeners. There was, for example, 'The Armenians: their history and suffering', 'John Ruskin and the social and political brotherhood', 'The poetry of John Bunyan' and 'The life and work of William Gladstone'. Alongside these largely secular subjects there was also a programme with a clearly religious theme. This was designed to address a range of philosophical questions, as well as questions of scriptural interpretation. There was 'Reason and faith', 'Individualism and religion', 'Evolution and God', as well as 'Who wrote the Gospels?' and 'The use and abuse of dogma'. The *Newcastle Daily Chronicle* described these lectures as 'intellectual treats', noting that they were always crowded, with an audience paying very close attention to everything that was said. They 'spoke volumes for the ability of Canon

Moore-Ede and for the thirst after knowledge possessed by so large a section of the population of Gateshead.'[4] Not all of these lectures were delivered by William himself but the choice of lecturers was clearly his, carefully selected to promote his own particular views and those of like-minded colleagues. Bridging between the social and the religious, and thus linking social reform to his own Christian Socialist interpretation of the gospel, was his own special mission.

Although William would claim his teaching was educationally neutral it is easy to see why his critics thought otherwise, for there was a common theme to these lectures. Beginning with an historical overview of industrial development in Britain they usually progressed to a description of the social problems which had arisen as a result. Invariably this was followed by an insistence that he proposed to address these as 'economic' rather than 'political' questions, although he often conceded that the one must affect the other. In truth the questions may well have been economic but the answers were undoubtedly both political and radical. In the Darlington Mechanics Institute on a February evening in 1899 he concluded as follows:

> The nineteenth century has been the period of the most rapid development the world has ever known. The work of the twentieth century will be the removal of the evils which the rapid change has condoned. Our slums must be removed and the poorer quarters of our towns rebuilt. There must be an extension of control over great masses of capital. We have developed great producing power by mechanical contrivances which assisted man's labour. In this century these have been utilised in the main for enrichment of the few. In the next we have to learn how to utilise the increase of our power of production for the benefit of the whole, making the life of all fuller and richer.[5]

---

4. 'Sunday Lectures at Gateshead.' BNA, *Newcastle Daily Chronicle*, 1 March 1894. William was made an Honorary Canon of Durham Cathedral in 1894.

5. WME, 'Lecture at Darlington Mechanics Institute. The Industrial Development of the Century,' BNA, *Northern Echo*, 9 February 1899.

In his pursuit of better 'social arrangements' there were some aspects of society that were particularly close to William's heart. One such was the need for an insurance system which would protect the working man from 'the evils to which he is subject . . . and did not fail him in time of sickness and old age.'[6] His promotion of this began in January 1889 with a lecture at a well-attended meeting, chaired by his now staunch ally Thomas Burt, at the local Mechanics Institute in the colliery village of Shankhouse. William's ideas on the subject had distant echoes of his experiences in Alston, but they also drew heavily on those underpinning a system that already existed in Germany, a country that he considered to be distinctly more socially advanced than England. All working men, he argued, should be automatically enrolled into something resembling a National Friendly Society, one that was legally guaranteed by the State. For, as he pointed out, 'thousands of honest men become paupers every year because they have put their savings into unsafe clubs . . . and many others have no savings because they distrust such clubs.' In a national society every workman would be required to join the society of his trade, he must pay in between 1 per cent and 3 per cent of his wages, according to the risk or unhealthiness of his trade and his employer must pay in an equal amount. The scheme would cover sickness benefits and death benefits for survivors of workmen who died. It would, he considered, go a long way towards addressing the problem of pauperism and maintain the essential independence of the working man (always important in William's thinking). He would, after all, 'only receive what he was entitled to.'[7]

The following September William delivered a detailed exposition of his 'Proposal for a National Pension Fund' at the Annual Conference of the British Association for the Advancement of Science (Economic Science and Statistics Section) held that year in Newcastle on Tyne. And during the next few years he presented the same lecture to a

---

6. WME, lecture at Shankhouse. 'The Poor Ye Have Always'. BNA, *Shields Daily Gazette*, 28 January 1889.

7. ibid.

wide variety of enthusiastic audiences ranging from the Mutual Improvement Association in Bedlington and St Oswin's Literary Society in Tynemouth to the Co-operative Hall in Consett and the Zion schoolroom in South Shields. Venturing a little farther afield, just before Christmas in 1889, he addressed another crowded meeting at the York Railway Institute where he painted a frightening picture of what might lie ahead, even for those who, like his audience, were fortunate enough to belong to the 'wage-earning class.'[8] He informed them that,

> The multitude of the working population are living on the edge of a precipice of poverty, always in danger of being pushed over, the circumstances which might cast them into the abyss being for the most part beyond their control. About half of the population who reach the age of sixty will be driven into the degrading charity of the Poor Law.[9]

As William frequently pointed out, benefit provision for those suffering from ill-health or the effects of accidents at work had been established in Germany in 1884 and four years later had been extended to provide old age pensions for workers reaching the age of seventy.

> We allowed Germany to establish a national system of education many years before we grappled with that important question ourselves. I hope we shall not allow an equally long period to elapse before we follow in her steps in securing for our working classes a sound system of national insurance.

In this he was to be rather disappointed for the direction of politics which underpinned Bismark's welfare reforms in late nineteenth-

---

8. This was established in 1889 by Henry Tennant, general manager of York station. The building contained a reading room, library, three classrooms, a games room and a large dining room. It remains today in the original building and is the centre of a range of recreational activities.

9. WME, 'Lecture at the York Railway Institute. National Insurance.' BNA, *Hartlepool Northern Daily Mail*, 7 December 1889.

century Germany had taken hold much earlier.[10] It would be over twenty years before such a scheme was introduced in Britain.[11]

William's desire for a national system of old age provision did not imply a blanket criticism of Friendly Societies and similar organisations. On the contrary, as prominent examples of self-help they met with his general approval, provided they were well run, honest and looked after peoples' money properly. One such organisation which gained his enthusiastic support was the Independent Order of Rechabites (IOR) which also espoused another cause close to his heart, that of temperance. The distinctive feature of the IOR as a Friendly Society was its founding principle of total abstinence from alcoholic drink. The Society took its name from a biblical story recounted in the book of Jeremiah which described how the descendants of Jonadab, the Rechabites, were instructed 'you shall drink no wine, you nor your sons forever.' Another element of the story which required adherents to lead a nomadic life, 'build no houses and dwell in tents' provided the inspiration for the organisation of members into regional groups known as 'tents', each under the direction of a 'High Chief Ruler'.[12] It is not entirely clear when William first 'took the pledge'. His upbringing, surrounded by seafarers and military men, and his student days at Cambridge with its renowned cellars of fine wine, seem unlikely breeding grounds for a fierce moral disapproval of alcohol. However, his time at the Methodist stronghold of Alston, where the IOR had a major presence, would have introduced him, possibly for the first time, to the idea that strong drink was responsible for many of the ills of contemporary society and as such should be severely censored. His subsequent curacy at the sailor town of South Shields would, no

10. Chancellor Bismark in Germany is widely viewed as being responsible for the development of the first Welfare State in Europe. Although politically conservative he astutely introduced a number of social welfare measures to stave off the growing threat from socialist movements in Germany. Historians have argued that the same political processes ultimately led to the introduction of the Welfare State in Britain some years later when the Liberals confronted the growing socialist threat emanating from the Independent Labour Party established in 1893.
11. National Insurance Act 1911.
12. Jeremiah 35:6, King James Bible.

doubt, have provided some good examples of this. What is certainly clear is that by the time he moved to Sheffield he was already a devoted follower of the cause, involving himself in the establishment, as a founder member and chairman, of the pioneering temperance Sheffield Café Company, with its numerous Coffee and Cocoa Houses.

William was 'initiated' into the IOR (County of Durham tent) in 1883 and campaigned enthusiastically on their behalf. Alcohol was a huge problem in nineteenth-century Britain. It was readily and cheaply available from innumerable outlets at any hour of the day, and its inclusion in a variety of widely accepted medicaments served to increase its potential for addiction in all classes of society. Against this background the temperance movement as a whole which originated during middle of the nineteenth century was by now enjoying considerable success, particularly in strongly non-conformist areas such as Gateshead. Regular Saturday temperance processions attracted hundreds of people who marched with gaily coloured banners, singing enthusiastically, invariably to the accompaniment of the Windy Nook Temperance Brass Band. Rousing speakers to rally the crowds were a particular feature and William, with his considerable talent for public address, was much in demand at these popular events. He was also a prominent active member of the children's branch of the organisation, the Band of Hope, where children were treated to picnics, music and other entertainments of various sorts.

Even the Anglican church had its own temperance society, the Church of England Temperance Society (CETS) although its influence was somewhat diluted by the fact that it maintained two branches, one espousing total abstinence and the other a more convenient position of 'moderation' in drinking. This of course required no 'pledge' of its members who were trusted to moderate their own habits, a proposition infinitely more attractive to many members of the Church of England.

The CETS campaigned largely for the restriction of the opening hours of Public Houses and in particular for a ban on Sunday opening. William, however, seems to have gone one step further, making it his special mission to campaign against the opening of any new public houses. Invariably he would turn up at the regular Brewster Sessions of the Magistrates Courts either to argue the case against the proposed licensing of new premises or the case for the closure of existing ones. In both cases the argument was the same, that the premises in question were superfluous to the needs of the district. On many occasions he was successful, although sometimes he was out manoeuvred by aspiring landlords. In 1903, for example, he attempted to reduce the number of drinking establishments in Cleadon, a village which fell within his parish. Cleadon contained two large public houses, the Britannia and the Ship Inn, but there was also the popular Cottage Tavern, a tiny and somewhat decrepit 'beerhouse', a relic of earlier, rather more relaxed times. The authorities were quite keen to gradually remove these somewhat insanitary establishments and the owner, a Mr Ernest Vaux, who was probably aware that his legal days were numbered, applied to develop his tavern into a much larger modern establishment. On 10 March at the Brewster Sessions for South Shields he submitted his plans for approval. William arrived to argue that there were only seventy residences in Cleadon in what might be termed 'drinking distance' of public houses and two were quite enough. After much argument the magistrates granted Mr Vaux, a stay of execution in the form of a provisional licence for a year to complete his development, after which time he must close his existing 'beerhouse'. The magistrates presumably expected that Mr Vaux's ambitious plans for the Cottage Tavern would never come to fruition, and William no doubt thought the same. In this, however, they were sadly mistaken, as a photograph of the much improved and rather attractive tavern, taken a few years later, confirms.

The Cottage Tavern, Cleadon, early 1900s. (Courtesy of South Tyneside Libraries.)

Chapter Ten
STORMY EDUCATIONAL WATERS

It might be supposed that William's most sceptical and critical audiences were those he encountered at the Newcastle Literary and Philosophical Society where members were more likely to belong to the business and professional classes of the area. Socialism, as currently defined, seemed unlikely to find favour in this section of society. Even here, however, he found growing support for his views with earlier fears of a 'radical dodge' now largely confined to its older members. This was amply demonstrated when, in the autumn of 1895, he and a group of like-minded enthusiasts decided to set up an Economics Society in Newcastle 'for the purpose of the study and discussion of economic questions.' Basing itself at the headquarters of the Lit and Phil. where it was formally approved as a sub section of the society, a programme of lectures was arranged covering controversial topics such as 'foreign trade', 'bimettalism',[1] 'land prices', 'municipal finance' and 'the sources and distribution of national income'. William, as its first president, gave the inaugural address on the evening of the 2 October that year. Entitled 'The Economic Aspects of Merrie England', it painted a less than 'merrie' picture of the state of the nation.[2] Perhaps unsurprisingly it attracted a blizzard of criticism in local newspapers, much of it quite personal. He does not tackle *Das Kapital* opined one correspondent but prefers to demolish 'Merrie England'. 'Anyone who knows anything about socialism is not deceived, and knows he

---

1. The proposal that gold as the basis of legal tender should be replaced by a dual standard of gold and silver.
2. 'Canon Moore-Ede on Socialism,' BNA, *Newcastle Courant*, 5 October 1895.

is not taken seriously even by his own friends.'[3] Another wrote that the Canon had made 'a bumptious parade of his ignorance.' He was 'feeble and foolish . . . why did God make so many stupid people?'[4] William, it seems, had hit a sensitive nerve, something that was not lost on the editor of the *Newcastle Daily Chronicle* who wrote an altogether more thoughtful piece on William's inaugural address and noted that 'the advent of the young association may be accepted as evidence that a number of thinking persons, struck by the progress which the novel gospel is making, have become convinced of the necessity of examining its tenets.'[5] The *Northern Echo* was similarly supportive, describing William as someone

> who once more has with all his heart and soul managed to put into words, the vague unrest, the restless desires and the aspirations which move, and always will move, the poorer classes of nations so long as the distribution of the good things of the earth is not in accordance with some scale of approximate equality.[6]

The society's first series of lectures came to an end in the middle of April 1896, at which point a meeting was held to review the situation. The society, it was reported, now had seventy-eight members and an impressive committee composed of two knights of the realm, a local JP and various other local professional men. Three lectures had been delivered and five papers read, each of which was followed by a discussion session. So 'animated and interesting' had been these discussions that 'three were not concluded by closing time and further meetings had to be arranged for their continuance.' All agreed that the papers had been of a very high standard and one had even included 'statistical data that promised to be of national importance.'[7] It was all very encouraging.

3. Letter from Mr M. Maltman Barry. BNA, *Newcastle Daily Chronicle*, 9 October 1895.
4. A Correspondent. BNA, *Newcastle Daily Chronicle*, 16 October 1895.
5. 'The Dismal Science'. BNA, *Newcastle Daily Chronicle*, 3 October 1895.
6. 'Moore-Ede on Numquam.' BNA, *Northern Echo*, 4 October 1895.
7. 'Local News.' BNA, *Newcastle Chronicle*, 18 April 1896.

A month later, however, came a significant backlash in the form of the formidable figure of Lord Armstrong, major industrialist, employer and benefactor of the city, whose influential tentacles extended across much of Tyneside. He was also the president of the Lit and Phil. Lord Armstrong issued a statement that he considered the subjects discussed at the Economics Society were 'political' and that this contravened the rules under which the Lit and Phil operated. Unless the Lit and Phil ended its association with the new society he proposed to resign his presidency.

Interestingly, in the course of this dispute, it emerged that Lord Armstrong's major objection was specifically to the lectures of the Reverend Moore-Ede. One subject in particular that had provoked his disapproval was that of the 'unearned increment'.[8] This was an area of current political concern and a subject that William had lectured on many times before to different audiences, describing how, throughout the agricultural history of England, there had been a progressive transfer of land ownership into the hands of a relatively small number of individuals or institutions. Invoking the concept of the 'unearned increment', derived from the writings of the political economist John Stuart Mill, William maintained such landowners were in fact the sole beneficiaries of any increase in the value of the land, robbing the people of any benefits, despite the fact that, in agricultural settings, this increase was due not to the landowner but to the labour of the people themselves. It was, Mill argued, the community not the individual who should reap the benefits. In towns and cities, meanwhile, 'unearned increments' might accrue when increases in value occurred due to the discovery of mineral deposits or other assets, or to population growth and the ensuing demand for housing. Near his own house, he noted, the value of land had increased from £30 per acre to £1,000 per acre over the previous forty years. If land was in the hands of local corporations rather than individual landowners, or if limits were placed on the profits of such 'unearned

---

8. 'Lord Armstrong's Presidency,' BNA, *Newcastle Chronicle*, 11 July 1896.

increments', these could be used for the benefit of the community as a whole, rather than contributing to the individual wealth of a few. With an observation that has a certain resonance for twenty-first-century social commentators he also added that

> speculative builders who kept land idle until its price should be raised far above what they gave for it – and under existing laws they are perfectly justified in doing so – would cease their operations; the gain which they were looking forward to would pass to the community.

Lord Armstrong's ultimatum was a major threat to the Economic Society, but on this occasion, it seems, he had misjudged the extent of his power and influence. At a hastily convened emergency meeting of the Lit and Phil it was agreed (by 112 votes to 64) that the Economics Society should continue as a sub section of the society – and that Lord Armstrong should be asked to reconsider his decision to resign, something which he resolutely refused to do. Having survived these early stormy waters, therefore, the Society proceeded successfully on its way. William stepped down as president after twelve months but remained an active and enthusiastic participant, occupying a joint position as one of a group of vice presidents. Lord Armstrong meanwhile could have been forgiven for pointing out that his fears had been entirely justified. In October 1898, for example, the sessions included 'The New Economic Movement in Ireland' by Horace Plunkett MP, supporter of Home Rule for Ireland and founder of the agricultural co-operative movement in that troubled isle. This was followed by a series of radical writers and speakers on subjects such as 'Karl Marx: a criticism and an explanation'; 'Socialism analysed and an alternative social theory proposed'; and 'Methods for the prevention of industrial war'. The final session that year was a lecture by William himself on one of his favourite subjects 'Old Age Pensions'.

Given his passion for mass education it was perhaps predictable that William would put his name forward for membership of the Gateshead School Board. The Education Act of 1870 had required the creation of local authority school boards, funded by a combination of local rates and government grants, to oversee the development of free and compulsory education for children between the ages of five and thirteen.[9] Prior to this the provision of primary education had been very patchy, with most schools either privately run or provided by religious organisations and rather sparsely funded. Gateshead was fairly typical in this respect, with a total of twenty-six private schools, two Church of England (National) schools, two Roman Catholic schools and one Wesleyan school. Together these catered for just over four thousand of the town's school age children, which in the early 1870s numbered around ten thousand. Gateshead was also typical in another way, for its population of industrial workers was predominantly non-conformist, rendering Anglican and Roman Catholic schools unattractive to many parents. After 1870, however, the local school boards were empowered to build additional schools, known as 'Board Schools'. which, in order to satisfy the demands of non-conformist and non-religious parents, were deemed 'non-denominational'. In these schools there was only a minimum of basic religious teaching and an option for parents to withdraw their children from this if they so wished. The Anglican and Roman Catholic churches were never really reconciled to this situation which, they felt, reduced their funding and essentially undermined their already tenuous hold on the religious allegiance of the population. In the years that followed, school boards across the country were engaged to differing degrees in religious battles as Anglican, non-conformist and Roman Catholic representatives (as well as the 'independent' non-religious) struggled to assert their claims on educational funding and provision. It was a controversial time in the history of primary education with religious matters at the centre of almost every argument.

Elections for the board, which in Gateshead consisted of eleven

---

9. From 1870 local authorities were empowered but not required to provide free education. Some charged a small fee until 1891 when they were legally required to abolish any fees. In 1881 education between the ages of five and ten years was compulsory. By 1900 the school leaving age was fourteen.

members, were held every three years. William seems to have been co-opted as a member immediately on becoming Rector in 1881, presumably since his predecessor Archdeacon Prest had been the board's chairman for many years. This, however, was not a helpful start. The delicate balance in the membership, first between representatives of the various religious (and non-religious) groups, and second between those dubbed 'educationalists', who claimed to prioritise educational aspirations, and economists who, it was argued, focussed largely on saving money for the ratepayers, was maintained with great difficulty. In particular the minority of Roman Catholic members, who at every election struggled to maintain their representation on the board,[10] resented the longstanding Anglican chairmanship, first of Archdeacon Prest and subsequently of Anglican clerics George France and then Henry Riley, who between them presided from 1881 to 1894. Roman Catholic resentment simmered constantly, on occasions breaking out into heated and abusive arguments. One such occurred in May 1883 when Father Patrick Matthews gave vent to longstanding Roman Catholic concerns accusing the 'Church Party' (i.e. the Anglicans) of acting illegally and dishonestly in interpreting the terms of the Act. For the last ten years, he said, they had striven to make Board Schools 'church schools' and 'to teach the catechism and formularies of the Church of England,' remarks described by another member as 'savouring of malice and ill-feeling.' The escalating row with accusations of 'blackguardly conduct' and 'unmanly and un-English language' culminated with a Roman Catholic member, Charles Redmond, accusing the Anglican vice chairman Henry Riley of being 'a liar who deserved to be kicked downstairs.'[11] At the heart of these 'lively discussions' as the local press described them, lay the unresolved and deeply felt issue of religious freedom. This was particularly true of Roman Catholics, who had long been engaged in a battle with the Church of England over the preservation of their rights, and in particular their right to educate

---

10. Since Roman Catholics tended to live in the poorer parts of the town fewer of their supporters were ratepayers and thus entitled to vote in elections.

11. 'Gateshead School Board. Unfounded Charge'. BNA, *Newcastle Courant*, 11 May 1883.

children in the way they saw fit. In Gateshead, unlike many other places, non-conformists seemed to be broadly content with what Anglicans proposed as a reasonable educational compromise, i.e. the daily singing of one hymn and no more than forty-five minutes of 'Bible Study'. Their criticisms were confined to occasional objections about the choice of hymn or of a Bible passage. For Roman Catholics, however, what was proposed was nothing short of a travesty of proper religious instruction. The perceived failure of the board to allocate adequate funding for the development of specifically Roman Catholic schools, left their children bereft of what they considered to be an appropriate education.

William, himself, acquired an increasing share of the vote in successive board elections as he gained a reputation as a dedicated supporter of mass, non-sectarian education, although in this he attracted some criticism from members of his own church who considered that he gave too much ground to non-conformists. However, he seems to have gained the support of most board members who elected him as vice chairman in 1891 and as chairman in January 1894. Both these appointments, however, were vigorously but unsuccessfully opposed by the Roman Catholic contingent who continued to feel that board decisions were made largely in the interests of the 'Church party'. It was obviously not an easy role, negotiating the funding arrangements for new schools, organising their construction and development, appointing staff, overseeing the curriculum and monitoring pupil performance, all in an atmosphere of religious controversy which constantly threatened to destabilise the whole decision-making processes. This was by no means a problem unique to Gateshead. In other parts of the country some boards even found themselves completely dismantled following the mass resignation of their members. The fact that Gateshead managed to avoid this and achieved so much in the thirty-one years of its existence is due in no small measure to the skilful leadership of its various chairmen, including William who served from 1894 until the board's abolition under the new Education Act of 1902.

Throughout his period as chairman, however, William was determined that the development of educational provision in Gateshead should 'proceed without recourse to religious feuding.' In November 1894 as the election of board members approached he wrote a strong letter to the editor of the *Newcastle Evening Chronicle* urging people to understand that there was 'no such thing as the Church party or anti-Church party on the Board.' There was, he said, 'an attempt being made to revive the evil sectarian spirit which, if successful, must be detrimental to the interests of education.'[12] The editor of the *Newcastle Courant* meanwhile had already noted that 'it goes without saying that the reverend gentleman holds rather advanced views not usually held among parsons of the Established Church persuasion . . . one might well call him A Radical Parson.'[13] By 1902, however, when the new Education Act disbanded the local school boards, educational provision in Gateshead had increased substantially. There were now twenty-four elementary schools, serving an increased population of nearly ninety thousand and providing school places for all of its twenty-five thousand children. Of these eighteen were new non-denominational Board Schools. The two Church of England schools and the Wesleyan Methodist school remained, and the Roman Catholic provision had in fact increased from two to three schools. This last addition rather gave the lie to the continuous accusations of neglect from Roman Catholic board members, as well flying in the face of vehement opposition from Anglican ratepayers, the majority of whom wanted no Roman Catholic schools at all.[14] Added to this there was an 'industrial school', a reform establishment which catered for children whose 'moral welfare was considered to be at risk', most of whom had been removed by magistrates from parents who had been convicted of

---

12. WME, letter. BNA, *Newcastle Evening Chronicle*, 17 November 1894.
13. 'Local and District Notes.' BNA, *Newcastle Courant*, 4 March 1893.
14. However, there was a prolonged dispute about the inclusion of the new Roman Catholic school in the government grant scheme. This was eventually resolved in the Catholics' favour.

crimes.[15] Two 'higher grade' schools were also constructed which offered three years of more advanced free education for abler girls and boys, as demonstrated by examination. These schools gradually increased the range of subjects on offer, particularly following the Technical Education Act of 1889 which provided that higher grade schools could apply for local authority grants to fund courses in subjects such as modern languages, shorthand and typing and various technical subjects. Finally, there was a hugely popular 'evening school' which, for a very modest fee of 1½ pence, offered basic education classes for young men and boys above the age of fourteen who were in employment and who, for one reason or another, had left school deficient in basic skills. Over the years this developed into what was known as the 'continuation school' offering to both men and women a wider range of subjects, including those that might be classed as 'recreational'. Certainly, by the standards of the time, this was an impressive package of educational opportunity for the children and young adults of a poor, industrial nineteenth-century town.

---

15. This was the Abbot Memorial School originally founded in 1867 by Mrs Catherine Abbot, in memory of her husband, as a 'ragged school' for poor children. Later it also began to function as a 'reform school' taking in children whose parents had been imprisoned or children who had themselves been convicted of a crime.

Chapter Eleven
THE GOSPEL OF PENNY PIES

The last years of the nineteenth century were not prosperous times for the British Isles. Intermittent downturns in trade hit areas of heavy industry such as Tyneside particularly hard and the area suffered frequent periods of high unemployment. By 1885 it was estimated that around thirty thousand men were out of work in the wider Tyneside area, of which two thousand were in Gateshead. Appointed as Rector in 1881 William soon found himself at the centre of efforts to provide food and shelter for the increasing numbers of destitute unemployed men and their families. It was clear from the beginning that he was expected to be a member of the Board of Guardians which administered both the Gateshead Workhouse and the administration of 'outdoor relief' for others requiring help. The reason for this appointment was rooted in history, a system still honoured in the observance but in practice a source of considerable tension. For centuries the town had been governed by a 'Select Vestry of 24' which included the Rector of St Mary's, four churchwardens and a number of leading citizens. These self-co-opted men proceeded to appoint various local officers including the overseers of poor relief. By the middle of the nineteenth century this form of government had been abandoned in favour of elected Mayors and town councils but in Gateshead it seemed that elements of the Vestry were still very much alive.[1] The Rector's automatic presence on the board and, more particularly, the role of the churchwardens in administering the collection of rates were clearly sources of considerable

---

1. 'The Powers of the Select Vestry,' BNA, *Newcastle Evening Chronicle*, 29 April 1889.

resentment, just one of the tensions that beset this somewhat tetchy and argumentative committee. There were acrimonious demarcation disputes between the churchwardens and the 'overseers', the men who were officially employed to run the workhouse and the system of rate collection. There were furious arguments about whether Anglican lady visitors were 'troubling the consciences of Roman Catholic inmates' by preaching the doctrines of the Church of England and angry exchanges about whether residents in the workhouse should be allowed their customary allowance of beer on Christmas day, especially since, as was popularly imagined, that was the reason most of them were there in the first place. In April 1889 William diplomatically suggested that there should be an historical enquiry into the current legitimacy of the Vestry, the results of which confirmed that the rights conferred on Vestry members were in fact no longer legitimate. He was happy to accept this and duly submitted himself at the next election for formal (legitimate) membership of the board. In the election of 1890 he was duly elected, gaining a huge share of the vote.

William's growing popularity in the town, it seems, rested on his practical actions, particularly in relation to the social distress now so prevalent in Gateshead. An early example of this concerned the so-called Test workers who were offered 'outdoor relief 'in the form of food, clothes and a miserable wage in exchange for manual labour.[2] The work, which very often consisted of stone breaking in the workhouse yard, was hard and soul-destroying, intentionally designed to be a deterrent to any but those in the greatest need. Many of these labourers were young skilled workers with families to support who had been laid off as a result of the economic depression. They were angry and restless, seething at the humiliation of their position and complaining frequently and bitterly about their working conditions which, they considered, amounted to slave labour. William was inclined to agree with them and was deeply sympathetic to their plight. In February 1886 he met with the equally sympathetic Mayor of Gateshead, John

---

2. The Outdoor Labour Test Order had been issued in 1842.

Lucas, to discuss the grievances of the men which currently centred on the fact that they were paid less than similar workers in neighbouring Newcastle and were provided with 1*d* per day less for the upkeep of their children.[3] In addition, they were prevented from taking a day off from the stone yard (on pain of dismissal) if they had managed to obtain a day's work elsewhere. The following evening William addressed a mass meeting of the men gathered at a popular assembly point, Windmill Hills, on the outskirts of the town. It was an unusual course of action by a clergyman and what he said was even more unexpected. He agreed, he said, that the rules by which the Board of Guardians operated were ambiguous and unclear and he promised to make representations to the board on their behalf. Later that week the Guardians agreed to the men's demands and increased their pay such that they now, at least, had parity with those in Newcastle.

In December 1884 William had also persuaded a local industrialist to give the Test workers free tickets which they could exchange for coal, for these families were cold as well as hungry. The same month he was formally thanked by the Board of Guardians for 'finding free dinners for the men', who currently numbered about ninety.[4] This particular achievement, however, was not a single act of charity but part of a much larger scheme, which would turn out to be William's major legacy both within and beyond Tyneside. This was his scheme of Penny Dinners. In April 1884, in the midst of one of the periodic depressions that beset the North East, he read an article in the *Pall Mall Gazette* by a Swedish man going by the name L. O. Smith. Mr Smith (whose real name was Lars Olsen Persson) was a wealthy Swedish entrepreneur. Popularly known as 'The Brandy King of Sweden' his business empire was built on the vodka and brandy trade and he was perhaps an unlikely source of inspiration for a devotee of the temperance movement. In later years, however, Mr Smith had turned

---

3. John Lucas, best known for his support of the development of Saltwell Park (The People's Park) was a brickmaker by trade and had great sympathy with the plight of skilled men out of work.

4. 'Gateshead Board of Guardians,' BNA, *Newcastle Journal*, 17 December 1884.

his attention to social improvements including the diet of the poor. His article entitled *My Social Revolution*, emphasised the importance of the provision of food at affordable prices as the first essential step towards any form of social reform.[5] Smith's emphasis was not just on food but on nutritional food. He based his ideas on 'Koenig's Tables' which detailed the constituents of different types and amounts of food required for different groups in the population (older and younger, men and women, manual and non-manual workers, warm and cold climates).[6] So inspired by this article was William that he took a trip to Stockholm to talk to the man himself, returning with a definite plan to implement Smith's ideas in conjunction with those of a certain Dr Thomas Nichols, who promulgated the virtues of the vegetarian diet as a means of providing cheap food and also 'enhancing the moral and physical progress of the population.'[7] William retained an interest in vegetarianism all his life, often attending and even presiding over meetings of the Vegetarian Society, although he never seems to have fully accepted its doctrines in the way, for example, he endorsed and promoted his other major passion, that of temperance. However, Penny Dinners, if not entirely vegetarian, would certainly include plenty of fruit and vegetables.

In 1884 William's primary concern was to provide food at affordable prices for the large numbers of children who were arriving at school hungry each morning. To this end he worked out, in exhaustive detail, varied menus of nutritional and seemingly appetising dinners to be provided each weekday at school to every child of 'widows or those whose parents were out of work or on short time.'[8] A typical example served on one day for instance was pea soup, meat roly-poly pudding,

5. L. O. Smith, 'My Social Revolution by the Ex-Brandy King of Sweden', *Pall Mall Gazette*, 3 April 1884.

6. Karl Koenig was a pioneering Austrian nutritionist based at the University of Vienna.

7. Dr Nichols, *Penny Vegetarian Cookery. The Science and the Art of Selecting and Preparing a Pure, Healthful, and Sufficient Diet* (Franks & Co, London, 1888).

Dr Nichols and his wife, Mary Gove Nichols, opened the first vegetarian restaurant in London, the Alpha in 1879.

8. W. Moore-Ede *Cheap Food and Cheap Cooking to Which is Added Hints for the Management of Penny Dinners for School Children* (Walter Scott, Newcastle Upon Tyne, 1884).

carrots, onions and potatoes, rhubarb pudding and custard. Each child was encouraged to bring 5d each Monday morning to cover the cost of one week's meals.[9] William, with his strong belief in the inherent dignity and self-respect of the poor was always unwilling, in principle, to distribute anything that might be construed as 'charity', but even he, in these circumstances, was prepared to recognise that many children would not be able to bring the whole week's amount on one day, or in some cases on any day. It is a sobering window on the depths of extreme poverty which prevailed at the time. Teachers, who recorded weekly payments, were encouraged to waive the fee in cases where they knew the family was completely destitute. The economics of the whole enterprise were calculated with great care, from the price of each item of food and the cost of crockery and cutlery to the renumeration for the school caretakers who were required to do the cooking. Central to the whole enterprise was a cooking device based on the idea of a simple steam boiler, known as a Warren Pot. The pot was a simple iron box, lined with felt and heated by two powerful burners. Various types of food were placed at different levels in an inner chamber while water was poured into the outer chamber and maintained at a high temperature. In this way the food was steamed, retaining its taste and nutrients. As William was keen to emphasise, 'it could be placed in any room without requiring any arrangements of flues . . . there is no smell of working or heat within a yard of the operation.'[10] He had already persuaded a firm of ironmongers to produce these boilers at the very reasonable cost of £5–£8 each depending on the size required. Messrs Walker & Elmley of Newcastle had hitherto specialised in the design and construction of ornamental fountains and in the midst of a depression were no doubt finding a somewhat limited market for their usual wares.

The Penny Dinners scheme was first rolled out in the autumn of 1884 at St Mary's National School situated in Barn Close, one of

9. 1d = 1 penny in pre-decimal coinage. This was worth much less than today's decimal one pence. i.e. £1 is equal to 100 decimal pence but 240 pre-decimal pennies.

10. op cit., *Cheap Food and Cheap Cooking*.

the poorest parts of Gateshead. Here nearly one hundred children were soon being provided with dinners on a weekly basis. This was soon expanded to include all the elementary schools in Gateshead, in what became a large and highly organised operation. By December 1884 an average of 1,200 dinners were being provided each weekday in Gateshead. William's prediction that the dinners could be run without financial deficit appeared, surprisingly to some, to be correct.

A Warren Cooking Pot.
(Courtesy of www.chestofbooks.com)

However, there were undoubtedly a considerable number of charitable donations forthcoming, both in money and in kind, which cushioned the scheme from any sort of financial collapse. Residents with garden produce, for example, were encouraged to bring this to the centres (rhubarb seems to have been a particular favourite, with plums not far behind) and the whole effort, focussing as it did on vulnerable children, was a great success. An initial audit of the situation showed that, even without donations, when 150 dinners were provided the scheme just broke even, and when 300 were provided there was a small financial surplus. A year later, when the scheme had been expanded to the whole of Gateshead, William attended an Education Conference in Manchester and presented detailed figures which 'showed conclusively that good substantial meals can be provided at a cost not exceeding 1d per child.' This was, he added 'if the management was in the hands of zealous and capable ladies.'[11]

It was not long before other areas became interested in the scheme not only in and around Tyneside but farther afield. Sunderland School Board was the first to adopt it, during the winter of 1884–85, giving

---

11. 'The Rector of Gateshead on Feeding School Children,' BNA, *Shields Daily Gazette*, 16 April 1885.

THE "PENNY DINNER COOKER"

IS MANUFACTURED BY

WALKER & EMLEY,

Heating, Ventilating, and Sanitary Engineers,

GALLOWGATE, NEWCASTLE-ON-TYNE.

CIRCULAR PATTERN, WITH FLETCHER'S RADIAL BURNERS,

COMPLETE, READY FOR FIXING.

								£	s	d
A size with inner pan to contain	15 gallons	...	...	...	...	5	0	0
B ,,	,,	,,	20	,,	...	...	...	5	10	0
C ,,	,,	,,	25	,,	...	...	...	6	0	0
D ,,	,,	,,	30	,,	...	...	...	6	10	0
E ,,	,,	,,	35	,,	...	...	...	6	17	6
F ,,	,,	,,	40	,,	...	...	...	7	5	0
G ,,	,,	,,	45	,,	...	...	...	7	12	6
H ,,	,,	,,	50	,,	...	...	...	8	0	0

Each 5 gallons will be found sufficient for about 40 children.

Advert for Penny Dinner Cooker, in *Self-Supporting Penny Dinners for School Children*. (Courtesy of the Wellcome Library.)

out an average of 450 dinners each day, followed by Newcastle, North and South Shields, Wallsend, Monkwearmouth and Alnwick who reported comparable numbers. Liverpool and Sheffield introduced similar schemes and in Birmingham Mr George Herbert Sargent went one better and provided children with thick nourishing soup and bread (cooked in a Warren Pot) for one farthing (a quarter of 1*d*). William must have been particularly moved to hear about the introduction of the scheme near the place of his birth, Deptford, East London. Here an empty school building near Laing's shipbuilding yard had been taken over (by Mrs Laing and a team of helpers) and during the eight

Self-Supporting Penny Dinners for School Children, published by the Central Council for Supporting Penny Dinners in 1886. (Courtesy of the Wellcome Library.)

weeks up to the beginning of December 1884, 2909 children had been provided with a meal each day with an extra 701 on Sundays. Clearly the poverty of his youth in this place had not significantly abated.

Meanwhile, back in Gateshead William had begun to expand his operations to include cheap food for adults in the form of what became known as the Nelson Street Restaurant. This was a profit-making concern run by the Gateshead Public Dinner Company with William as its chairman and, like the Penny Dinners scheme, it relied on cooking in bulk to keep its costs down. It was also largely vegetarian. During 1886 William let it be known that the company was ready to establish other similar restaurants in any place where five hundred shares at one shilling each could be taken up locally. As a result, similar 'peoples' kitchens' were established across Newcastle, North and South Shields and Sunderland. Some were classical soup kitchens offering nourishing broth and bread, others provided full meals. These kitchens were a curious hybrid, in once sense a charity providing cheap food for the poor, but in another a profit-making concern which paid a dividend to its shareholders. Any remaining profits, however, were donated to the more general relief fund of the area.

Throughout the 1880s and 1890s the peoples' kitchens were a constant welcome presence across Tyneside, providing sustenance to hundreds of people especially during the winter months when the frost and snows of the North East exacerbated the gnawing pangs of hunger amongst the poor. And there can be no doubt that many a child was saved from starvation by the safety net of the Penny Dinners. In the freezing January of 1893 as the biting north-east winds battered the area the Gateshead School Board recorded that they had supplied almost four thousand dinners to children the previous week and needed to increase this to cover an ever- growing need. For the first time the coffers were getting low. The board agreed an increase to 4225 for the ensuing week but also decided to launch an appeal for donations from the public to make up a threatened shortfall in funds. Inevitably, even in this situation, there was some periodic grumbling from the more comfortable about 'the undeserving poor'. Surely, it was argued, there were people receiving help who did not need it, or would not take steps to help themselves? As William recounted in an address at the Wesleyan Chapel in the colliery village of Brunswick, there was much talk in some circles of the danger of 'weakening character rather than strengthening it.' And there were plenty in the Anglican church who were ready to disparage this 'gospel of penny pies' as one church dignitary put it.[12] Set against this, however, were the hundreds of pounds of donations and the numbers of volunteers, many of them local clergy, together with armies of 'local ladies' who quietly and efficiently administered the scheme on the ground. In North Shields the 'indefatigable Reverend Charles Woosman', chaplain at the Seaman's Mission, handed out over one hundred dinners every day at St Peter's Church, while in January 1891 the *Newcastle Daily Chronicle*

---

12. Recounted by WME at an address at the Brunswick Wesleyan Chapel, Newcastle, on the occasion of the inauguration of the Wesleyan Union for Social Service. BNA, *Hartlepool Northern Daily Mail*, 13 September 1906.

described a typical scene where the Reverend Charles Seymour and Mr Robert Aitken and his wife doled out broth at St Jude's mission room in Stoddart Street, Newcastle. The recipients were:

> hundreds of poverty-stricken children, women and aged persons who stream out of their poor dwellings to stand in the kitchen with their pots and pans and wait their turn to gratefully partake of a wholesome meal of bread and soup, cooked in Messrs Elmleys cookers and supplied for one penny.[13]

To those inclined to be critical William offered a swift rejoinder. 'Those who say this is none of a clergyman's business I would say this. Christ cares for our bodies as well as our souls. We set forth a religion that embraces every area of human activity – all that is good is God's.'[14] William was ever ready to recognise that there would always be people who would take advantage of this sympathetic giving. He said so frequently in various sermons, something that was picked up vociferously by those inclined to write outraged letters to the local newspapers. Less well reported, however, was what he invariably said next '. . . and where the children are concerned there need be no fear of helping the undeserving, for whatever may be the motives of some parents the children cannot be responsible.'[15]

The need to address an immediate problem whilst knowing that to do so through charitable means might simply serve to perpetuate the unjust society, of which such distress was a symptom, was a dilemma familiar to William. In 1887 he preached a sermon at St Mary's on the occasion of Mayoral Sunday when the members of the council, largely successful local businessmen and manufacturers, gathered for their annual service. This congregation was essentially the power base of nineteenth-century Gateshead. Noting that the previous Sunday

---

13. 'St Jude's Soup Kitchen'. BNA, *Newcastle Daily Chronicle*, 17 January 1891.
14. WME, 'Cheap Food and Cheap Cooking'. Lecture delivered at Victoria Hall, Sunderland. *Sunderland Daily Echo and Shipping Gazette*, 9 October 1884.
15. ibid.

the church had been filled with 'a large number of unemployed,' he went on as follows:

> I cannot content myself with a statement of Christian principles and not endeavour to indicate certain lines of practical application in relation to present questions... men may talk of the love of God, but if they don't show practical sympathy with the sorrowing and sufferings of their neighbours they are, notwithstanding the orthodoxy of their language, atheists. We cannot look at modern society with some so rich and some so poor without being painfully conscious that we do not see around us a realisation of Christ's ideal of universal brotherhood. When we see the uncertain employment and miserable pay of some men, and more women, and the consequent moral and physical degradation of their lives, we can scarcely salve our conscience by pleading the operation of economic laws, for these laws are but the expressions for the tendencies of the actions of men, and men are masters of their own actions, and can alter them.[16]

In his address at the Brunswick chapel in 1906 he expressed similar views when he considered 'the causes of the Church turning to social questions.'

> ... it is the failure of the gospel of individualism, the increasing complexity of society causing the individual to become less and less an independent unit. It was not just for the few to be rich beyond the dreams of avarice, and millions to be hardly able to keep body and soul together. The Churches must proclaim the Christian ideal of society and uphold the idea of universal brotherhood; they must draw attention to the slums, worry the conscience of the community.[17]

'Brotherhood' was something he would return to again and again as he involved himself in other fields of work such as industrial conciliation, and much later when, following the horrors of the Great

---

16. 'The Rector on the Unemployed,' BNA, *Newcastle Daily Chronicle*, 14 November 1887.
17. op cit., WME, address at Brunswick Wesleyan Chapel.

War, he became an ardent supporter of the Peace Movement. For William 'brotherhood' was not a specifically male concept but defined in terms of its wider meaning of 'fraternity' a loyal friendship between people working co-operatively together for a common purpose. To him it represented the very opposite of a society where people worked individually and competitively to further their own interests.

There is a strong memory of William among the people of Tyneside. However, his wider and longer-term legacy may not have been fully appreciated. In May 1906 he was invited to give evidence to a House of Commons Committee in the process of considering the Education (Provision of Meals) Bill, a proposal to introduce school dinners for all children and free school meals for those in need. This was a Liberal reforming government, mindful of what had come to light in recent years about the poor state of the nation's health and physique. During recruitment for the Boer War the lack of nourishment of large numbers of children over previous years had produced a population of puny, unhealthy individuals, largely considered unfit for military service. By now the scheme William had introduced in Gateshead had been running successfully for many years and had been replicated by numerous voluntary bodies across Tyneside and in many other areas of the country. Having acquainted the committee with the practicalities and the economics of the scheme he was asked particularly about the means by which the children were selected to receive meals and, of course, about the problem of overuse of the scheme by those who might not need it. He considered, he said, that this was a very real difficulty which could only be overcome if the scheme were administered, not by willing volunteers as now, but by local authorities with the power and facilities to administer a system of selection of those in need, and a system of payment by those who could afford it.[18] In December that year the Education (Provision of Meals) Act was passed authorising (although not requiring) the provision of cheap, nutritionally balanced school dinners by local authorities, including free school meals for

---

18. 'Free Meals for School Children,' BNA, *Newcastle Evening Chronicle*, 11 May 1906.

those that could not afford to pay. The system introduced by the Act of 1906 was essentially that of state funded Penny Dinners. Today the basic principle of the scheme, as originally designed and instituted by William, is still in operation. Many schools in the UK still offer children inexpensive food at lunchtime and children from low-income households receive free meals, offering an essential lifeline to struggling families. In 2021 it has been observed that the number of children falling into this category has increased substantially and many now argue that the scheme should continue to provide such assistance during school holidays.[19] More recently surveys have drawn attention to the number of children arriving at school each morning without breakfast, with inevitable adverse effects on their behaviour and their ability to learn. As in the nineteenth century, a variety of charitable initiatives have developed in an attempt to address this situation.[20] The scheme inherited from Penny Dinners, therefore, continues to go through a range of modifications, and to provoke controversy as it is variously administered by different governments.[21] It remains, however, a significant part of the British education system.

---

19. In March 2021 this was one of the first proposals of the newly appointed head of the Children's Commission for England, a body responsible for promoting and protecting the rights of children under the United Nations Convention on the Rights of the Child.

20. See for example the 'Magic Breakfast Project', launched in 2016 to provide free nutritious breakfasts to children in schools where at least 35 per cent of the children qualify for free school meals.

21. A. Finch, *The Provision of School Meals since 1906: Progress or a Recipe for Disaster? History and Policy* (History and Policy, 2019) www.historyandpolicy.org

Chapter Twelve
INDUSTRIAL MATTERS

William's first tentative steps into the field of working conditions had been provoked by his encounter with James Gray on that Sunday morning in April 1882 when he learned of the death of Mary Jane and wrote an outraged letter to Thomas Burt. Thomas had, for some time, been pressing the government to address the matter of lead poisoning in the white lead industry. He had, for example, recently highlighted the death of Hannah McCarthy, another young woman who had died in the Shoreditch workhouse just a few days before Mary Jane. Hannah, aged just twenty-seven, had worked at the Millwall White Lead Company in East London and the medical officer of Shoreditch had given evidence at her inquest that deaths from lead poisoning were a frequent occurrence in London workhouses. Now both the Rector of Gateshead and John Caris, a member of the Gateshead Board of Guardians, had written to him to express their concern. He immediately forwarded their letters to the Home Secretary, Sir Vernon Harcourt, expressing the view that lead poisoning was also a widespread problem on Tyneside, largely concealed by the habitual failure there to conduct inquests into the deaths. In response Sir Vernon instituted a comprehensive enquiry into the matter and in January 1883 a Bill containing some initial regulations for the protection of workers employed in the production of white lead began its progress through Parliament. It became law in August of that year.

Factory regulations during this period were somewhat thin on the ground. Most had been developed in response to concerns about the long working hours of children or about the shocking accidents and terrible injuries occurring in cotton mills. By the standards of subsequent twentieth-century workplace health and safety regulations, the Act of 1883 was clearly deficient in many respects, not least in terms of the impracticability of the measures proposed or the adequacy of monitoring and enforcement. Despite this, however, it is regarded as a highly significant step forward in the development of workplace health and safety, for it represented a first, if somewhat limited, attempt to control a specific industrial disease by means of workplace legislation. As such it marked the beginning of a conversation about the role of workplace conditions, not only in the incidence of accidents and injury, but also in the development of ill health.

William, who had first become aware of such effects during his time in Alston, would have followed the developments in this story with interest. The adverse effects of exposure to lead, whether in mining or manufacture, was an issue that seemed to haunt him. And it seemed he was destined to have one more brush with the question of white lead manufacture on Tyneside. In 1893, ten years after the death of Mary Jane and Hannah McCarthy, nineteen-year-old Annie Case died. Like Hannah she was employed at the Millwall White Lead Works and, like Hannah, she died in the Shoreditch workhouse. Annie's death was the catalyst for another formal enquiry, this one conducted by the first female factory inspector, May Abraham, newly appointed that year. May collected statistics that she felt showed 'beyond all reasonable doubt' that women were far more susceptible to lead poisoning than were men.[1] As a result she recommended that women should be excluded from employment in the white leadworks. In 1895, therefore, the government finally proposed legislation allowing the prohibition of 'vulnerable groups' from white lead production 'where this was considered to be necessary.' The move released a storm

---

1. Report of May Abraham on the results of her enquiry into the employment of women in the white lead trade in Newcastle. 1895. NA. HO45/9848/B12393A. Although May Abraham's report was highly influential this conclusion was, in fact, erroneous. She had failed to take into account that women were employed in the most dusty parts of the workplace. Exposure to lead dust was much lower where men worked and the effects on their health was correspondingly less. When men took over the work previously carried out by women the incidence of lead poisoning in men increased significantly.

of protest on all sides. Feminists groups insisted that women should never be excluded from any employment on the basis of their sex. For many women, they argued, their exclusion from the leadworks would deny them the only employment available to them. Manufacturers, meanwhile, considered that employing men as replacements for women would enormously increase their costs. We will be ruined they all cried. One manufacturer in the North East dragooned his female workforce of over five hundred to add their signatures (or at least their X marks) to a petition demanding that their jobs should not be put at risk. Negotiations between the government and the manufacturers dragged on until the spring of 1896 with, it seemed, no end in sight. One Tyneside firm, however, bucked the trend. Messrs Cookson & Co, had already changed their processes in an attempt to reduce lead exposure but, following a further female death, they decided to remove women from employment in this area altogether. In April, therefore, they informed the Home Office that they had replaced all women employees with men. Moreover, they said, this had been achieved at no economic cost for, in such heavy manual work, fewer men than women were required. Even more encouragingly, however, no women had lost their jobs, for they had all been redeployed elsewhere in the works and they were pleased to report that all had reported improvements in their health. Edward Troup, permanent under secretary at the Home Office, wrote immediately to Home Secretary Herbert Asquith. 'We are now in a strong position,' he said. 'One of the leading firms Messrs Cookson has accepted and will give evidence in favour. Now the others, particularly the smaller ones, are likely to back down.'[2] In this Edward Troup was proved entirely right and he was no doubt justified in taking some credit for an ultimately successful negotiation. It is just possible, however, that there were influences at work of which he was unaware. For Messrs Cookson was now run by Norman and George Cookson who under the tutelage of their Uncle Edward had shared a schoolroom with their

---

2. Edward Troup. memo to the Home Secretary. April 1896. NA. HO45/9856B12393AC.

cousin Eleanor, all those years ago in the vicarage at Kirkby Thore.[3] It is purely speculative to suggest that William and Eleanor could have exerted some sway over how the Cooksons conducted matters in their workplace. But it is hard to imagine that William would have allowed such an opportunity to pass him by.

During the next few years labour issues and, in particular, the problem of labour disputes, became another of William's central preoccupations. In 1886, at a meeting in Newcastle, Edward Pease of the Fabian Society launched the National Labour Federation, a general union which allowed workers of any trade to join, essentially providing a home for those whose work did not qualify them for membership of any of the established unions. William, together with MPs Thomas Burt and Charles Fenwick became trustees of the Federation which soon attracted thousands of workers.[4] By 1890 it had a membership of over sixty thousand and branches had been established all over the North East.

Labour disputes were a common feature in the area and William was concerned about the need for better worker representation. However, he was also exercised more generally about the regularity of these damaging conflicts, which so often brought an already fragile economy to a standstill. In 1889 the way opened for him to become more actively involved in this situation. In December that year J. B. Lightfoot, the Bishop of Durham, died suddenly from coronary failure and was succeeded by the Reverend Brooke Foss Westcott.[5] It was a controversial appointment that provoked several months of argument before the Reverend Westcott was finally enthroned. His reputation was that of a quiet, studious intellectual, a Cambridge professor whose major claim to fame was his revision of the Greek text

3. Cooksons Leadworks was originally developed by William Isaac Cookson, brother of Eleanor's father, Edward Cookson. Control of the firm passed to his sons, Norman and George in 1876. Under their direction Cooksons became one of the largest and most technologically advanced lead manufacturing companies on Tyneside.

4. Charles Fenwick was an ex-miner who had been elected as the Liberal-Labour MP for Wansbeck in Northumberland in 1885.

5. Brooke Foss Westcott, Bishop of Durham, in office 1890–1901.

of the New Testament. Not unreasonably many people were sceptical of his ability to relate to the colliers and other industrialists of the North East. They had, however, overlooked elements of his make-up that were to prove central to his achievements on Tyneside and which, ever after, would earn him the title of 'the Miners' Bishop'.[6] Although some argued that he was reluctant to pin his colours overtly to the Christian Socialist mast, his attitudes and behaviour were in many ways entirely in keeping with such beliefs. He had, of course, worked with Frederick Maurice years before during the foundation period of the movement, and more recently, having read Maurice's biography, he had reportedly said 'I never knew before how deep my sympathy is with most of his characteristic thought.'[7] Bishop Westcott was himself a surprisingly (to some) practical man and a humble one who disliked the pomp of high office and enjoyed the company of the miners and their families. (He particularly liked brass bands and would always prefer to attend events where these were a feature). It was said that he hated using the episcopal carriage and when forced to do so 'sat miserably with his back to the horses.'[8] In an earlier part of his life he had taught at Harrow School and while there, to the apparent derision of some of the boys, he often intoned a favourite prayer: 'Help us by thy great love to succour the afflicted, to relieve the needy and the destitute, to share the burdens of the heavy laden, and ever to see Thee in all that are poor and desolate.'[9] Despite his obvious sympathies with the disadvantaged, however, his more recent life experiences had left him ill-prepared for the social conditions of places like Gateshead and Newcastle and in this he was helped enormously by William who proved an invaluable source of information, a bridge between the mean streets of Tyneside and the grandeur of Auckland Castle.[10]

In the spring of 1892, the latest in a series of damaging miners'

6. G. A. Patrick, *The Miners' Bishop* (Epworth Press, London, 2004).
7. D. L. Edwards, *Leaders of the Church of England 1828–1944* (Oxford University Press, Oxford, 1971).
8. ibid.
9. ibid.
10. Auckland Castle was the official residence of the Bishop of Durham.

strikes began in the North East. By June over ten thousand miners had been out on strike for nearly three months, rendering many of them destitute and paralysing the economy of the whole area. Like so many disputes this one was essentially about wages. As a result of a fall in the price of coal the colliery owners had decided to reduce the miners' pay by 12½ per cent. The miners would only accept a reduction of 7½ per cent. It seemed that the situation was deadlocked with neither side willing to compromise. Much to everyone's surprise Bishop Westcott decided to intervene. He proposed a return to work on two conditions, that there should be an immediate reduction of only 10 per cent and that any further reduction should be referred to a properly constituted Wages Board, which would remain in place to settle any future disputes. Over one weekend at the beginning of June he travelled to each of the collieries in turn and obtained the consent of the miners' groups and the colliery owners, as a result of which the strike came to an end.

With some justification much has been written about this major success, but perhaps rather less attention has been paid to its longer-term consequences. For what Bishop Westcott referred to initially as a 'Wages Board' would turn into the rather more ambitious concept of the 'Conciliation Board'. Late in October 1893 he convened one of his, by now, regular private meetings at Auckland Castle 'for friendly discussion of social problems by men representing diverse views and diverse interests.'[11] Following this, a notice signed by William appeared in the *Newcastle Daily Chronicle* inviting representatives of the coal, iron and steel trades of Northumberland and Durham to a conference at the Miners' Hall in Durham in order to have a 'full and frank discussion on the desirability of forming Conciliation Boards to operate as forums for mediation and co-operative agreement where disputes arose.'[12] Over two days the delegates discussed the nature of the boards, the type of people who would be members and how they

---

11. WME, letter to the editor. The Bishop of Durham and Boards of Conciliation. BNA, *Newcastle Daily Chronicle*, 11 December 1893.

12. ibid.

would operate. After a further meeting at Auckland Castle, attended among others by Alfred Marshall, the first Conciliation Board was established in February 1894 in the Northumberland coalfield with several more to follow.

William, who was a central player in these discussions, had obviously been considering the whole question of dispute resolution for some time. On a Sunday in May 1892 as the miners' strike raged on, he preached on the subject in Dunston Parish church, returning to his recurring themes of 'brotherhood' and the peaceful resolution of conflict.[13]

> As far as trade unions realise the principle of brotherhood, they are sound in principle; but they sometimes forget there is a brotherhood within a brotherhood, the brotherhood of trade, the larger brotherhood of the nation. And nothing seems to me more regrettable in connection with the recent industrial conflict than the assumption that the object of a union was to gain by force as much as possible. The true object ought to be to gain what was just; and what was just could never be ascertained by an appeal to force, for when an appeal to force was made there was no security that justice would prevail. We might well say in the present industrial dispute to the coal owner and the miner, Sirs you are brethren; act like brethren; call in some outside authority, lay your case before him and let him determine what is just between brother and brother.[14]

For William the concept and practice of conciliation was the nearest he could come to his much larger vision of the co-operative organisation of industry. This, at least, had been achieved in a small way in 1891 with the construction of the Dunstan Co-operative Flour Mills, built to supply the Co-operative Societies of Tyneside. At the grand opening of this venture, which had cost £100,000 and

---

13. He based his sermon on Acts 7:26 (King James Bible) 'And on the following day he appeared to them as they were quarrelling and tried to reconcile them saying, men you are brothers, why do you wrong each other?'

14. WME, 'Sermon at Dunston Parish Church,' BNA, *Newcastle Daily Chronicle*, 3 May 1892.

employed about eighty workers, he gave an inspiring speech in which he declared that, 'should we see the development of other industries on similar Wholesale Society lines we should see a very great revolution in the methods and systems of productive organisations, and that the changes would hurt no-one and benefit all.'[15] During the following years he worked as closely as he could to his ideals of 'brotherhood' and 'co-operation' acting as the practical arm of Bishop Westcott's initiative and featuring prominently as the chairman of numerous Conciliation Boards as they developed across the region. Such boards were often convened reluctantly as a last resort when all else had failed, but invariably they resulted in a successful settlement. Some of the disputes involved different groups of workers while others were between workers and employers. In June 1894, for example, there was a bitter protracted demarcation dispute between bricklayers and plasterers who fiercely defended their right to ring fence certain areas of work for their own skilled trade. It was a dispute that had effectively closed down the building trade as a whole such that joiners, plumbers and general labourers were all out of work. A month later there was a complicated wage dispute lasting over eighteen weeks between the moulders and employers in the engineering and shipbuilding works, another argument that inevitably drew in numerous other trades. And in December the wherrymen who transported goods and passengers along the River Tyne went on strike when the boat owners refused to increase their wages. Fifty small boats lay idle on the river for ten months. Just as in his role as Chair of the School Board, William appears to have had a particular talent for reconciling opposing factions in these various disputes. Unlike the School Board this was a field in which he often had little direct knowledge of the daily experience of the participants, or of the way in which a particular industry was organised. Despite or perhaps because of this, however, he seems to have been a much sought-after choice of mediator.

A few months later, in 1895, William was invited to deliver the

15. WME, address at the opening of the Co-operative Flour Mill, Dunstan. BNA, *Shields Daily News*, 20 April 1891.

Hulsean Lectures at his *alma mater*, the University of Cambridge. The Hulsean Lectures, established by an endowment of a man called John Hulse in 1790, consisted of four theological lectures, to be given over a period of one year, by a graduate of Cambridge on a subject of the lecturer's choice. Unsurprisingly William elected to talk about the basic principles of Christian Socialism and some of its practical applications. The lectures were published in book form in 1896 and, as such, they represent one of the very few published writings of William Moore-Ede.[16] In these lectures he provided a detailed exposition of the practical theology which underpinned his life and work, drawing in particular from the Old Testament book of Isaiah.

> Whether the book of Isaiah is the composition of one writer or more is a question I am not competent to determine ... but this I do know: Never has faith been exhibited in stronger form; never have social evils been more bravely and decisively tracked to their ultimate source, more clearly shown to be the result of neglect or defiance of the Divine principles of righteousness; never has man had more clear vision of the glories of the golden age which will be when society is constituted according to the Divine order; never has faith found more confident expression than in this book of Isaiah.[17]

In his first lecture, entitled 'The function of the Church in the work of social reform' he presented the justification for involvement of the Church in social issues. Having traced the historical development of industrialisation and its consequences for the population, he describes the resultant growth of individualism and competition, arguing that 'the restless striving of each to do the best for himself, while productive of marvellous activity, has not conduced to a well-organised community, has not secured the well-being of all.' Quoting Alfred Marshall, he noted that

16. op cit., W. Moore-Ede *The Attitude of the Church to Some of the Social Problems of Town Life*.
17. ibid.

we are now setting ourselves to seriously enquire whether there is a need for large numbers of people to be doomed from birth to hard work in order to provide for others the requisites of a refined and cultured life, while they themselves are prevented by their poverty and toil from having any share or part of that life.

This, he maintained, is not living according to the divine principles of life as revealed through Christ.

> The subject of Christ's preaching, the object of His desire, is the Kingdom of Heaven being set up on earth, and the work of the Church is to labour for the realisation of this idea . . . the Church cannot ignore the economic and social surroundings of men . . . we are all influenced by our surroundings, they make their mark on us and our character.[18]

In subsequent lectures he enlarged on this theme, discussing in considerable detail 'The problems of the unemployed' and 'The homes of the people'.

> The struggling poor have in them capacities for appreciating beauty of sight and sound, capacities of mind whereby they might find pleasure in literature and science . . . but these are undeveloped, crushed out by the constant anxiety concerning daily food.
>
> The poverty of the unemployed degrades his children. It enervates them also. They do not obtain sufficient air light or food and so they grow up feeble and puny . . . and their feeble constitutions make them subject to more than the average amount of sickness.
>
> For us our home is a place into which we can retire . . . a place of rest and peace . . . where with books, music, games, or our hobbies, we can occupy ourselves and enjoy the society of our families. But in poor districts, where a whole family is crowded into one room, there is neither rest nor peace.

---

18. ibid.

> The influence of overcrowding shows itself in the death rate of children, which is about three times greater in poor districts than in better quarters of our towns.[19]

In each lecture he goes on to discuss the various causes of unemployment and poor housing, concluding that:

> ...the problems are complex, the product of many causes and influence, and therefore the remedies will be many but it is the duty of the Church, in its care for Christ's poor, to study carefully the causes which produce the evil conditions under which these brethren of ours labour.[20]

Throughout it all the message is one of Christian responsibility, the call to be actively involved in the problems of 'town life'.

> There is a deep hypocrisy in our being at our ease in Zion, as we sit in some church, where we utilise every external accessory to aid the devotion of the spirit, or sit in some comfortable pew and pray 'Thy will be done on earth as it is in heaven', if we do nothing to remove the causes of degradation in the courts and alleys which exist, perhaps within a stone's throw.[21]

William dedicated the book to the 'stimulating teaching' of Alfred Marshall which he said, 'first aroused the interest of the author in social questions'.[22] Meanwhile a 'Prefatory Note' (seven pages long) was provided by Bishop Westcott who concluded,

> No-one, I believe, can study Canon Moore-Ede's lectures and look with open eyes on the common life of men, without feeling the range and gravity of the problems of great towns by which his attention

---

19. ibid.
20. ibid.
21. ibid.
22. ibid

is necessarily arrested; and without finding some fragment of work which he can do.[23]

During this period a close and supportive relationship developed between Bishop Westcott and William, who has been described as 'the Bishop's principal lieutenant in industrial matters.'[24] Their contrasting backgrounds and careers meant they often brought different skills and influences to bear on the problems they encountered but, throughout it all, they shared a common mission to involve themselves fully in the lives and the problems of ordinary working people. The strength of the friendship between the two men was touchingly referred to by Thomas Burt at the memorial service following the death of Bishop Westcott in 1901. Thomas's admiration for the Bishop's work concluded with the following observation.

> He always had a willing capable helper in Canon Moore-Ede who brought to all social and labour questions great knowledge and sympathy, a clear head and a facility to give fitting form and shape to the decisions. Between the Bishop and the Canon – kindred spirits – the relationship was beautiful, like that of a father and son when at their best.[25]

---

23. ibid.
24. G. Best, *Bishop Westcott and the Miners. The Bishop Westcott Memorial Lecture*, (Cambridge University Press, Cambridge, 1966).
25. A comment by *The Times*, reproduced BNA, *Shields Daily News*. 24 July 1908.

Chapter Thirteen
ABUSE AND NEGLECT

One Saturday evening in July 1893 a young woman called Elizabeth Levy attempted suicide by jumping into the River Tyne. Fortunately, twenty-year old Elizabeth was rescued by the crew of a steamer which had just left the landing stage on its way to South Shields. Attempted suicide, however, was a criminal offence which meant that the following Tuesday, having recovered from the effects of 'pleurisy caused by immersion in the water' Elizabeth appeared at Gateshead Police Court.[1] Mindful of the risk of imprisonment she expressed great remorse for her conduct and indicated that she was willing to go into 'a Home'. She had apparently been seen by the Reverend Moore-Ede that morning and the 'Home' referred to was a hostel called the Lodge run by the Association for the Care of Friendless Girls, the president of which was William's wife, Eleanor.

Eleanor had set up the Association shortly after arriving in Gateshead. In Sheffield she had contributed financially to the establishment of a branch of the Girls Friendly Society (GFS) an organisation that had been established in the 1870s with the broad aim of assisting working class girls to develop their 'potential' by means of training and other educational programmes. It also specialised in providing safe places for young women to stay when they arrived alone in an unfamiliar town, looking for work. However, the ethos of the GFS, as it existed in the late nineteenth century, contained elements that would probably have jarred with Eleanor, in particular

---

1. 'Charge of Attempted Suicide,' BNA, *Newcastle Evening Chronicle*, 10 July 1893.

the requirement that girls who enrolled should have an 'unblemished character'. Those found wanting in this respect were summarily ejected. Certainly by the time Eleanor arrived in Gateshead she had shifted her aspirations towards the establishment of a rather different organisation with a very different clientele. The objectives of the Association for the Care of Friendless Girls were described in an article which appeared in the *Newcastle Daily Chronicle* just before Christmas 1887. The article written by 'a Gateshead lady' was intended as a fundraiser for the Association and described the fundamental principles of the organisation which were 'to attack the causes of the degradation of women . . . attaching paramount importance to preventative work and seeking out those whose lives are so bad as simply to set them apart for ruin.'[2] Ruin, of course, referred primarily to issues of sexual purity rather than material destitution, but for a woman in the nineteenth century these two aspects were invariably linked. 'Ruin' essentially barred the way to any occupation likely to be open to a respectable working-class girl. William may have been particularly sympathetic to Elizabeth's case when he discovered that she had formerly been employed in a white lead works, apparently the occupation of choice for those 'whose character did not bear scrutiny'.

The Association, therefore, was primarily an organisation that offered rehabilitation and training. Magistrates faced with young or vulnerable female offenders like Elizabeth, who otherwise faced the prospect of a period in prison, often made use of the Lodge as a more humane alternative to a custodial sentence. The Annual Report for 1896 recounted that seven women had arrived at the Lodge by this route. Some of these appeared to have been 'inebriates' a condition that often had a bearing on the offences with which they had been charged. Others taken in by the Association were children found sleeping rough on the streets, either because their parents had died leaving them homeless and without any means of support or had run

[2]. 'Friendless Girls, by a Gateshead Lady'. BNA, *Newcastle Daily Chronicle*, 6 December 1887.

away from home because of sexual or physical abuse. The 'Gateshead lady' described one such case.

> The mother, a delicate consumptive woman had passed away, leaving a little pinched starved-looking girl of thirteen behind her. This child had now to bear the brunt of the drunken father's temper and brutality. The neighbours told me he would frequently twist his hand in the child's hair, lift her off her feet and strike her with his clenched fist. She was bruised black and blue when we found her.[3]

It was recommended that women stayed for at least eighteen months at the Lodge, with the ultimate objective of finding them a suitable work placement. Inevitably most of these placements were in service, as maids or other house staff, taken on by sympathetic members of the middle-classes. From the perspective of the twenty-first century it is easy to criticise this type of rescue package. The limited placements on offer and the strong emphasis on the necessary formation of an obedient and submissive character, such as that required by the typical downstairs maid, can sound depressingly controlling to modern ears. In Victorian England, however, there were few options available to young women, or children, who had grown up in desperate poverty or become the victim of hard times. In her book *The Five* which follows the tragic back stories of the victims of Jack the Ripper Hallie Rubenhold describes in shocking detail the procession of misfortunes that lead each of these women to become the victim of a murderer.[4] The sacrifice of certain freedoms was often a necessary price to pay to keep body and soul together. A story recounted by 'the Gateshead lady' underlines this rather poignantly.

> I remember one child of thirteen who had an intemperate father, and her mother was dead. She had a miserable home and was fast becoming

3. ibid.
4. H. Rubenhold, *The Five. The Untold Story of the Women Killed by Jack the Ripper*, (Transworld Publishers, London, 2019).

a little street arab. She entered the lodge and accepted help very gladly, but one day the longing to have a run through the old familiar streets in absolute freedom became too much for her. She was missing for a few hours. It transpired that she had spent an hour with her drunken father. She had sat on the doorstep in the old-fashioned way and nursed a neighbour's poor little dirty baby. She had paid flying visits to several old acquaintance and given a glowing account of her new surroundings. She had enjoyed a good gallop up and down two or three streets with her hair flying in the wind, then, perfectly satisfied and happy, she returned to the lodge 'as good as gold'. She has now been more than two years in one situation, is comfortably clothed and has a little money in the savings bank.[5]

Many women were fully aware of this trade off and some did make the choice to reject what was on offer for, unlike the more sinister Magdalene Homes which took in 'fallen women', this was in no sense a prison or a place of forced labour. In 1896 a total of forty-six women and girls were admitted to the Lodge of whom, it was reported, nineteen remained there at the end of the year. Of the remainder, situations had been found for eleven, six had been transferred to other homes and eight had 'left by their own wish'. One child and one woman had been removed by relatives.

In common with many middle-class women of the period Eleanor's public profile was relatively low. Known predominantly as the wife of the Rector she would no doubt have fulfilled her fair share of public duties as an 'accompanying person'. And as a mother of eight she would have had plenty to occupy her at home.[6] Her life with William, however, would have been very different from the one she experienced with her first husband. In Alston, as the wife of a conventional country parson, she would presumably have dabbled in good works (including

---

5. op cit., 'Friendless Girls'.
6. Eleanor and William had seven children (William, Alfred, Laetitia, Stuart, Oswald, Cuthbert and Elizabeth) to add to Eleanor's two children from her first marriage. Oswald, however, died in infancy.)

of course the fund raising for her husband's new church) but she would probably not have experienced the abuse, drunkenness and violence she encountered at the hands of some of those who arrived at the Lodge. The 'Gateshead lady' was frank about this aspect of the work and described the success of the organisation as due largely to the 'tact and energy' of its president. In the Association for Friendless Girls, Eleanor seems to have fully embraced the ethos that was the driving force of William's own life and interestingly, from the outset, she added a new dimension to the Lodge, one which rarely if ever featured in similar organisations. Alongside the inevitable training in cleaning, cooking, washing and needlework the women and girls had the option of attending 'educational classes' given by Eleanor herself and a team of local lady volunteers. Eleanor was well suited to this role as she had, for several years, been giving lectures on history (to women only as sanctioned by the committee) as part of the University Extension Scheme. The classes offered to the Friendless Girls were also available to women from outside the home at a modest cost. Most attendees, it was reported, were 'factory and warehouse hands' with about 250 being present on each evening.[7] By 1901 these classes were supplemented by an extensive library of more than 120 books given by the girls of the Sunderland High School who seem to have taken a particular interest in the Lodge. It is probably no coincidence that William, on being asked to present the annual prizes at the high school, had taken the opportunity to remind these middle-class and relatively privileged young women of their obligations to the less fortunate. Addressing the assembly, he told them that they were currently forming the opinions that would govern their later lives. He would, therefore, wish them to ask themselves what they were going to be? Were they aiming 'to become a butterfly or an ornamental clothes prop?' He noted that women who had their living to earn had finer characters and were on the whole pleasanter companions 'than those whose life was made up of cycling, tennis, afternoon teas and ping pong.' Returning to his

7. M. A. Jepson *The Beginnings of English University Education – Policy and Problems*, (Michael Joseph, London, 1973).

familiar theme he urged on them a sense of duty and purpose. 'Each should have some aim in life and should, like Christ, be ready and willing to serve.'[8]

Many of those taken in by the Association were aged around twelve or thirteen or perhaps a little above. Variously described as 'young girls' or even 'young women' it is clear that they were considered to be ready to be trained as part of the workforce rather than as children, and their rehabilitation was based on this assumption. In most industrial towns and cities, however, there were many younger children who slept rough on the streets, or suffered at the hands of abusive, neglectful parents. In Gateshead a variety of solutions to this problem were pursued and predictably William was involved in various ways with most of them. One group of such children, first highlighted by Henry Mayhew in 1840s London, were still a common presence in many industrial cities. These were known as the juvenile street vendors who lived by selling their various wares on the streets, sometimes on behalf of handlers, sometimes on behalf of their parents and often simply for their own sustenance. These children (often referred to as 'street arabs') lived a hand to mouth existence, ragged, under-nourished and, to Victorian eyes, worryingly streetwise. Criminality, actual or assumed, was part of the juvenile vendor's persona, and concerns about sexual activity and prostitution added to the general horror with which they were regarded. Whenever they could afford to many slept in squalid lodging houses, sharing rooms and beds.

In the style of the age a group of concerned individuals formed a committee entitled the Waifs Rescue Agency and Street Vendor's Club which gathered funds to provide material help for these children, together with a meeting place and safe accommodation. Essentially the ultimate objective was to persuade them to abandon their life on the streets and 'settle down to a regular trade'. William, a prominent member of the Waifs and Strays Agency who often chaired their meetings was also a member of the Gateshead School Board and was

---

8. 'The Girls' High School. Distribution of Prizes.' BNA, *Sunderland Daily Echo*, 23 July 1901.

acutely aware of the numbers of these children who did not attend school at all or whose behaviour could not be coped with if they did. Perhaps sensitive to the same issues that the 'Gateshead lady' had described, he noted that there was 'a strange fascination in it for those who once took to this irregular life and the longer they followed it the more difficult was it to get them from it.'[9]

In the late nineteenth century, a common answer to the problem was the industrial school of which there were two different types, both of which existed in Gateshead. Certified industrial schools catered for children referred by the magistrate because of some form of criminality. This was essentially a residential reformatory and juvenile vendors often found themselves here.[10] In Gateshead the Abbot Memorial School, opened in the 1860s, fulfilled this function. The other type of school was the day industrial school intended for rehabilitation, education and training of children under the age of fourteen, who had been referred by the Magistrates for non-attendance at school or whose parents had been found guilty of neglect or abuse. The underlying ethos of this type of school was rather different, focussing on the rescue and protection of children who were not themselves considered to be guilty of criminality. In practice, however, this distinction was rather blurred, both in terms of the children admitted and the type of training on offer, for a day school was unlikely to be an appropriate placement for a child whose parents had already been convicted of abuse.

Numerous accounts appeared in the local newspapers of children who had been beaten, starved and sometimes killed by their parents. William, as a member of the School Board and presumably because, as a clergyman, he was trusted to be reliable, seems often to have been called to give evidence in such cases, recounting the injuries of the child and his interviews with defensive and evasive parents. In June 1888, for example, Samuel and Kate Kelley were charged at Gateshead

9. 'The Waif's Rescue Agency. Annual General Meeting. Taking Children off the Streets,' BNA, *Sunderland Daily Echo and Shipping Gazette*, 16 February 1903.

10. G. C. Gear, *Industrial Schools in England 1857–1933. Moral Hospitals or Oppressive Institutions?* (University of London Institute of Education, 1999). www.discovery.ucl.ac.uk

Borough Police Court with assaulting their nine-year old daughter Hannah. In court the child had stated that her injuries were caused by 'falling downstairs'. William, who gave evidence in the case, said that a 'female searcher' who had examined the child found her body to be covered in bruises and that the child had told this lady that her stepmother and father had 'caused them with a strap'. The parents were fined 10 shillings and the child was admitted to the residential industrial school.[11]

One of the things that constantly disturbed William was the leniency of the sentences handed out. In the case of Hannah Kelley the fine given to her parents was the equivalent of one day's wages for an average skilled worker. Moreover, it seems likely that those cases that actually came to court were the tip of a very worrying iceberg, for many parents viewed it as their unquestioned right to inflict severe physical punishment on their children. Added to this there was no sense that other children in the family might be at risk. Hannah Kelley had three younger siblings, the youngest only a few months old. Someone else who was seriously concerned about all this was a London clergyman called Benjamin Waugh who in July 1884 set up the London Society for the Prevention of Cruelty to Children.[12] His initial objective was 'to look after the children of drunkards, of the professional tramp, juvenile street hawkers, illegitimate children and children put out to the farm' by establishing hostels for the care of neglected and abused children.[13] In the early days he had considerable difficulty in garnering support or raising funds for a cause that many people apparently found too shocking to comprehend. Londoners, he remarked dryly, remained to be convinced that parents did not

---

11. 'Cruel Conduct of Parents,' BNA, *Newcastle Daily Chronicle*, 12 June 1888.

12. Benjamin Waugh was inspired by a similar initiative set up by businessman Thomas Agnew in Liverpool. The London Society eventually became the National Society for the Prevention of Cruelty to Children (NSPCC).

13. The 'tramper' was usually homeless and resorted to any means possible to pay for food and a bed for the night. Women 'trampers' were generally assumed to be prostitutes. 'Farm' referred to baby farms where numbers of children were left with childminders, inadequately fed and housed in poor conditions.

automatically love their children. As time went on, however, the Society began to shine an increasingly horrifying light on the range and extent of child abuse in Victorian society. It became clear that such abuse took many more forms and occurred in many more households than had previously been suspected. One particularly disturbing practice that emerged, for example, was that of child insurance, where the subject of such insurance was subsequently murdered by their parents. Increasingly, the Society began to involve itself in prosecutions which, by their sensational nature, invariably brought the subject to the attention of a much wider audience. By 1888 it had investigated and brought to court over 120 cases of abuse and neglect resulting in terms of imprisonment of between one month and fifteen years and had also set up a system of inspection and supervision to root out cases of child abuse. The Reverend Waugh was under no illusion that this was simply a London problem however. Keen to spread the word beyond the Capital, he began giving talks around the country, in part to raise funds, but also in the hope of establishing branches nationwide. The Society, he said, was willing to place a specially trained officer in each area to assist with the work.

William was an early convert to the cause, initiating the development of a branch in Gateshead in 1888 and, in typical style, he began to describe the Society and how it operated to anyone on Tyneside who would listen. In its first year the Gateshead branch had dealt with twenty cases where convictions of cruelty to children resulted in the imprisonment of the guilty parent. William was keen to emphasise that such cases were not just about parental punishment but about 'the additional benefit of a deterrent effect on the whole neighbourhood.' His enthusiasm for the society's methods was derived not so much from its ability to bring cases to court, although this was important, but from its wider objective to 'engender obligation and responsibility' amongst parents whose children remained with them.[14] Inspectors not only inspected families but attempted to work co-operatively

---

14. 'NSPCC Meeting at Gateshead,' BNA, *Newcastle Daily Chronicle*, 24 March 1903.

with them and in this they needed to fully understand the difficulties of working-class lives. Benjamin Waugh commented that, unusually, in Gateshead a working man representative of each of the major industries was on the committee, an innovation that he attributed to William. In 1903 at a meeting of what had, by then, become the National Society for the Prevention of Cruelty to Children (NSPCC) William himself paid tribute to the work of the Society's workers in Gateshead where he said 'even amongst the parents under supervision there was no feeling of antagonism to the Society's inspector.'[15] The NSPCC remains a major player today in the field of child protection. In order to encompass the new concerns and demands of the twenty-first century its work has expanded and changed in ways that would probably be unrecognisable to those who worked in its early days. One suspects, however, that one of its current slogans would not be so far removed from the sentiments of its early pioneers, 'Every child is worth fighting for.'

15. ibid.

Chapter Fourteen
MARSDEN MINERS

In May 1891 the *Newcastle Daily Chronicle* published an article under the heading 'Local Gossip' in which it recounted the activities of St Mary's parish church, its Rector and his 'splendid band of workers'. What prompted this is uncertain, perhaps a dearth of copy that week, but it nevertheless served as a useful summary of the 'new agencies of usefulness directed solely for the good of the masses forthcoming in recent years.'[1] It was an impressive list encompassing a variety of schools and educational classes, as well as numerous organisations. There was the Band of Hope, the Brandling Street Club for Working Men, the Barnes Court Amateur Gymnastics Club, the Boys Brigade Home for Destitute Boys, the Church Institute, the Anchorage Working Girls' Club, the Newcastle Sunday Club, and the Nelson Street Restaurant with its supply of cheap wholesome food.[2] And this, the writer pointed out, did not include the Rector's 'strictly ecclesiastical' work of the Parish which encompassed not only his duties as a parish priest but also his post as master of the local alms house King James' Hospital with its forty-four residents. Focussing as it did on the parish church, the article also failed to include William's more 'secular' work of the type described here. Even this, however, is by no means an exhaustive coverage of the various projects in which he was involved. He was a diligent committee member prepared, it seemed, to endure an endless series of meetings and conferences in order to lend his support to a whole panoply of organisations, for

1. 'Local Gossip. St Mary's Parish, Gateshead,' BNA, *Newcastle Daily Chronicle*, 21 May 1891.
2. The Newcastle Sunday Club was a programme of Sunday afternoon lectures.

example the People's Dispensary, the District Nursing Association, the Young Men's Christian Association (YMCA) and the NSPCC. And somehow, in the midst of all this, he found time to open bazaars, present prizes at local schools and trophies at the local cricket and footballs clubs (of which he was of course the president). It is hard to imagine he spent much time at home.

By the summer of 1901 William had been Rector of Gateshead for almost twenty years. During that time he had worked tirelessly with varying degrees of success to address issues of education, poverty, housing, hunger and industrial strife. There seems to have been few areas of need where he had not been involved. Throughout it all, of course, he had also been a parish priest with all the usual duties that entails, as well as occupying the post of Rural Dean and, from 1894, serving as an Honorary Canon of Durham Cathedral. At home, meanwhile, despite the undoubted support of a loving and equally industrious wife, there had been a large family to raise and educate on a modest income. There could be little doubt that William, now in his early fifties, was beginning to feel the strain. During the previous few months he had experienced two bouts of unspecified illness, each sufficiently serious to keep him away from scheduled meetings for as long as three weeks.

Bishop Westcott would have been well aware of all this and when the current Rector of nearby Whitburn died that year he immediately recommended William for the vacant post. On the face of it this was a much less demanding job and in the short term, at least, it would provide an opportunity for rest and recuperation. (The Bishop was probably under no illusion that it would mark an end to William's activities). It was also better paid. The living at Whitburn offered a stipend of £1,150 per annum as well as a large handsome Rectory, as opposed to the £500 per annum provided by Gateshead. William was not of course a wealthy man. Unlike many nineteenth-century clergymen he was not in possession of private means, something that was underlined by the small (by the standards of the day) contingent of two servants maintained at the Rectory. William signalled his acceptance of the post at Whitburn in June and on 21 July he preached a farewell sermon at St Mary's on the text 'Fear the Lord and serve Him in sincerity and truth.'[3] His parishioners must not, he said, think that he would lay down his office with a light heart. He felt that he ought to make way for someone younger and more vigorous, someone who would bring more energy, new life, new methods, to the leadership of the parish. It was a statement that bore witness to the extent of his weariness at this point, only tempered by his concluding remarks. Whitburn, he said, would be no sinecure. He would not have accepted it if it had been. 'There is plenty to do in the future at Whitburn,' he said, 'I do not intend to stop working.'[4]

Having made his decision to leave Gateshead William would have been comforted by the assumption that he would still be working closely with Bishop Westcott and would continue to enjoy his companionship and support. What suddenly took place at the end of July therefore would have come as a terrible shock. His induction to Whitburn was arranged for 31 July but on the previous day, as arrangements were being put in place, the Bishop died suddenly at Auckland Castle. Instead of his induction William found himself preparing to attend the funeral of his close friend. It is hard to imagine his thoughts or those he harboured during his own ceremonials which were hurriedly re-arranged for the following Saturday afternoon. The Archdeacon, who at short notice took the Bishop's place that afternoon, dispensed with the usual introductory welcome address due, he said, to the 'extraordinary circumstances' of the event, and suggested that the congregation should instead spend some time in silent prayer.

Just before Christmas William was invited back to Gateshead to receive a range of expensive gifts and glowing testimonials from grateful parishioners and the people with whom he had worked over the years. William said he was most pleased that the presentations had been from the town and had been handed over by one of his Nonconformist

---

3. Joshua 24:14, King James Bible.
4. 'Canon Moore-Ede's Farewell,' BNA, *Newcastle Daily Chronicle*, 23 July 1901.

brethren for he had 'always been on the best of terms with them.'[5] He was clearly moved by the genuine and heartfelt admiration and gratitude offered in this meeting – and he was obviously recovering some of his old energy and enthusiasm. His friends noticed his appearance 'had a much healthier look', observing that 'his facial pallor is departing and he seems stouter and fresher.' As one person remarked 'Breezy, healthy, picturesque Whitburn seems to be doing the Canon a world of good.'[6]

Whitburn was indeed a pretty coastal village that offered a marked contrast to the industrial smoke and grime of Gateshead. It had its due quota of comfortably housed local gentry as well as its obligatory aristocratic family, the Hedworth Williamsons, who had been residents of Whitburn Hall since 1780. The Williamsons owned large tracts of land in Northumberland which, among other assets, contained vast limestone quarries which by 1900 were producing 50,000 tons of lime a year. The Rectory, situated next door to Whitburn Hall, was a large, elegant three-story house, its leafy garden enclosed by a high stone wall which abutted the grounds of Sir Hedworth's estate. It was a serene setting, the family's arrival disturbed only by a minor panic caused by the family's pet cat which, having attempted to scale the wall, fell into the unfamiliar depths of a large hollow sycamore tree of the type he would rarely, if ever, have encountered in Gateshead. He was rescued a full twelve days later, thinner but remarkably unscathed, by some of Sir Hedworth's gardeners who happened to hear its plaintive cries. Adjacent to the Rectory, meanwhile, the thirteenth-century stone church, with its monuments and memorials, had the settled air of a building that had, over hundreds of years, quietly observed the comings and goings of village life.

It was unlikely, however, that William would settle quietly into these agreeable surroundings. When he alluded to their being 'plenty to do in Whitburn' he had not been thinking of the congregation

---

5. 'Presentation to Canon Moore-Ede,' BNA, *Sunderland Daily Echo and Shipping Gazette*, 3 December 1901.

6. 'Local Gossip,' BNA, *Newcastle Daily Chronicle*, 18 March 1902.

that he encountered on an average Sunday morning but the miners of Whitburn colliery, a mile away along the coast. The village of Marsden had been built in the 1870s to house the miners and their families of the newly developed colliery. Perched on a windswept promontory overlooking the North Sea it was an environment that would have felt much more familiar to William with its tiny basic houses and backyards, its Methodist chapel, its Co-operative store and its primary school catering for upwards of three hundred children. This was a tough and resilient community, well used to hardship and tragedy. In the month before William arrived there were three separate fatal accidents in the mine, a fairly typical month for Marsden. And here of course it was the chapel, not the Anglican church, that was the centre of village life, at least for those of a religious inclination. What remained of any Church of England aspirations was an empty and neglected Mission Room which lay alongside the line of 'the Rattler', a notoriously uncomfortable and noisy railway that carried coal and passengers between Marsden and South Shields. Clearly any 'mission' had long since failed. William was informed on arrival that no services had been held there for many years.

The Mission Room, Marsden. (Courtesy of the Marsden Banner Group.)

His response to this was twofold. First, he restarted services in the Co-operative Hall, a large room above the shop in the centre of the village and second, he offered the Mission Hall as a site for a Miners' Institute. In recent years there had been much talk in Marsden of the need for a place of recreation in the village but no-one, it seemed, had been inclined to do much about it. Thus it was, on a Saturday afternoon in October 1902, the opening ceremony of the new 'Workmen's Institute' situated in the former Mission Hall was performed by Sir

Lindsay Wood, managing director of the Harton Coal Company which had largely paid for the refurbishment.[7] The necessity of such a place of recreation in Marsden, Sir Lindsay said, had not been realised until the Reverend Moore-Ede interested himself in the matter. 'It was largely due to his energy and influence that this had come into being.'[8] The building was described as comfortable and cosy, and fitted with a games room, billiard room and reading room. William, who had personally paid for the billiard table, had apparently made a kind of deal with the coal company, for his ultimate object was to build a new church in Marsden. Even William, it seemed, was not immune to prevalent Anglican thinking that the absence of worshippers was due, at least in part, to the lack of a large and beautiful building. To this end he had negotiated the donation of the Mission Room on the understanding that over the next few years the coal company would help to raise the necessary funds for the erection of such a church. In the meantime, Anglican services would continue, on a temporary basis, in the Co-operative Hall.

In the event Marsden eventually acquired not only a new church but also a larger and better Miners' Institute. A year after the refurbishment of the Mission Room the new Marsden Church, situated immediately opposite the colliery, was opened with considerable ceremony by the new Bishop of Durham, Handley Moule.[9] St Andrew's, appropriately opened on St Andrew's Day 1903, was 'a handsome stone building' constructed largely from local Marsden limestone, no doubt supplied by Sir Hedworth, with other dressed stonework around the doors and windows specially obtained from the Windy Nook quarry in Gateshead.[10] With its barrel-vaulted pitch pine roof, carved oak pulpit and altar rail, brass lamps, embroidered altar cloths, richly coloured stained glass and beautifully designed Minton floor tiles this was a

---

7. From 1891 the Harton Coal Company were the owners of the colliery, variously called Marsden colliery or Whitburn colliery.

8. 'A Workman's Institute for Marsden,' BNA, *Shields Daily Gazette*, 20 October 1902.

9. Handley Moule, Bishop of Durham, in office 1901–20.

10. 'New Church for Marsden Colliery,' BNA, *Shields Daily Gazette*, 1 December 1903.

building designed to emphasise not only the glory of God but also the importance and the value of those who came to worship there. For as William conducted his services for the gentry in the beautiful old stone church in Whitburn village, he would have been well aware of the message the draughty dilapidated Mission Room had sent to the miners of Marsden colliery. Looked at from this perspective it is perhaps easier to understand his determination to build a new church for the colliery village. And the church was not only beautiful but

St Andrews Church, Marsden. (Courtesy of the Marsden Banner Group.)

comfortable. It was, the reporter of the *Sunderland Daily Echo* informed his readers, constructed in 'the simplest form of thirteenth-century Gothic and as such was peculiarly suitable for the exposed position of the church, standing as it does fronting the sea.'[11] Probably because the opening ceremony took place on a typically cold North-Eastern day the reporter also made much of the building's advanced heating

11. 'New Church at Marsden,' BNA, *Sunderland Daily Echo and Shipping Gazette*, 30 November 1903.

and ventilation systems, which was, no doubt much appreciated by the large congregation of local clergy who attended the inaugural service. (A separate service was held for 'the working men' in the evening). Not only were there hot water pipes in the nave and radiators in the chancel but the roof contained an ornamental spirelet which contained the very latest extractor ventilator which drew off the 'vitiated air'.[12] This had been designed by a certain Mr Robert Boyle, a successful engineer and manufacturer who was also renowned for his promotion of the temperance movement.

It is unrecorded how successful St Andrews was in drawing the Marsden miners to the Anglican faith, although the congregation in the Co-operative hall had reportedly been growing significantly during the previous year. However, the new 'Institute' in the refurbished Mission Room was an unqualified success, such that by October 1904 it had been decided that a larger more substantial building was required. William pointed out to the coal company that the membership had risen during the previous twelve months from 82 to 138 and the old Mission Room was now completely inadequate for the purpose, whereupon the owners produced a substantial donation as did several local businessmen. The foundation stone of a new institute was duly laid by Sir Hedworth, who donated the site with the promise of a new larger, two-story building with games room, reading room, a billiard hall and a committee room. Meanwhile William repeatedly badgered the coal company to make good on their somewhat luke-warm promises to provide the remainder of the necessary funds. He said that he looked upon the whole venture as a religious duty. It was not, he said, the church's job to point out peoples' sins but to provide things in life that would help them to resist temptation! In this he was no doubt taking an opportunity, as he always did, to bang the temperance drum. The institute, when it was eventually opened in 1905, was

---

12. A contemporary term for air in which the oxygen content was considered to be reduced, or which contained harmful contaminants deriving from the breath of people or animals.

of course 'dry'. Much of the money, in fact, came from a recently deceased local lady called Eleanor Pollard Barnes who had left a substantial legacy for the purpose. Mrs Barnes was a wealthy widow in possession of a considerable fortune courtesy of her successful entrepreneurial husband. She chose to spend the bulk of this on local good causes of which the institute, subsequently known as the Barnes Institute, was an important example.

Rather curiously the new Miners' Welfare Centre, as it was known, was built not in the village of Marsden itself but in nearby Whitburn, a position presumably dictated by the location of the piece of land gifted by Sir Hedworth. Miners would have had about a thirty-minute walk to avail themselves of its facilities. In the longer term, however, this decision effectively saved the building for future generations, for during the 1960s and '70s the old Marsden village essentially disappeared, first with the gradual movement of people to better housing in Whitburn and later with the closure of the colliery. The Institute, an attractive building in the Arts and Craft style, remains today as a thriving local community centre. Meanwhile the old mission room gradually crumbled into dilapidation and decay such that in 1977 it was finally demolished, reputedly a victim of the desire to smarten up the area in advance of a Jubilee tour by the Queen and Prince Philip. By that stage, however, the coal company had closed and Marsden village itself had been largely abandoned. Sadly, in 1968, St Andrews church, opened with such pride and fanfare in 1903, was also demolished alongside much of the village itself.

Two of the men killed at Marsden colliery in June 1901 were Colin Atkinson and Preston Young who were aged sixty-nine and sixty-three respectively. These individual tragedies highlighted not only the dangerous and arduous nature of their work but also the age of those still working in the mine. Men frequently worked well into their seventies for without work they had no means of adequately supporting themselves. There were estimated to be between two and three thousand retired or disabled miners at any one time in the county of Durham. Currently they received, at most, four shillings a week from the Permanent Relief Fund.[13] It was an insufficient amount to pay for both rent and food which meant that many were left with no option but to continue working or to resort to the workhouse. William had long been concerned about financial provision in old age, often highlighting the subject of old age pensions in lectures all over the North East and beyond, but so far without any response from the government. Back in 1896, however, a man called Joseph Hopper had visited him at the Rectory in Gateshead. Joseph, a non-conformist preacher and former miner, wanted to hire the Parish Room for a meeting to discuss a scheme to provide rent free homes for 'aged miners'. He had noticed that as pits were worked out and miners moved on many unused and dilapidated houses were left abandoned across the district. It occurred to him that many of these houses could be rescued and reused to house retired miners. William was immediately interested in this idea and attended the first meeting, also attended by Bishop Westcott, County Councillor Henry Wallace and local MPs Joseph Johnson and John Wilson.

Over a period of a few years and many more meetings this group of men, led and inspired by Joseph Hopper, worked to develop these ideas in terms of raising the necessary finance and carrying out the renovation work. In what turned out to be a hugely successful fund-raising effort current miners were asked to make voluntary contributions to the scheme. William, who was treasurer of the scheme by the time he moved to Whitburn in 1901, was pleased to note that year that so far £6,812.14s.5d had been subscribed and that the major portion of funds had come from the miners themselves. Each cottage, he said, cost on average £17 to renovate. He also reported that the previous Christmas the health of the balance sheet was considered good enough to treat sixty-four aged miners of Marsden colliery to Christmas dinner at

---

13. This was a scheme initiated in 1862 following the Hartley Colliery disaster which killed 204 men and boys. The scheme was funded by voluntary subscription and provided some financial help for miners injured in mining accidents and for dependents of those killed.

the County Hotel in nearby Westoe and to give each of them a gift of 30 shillings. Inevitably funds were supplemented by some donations from benevolent well-wishers (William himself gave £20, as did Bishop Westcott) and some landowners who had previously benefited from colliery rents now donated their land and property. In particular a considerable amount of land owned by the Church of England was given up by the Ecclesiastical Commissioners as a free gift to the scheme. Importantly, however, the view prevailed that the scheme should belong entirely to the miners themselves. William was always inclined to stick rigidly to this principle and offers of funding from current mine owners, in particular, were initially refused. However, others on the committee were less adamant on this point and the rule seems to have been relaxed somewhat after a few years. During a period of acute financial stress, for example, the owners of Monkwearmouth Colliery in Sunderland had donated £1,000 and that same year (1907) William had to swallow his most fervent objections and accept a donation from the Public House Trust. No doubt fully aware of his disapproval, others on the committee pointed out that, by taking money given by the Co-operative Society, they were now operating in a completely even-handed way, supported by both 'teetotallers and drink sellers' alike!'[14]

One large house with four acres of land (White House) was acquired for communal use, accommodating sixteen people, but most were individual dwellings provided rent free for life. Most cottages had housed the miners of long closed collieries and as such were in large groups. There were, for example, sixty-six cottages on the site of the former Shincliffe Colliery and ninety-eight at Shotton. The first to be formally opened were a group at Haswell Moor where eventually a whole village of 110 cottages would be renovated, together with a reading room, a Chapel and eight acres of land. Allocation of the homes was determined by ballot across the whole of the Durham coalfield. The opening ceremony, attended by strong supporter Bishop Westcott

14. 'Aged Miners' Homes: Meeting of Durham Associates,' BNA, *Newcastle Daily Chronicle*, 8 April 1907.

and a large number of miners' representatives was held on a bleak and rather damp Saturday afternoon at the end of October 1899 when, according to a local reporter, 'the cold nor-easter swept the place and caused the gorgeous lodge banners to flap wildly as the ceremonial procession made its way across the moor.' The weather, however, 'was quite insufficient to quench the genial spirit that generally prevailed' but rather emphasised 'the bracing, strong independence of the Northern character.'[15] The Bishop, now in his seventies and not in the best of health, to his credit, seems to have been similarly unfazed by the conditions, thanking them 'for the honour and privilege they had conferred upon him in asking him to take part in that most memorable ceremony.' Addressing the large gathering, to loud cheers and much applause, he said he considered the enterprise to be 'epoch making', marking a new departure in which, it seemed to him, Durham had shown England the way. 'Some said that what they had achieved was unattainable,' he said, 'but no-one for one moment should listen to a vision of despair but cherish the vigour of hope.' It was, he said, 'representative of two great principles of labour and love, self-help and co-operation.' The miners had contributed most generously out of their own resources. They were building not just homes for themselves but homes for the common good, for the whole society of which they were members. 'Self-help guarded and developed personal independence, and co-operative sympathy developed fellowship, and these two together formed the sure and solid foundation of human happiness.'[16] William, listening to this, would have agreed entirely with these sentiments but would have known that at least some of the money had been provided by generous benefactors, among them mine owners. It was something that would always grate on him, cutting across his own deeply held principles, but on this day of celebration he was not prepared to strike a discordant note. Finally, the Bishop offered a dedicatory prayer where he asked for 'joy, light and peace in the evening time for those who

---

15. 'The Haswell Moor Retreat. Durham Miners' Scheme,' BNA, *Northern Echo*, 30 October 1899.

16. ibid.

have borne the heat and burden of the day' and with due formality amid loud cheers, the door to number 1 Wilson Street was unlocked with a gilt key by John Wilson MP.[17] No doubt with some relief the ceremonial party then adjourned for tea in an adjoining marquee which also, remarkably, had managed to weather the storm.

The Durham Aged Mineworkers' Homes Association (DAMHA) still exists today as one of the largest and oldest almshouse charities in the UK. Currently it has around 1,700 homes, predominantly bungalows, on 130 sites in 80 villages across the area which formerly covered the County Durham coalfield. Nowadays, with the demise of the mining industry, anyone over the age of fifty can apply for one of these homes, designed for older, less physically active or disabled people. Although the charity has a continuing building programme of new homes many of the original cottages have obviously stood the test of time since some of the properties are more than one hundred years old. Every year £1 million is invested in upgrading these to meet twenty-first-century standards. Like Joseph Hopper and his indefatigable committee DAMHA is keen to emphasise, on its website, that 'we never stand still.'

17. ibid.

Chapter Fifteen
THE HOUSING OF THE PEOPLE

In June 1899, a few months before the opening of the houses at Haswell Moor, a number of delegates from Miners' Lodges and local Co-operative societies had attended a conference in Blyth under the auspices of the Land Nationalisation League. The League was the latest in a series of organisations formed in the latter part of the nineteenth century to promote the belief that land, like all means of production, should be the collective property of the people. It had recently joined forces with the similarly motivated Land Restoration Society which argued that land should be returned to national ownership by those who had acquired it by inheritance in the past. This in turn had developed from the Land Tenure Reform Association founded by John Stuart Mill in the late 1860s. The League had gained a substantial following by the 1890s, not only in rural areas dominated by wealthy estates, but also in towns and cities. Its cheery promotional yellow vans became a familiar sight on urban open spaces and village greens across the country.

The specific object of the conference in Blyth was 'to take into consideration the housing of the people and the best means of improving it.'[1] It was certainly a subject in dire need of consideration. In common with many industrial towns and cities, Victorian Gateshead had a severe housing shortage. Government statistics published in 1896 indicated that conditions in the town were some of the worst in the country with 40 per cent of the population living in substandard housing. Many

---

1. 'Canon Moore-Ede at Blyth. The Housing of the People,' BNA, *Shields Daily Gazette*, 20 June 1899.

people, trapped in a never-ending cycle of poverty, were paying high rents for dilapidated and insanitary dwellings. William, the main speaker at the conference, had considerable sympathy with the aims of the League. He had given numerous lectures on the subject of land ownership, first under the auspices of the Extension Scheme and later at meetings of the Economics Society at the Newcastle Lit and Phil. He agreed entirely with his audience that land should not be in the hands of those who had simply inherited it and who proceeded to use it to exploit the poor and thus obtain their 'unearned increment'. Much as he sympathised with the aims of his audience, however, he was also a practical man. The revolutionary vision of the League, however desirable, seemed to him to be essentially unachievable at least at the present time. Instead, he suggested, they should campaign for the implementation of the existing law. Under the terms of the Housing Act of 1890, he pointed out, local authorities possessed the power firstly to condemn any houses which they considered to be slums and secondly to compulsorily purchase the land on which they stood in order to build new dwellings at affordable rents. Consequently, local authorities should be urged to use the powers they already possessed for the benefit of the people. This was the position adopted by yet another recently formed organisation, the National Housing Reform Council. His audience however was dubious about the efficacy of such an approach. The problem in mining areas, laid out by another delegate at the conference, Co-operative Society representative, Henry Aldridge, was the composition of the town councils which in turn, he argued, was the fault of the miners themselves.[2] They persisted, he said, in their 'wicked folly of electing mine managers to positions on the local authority, men who worked entirely in the interests of the mine owners and not the rest of the population.'[3]

William felt he understood the miners' reluctance to stand for

---

2. Henry Aldridge, a prominent housing reformer, was initially a member of the Land Nationalisation League but later became the secretary of the National Housing Reform Council.

3. op cit., Canon Moore-Ede at Blyth.

election. Many would have felt they lacked the education or the time to put themselves forward for positions on the town councils. But he was forced to agree that the inertia of the councils was a major stumbling block. In May 1900 he made a further attempt to make inroads into the housing problem helping to organise a further meeting of another interested party, the Durham Land and Labour Committee, bringing along some influential local figures, notably the MP for Mid Durham, ex-miner John Wilson and also Bishop Westcott. As ever William considered that the Church had a responsibility to play a significant role in tackling social problems such as housing shortages. He said:

> The first practical work is to rouse town councils, to make them feel that the reason of their being is not political but social, that their duty is not the salvation of the pockets of the rich, but the salvation of the poor and weaker members of the community. And surely it is the special function of the Church to create a righteous public opinion, to infuse it with a lofty ideal of duty.[4]

The Bishop agreed wholeheartedly, giving a rousing address to more than a hundred delegates, confessing that, 'since they have come to my knowledge, the figures on the state of overcrowding and poor housing in Gateshead have haunted me.' With distinct echoes of William's position, he went on, 'Given the existence of the Housing Act the solution is human, not mechanical. There is a need for energetic action, not new legislation.'[5] The Bishop asked for the help, support and co-operation of all those present and a few weeks later the routine meeting of Gateshead Town Council was duly confronted by a large formal deputation of men and women 'with reference to housing reforms in Gateshead.' They 'desired to do away with the slums which were

---

4. op cit., Reverend Moore-Ede. *The Attitude of the Church to Some of the Problems of Town Life.*
5. 'Housing of the Working Classes. Speech by the Bishop of Durham,' BNA, *Newcastle Daily Chronicle*, 14 May 1900.

a disgrace to civilisation.'⁶ In keeping with contemporary protocol the council members listened politely to the four speakers. Miner and 'Pitman's poet' Robert Elliott, non-conformist minister the Reverend Packer and a Mr Mackie of the Gateshead's Trade Council all variously described the appalling effects on the lives of those forced to live in the conditions currently prevailing in Gateshead. William, as ever armed with well-researched detail, described in particular the average height of children living in the slums compared to those living in other parts of the borough.⁷ The Mayor then thanked them all and said the matter would be given 'every consideration.' Formalities duly observed, the deputation then withdrew. There was no further action.

The inertia of the town council reflected the prevailing attitudes among those whose pockets might be raided to help tackle the housing problem in Gateshead. During the conference William had been unsparing in his detail of the squalid state of so many houses in the area, the alarming statistics that showed that the situation in the town was worse than that in London, and the effect of this on the rates of illness and death, particularly amongst children. The subject seems to have attracted an avalanche of outrage in the local newspapers, but much of this was unsympathetic. William had, apparently, 'brought a hornet's nest about his ears,' for the reputation of the borough was being 'besmirched'.⁸ Many thought that the blame lay entirely with the occupiers of these dwellings. 'There are persons whose slovenly habits would, in six months, convert the most respectable street into a slum – and I should like to know what is to be done with them,' declared one correspondent.⁹ Another was prepared to concede that 'the local authority might do something to mitigate the evil but it must ever be remembered they cannot be held responsible for the individual

---

6. 'Gateshead Housing Reform Council. The Housing of the Working Classes in Gateshead,' BNA, *Newcastle Courant*, 7 July 1900.

7. Poetry played an important part in Northumberland mining culture and Robert Elliott was one of the most famous of the 'pitman poets'. He was also very active in local politics.

8. 'Topics by Tyne and Wear,' BNA, *Newcastle Courant*, 1 July 1899.

9. 'A Gateshead Grumble,' BNA, *Newcastle Daily Chronicle*, 23 June 1899.

who cares neither for cleanliness or godliness.'[10] Prominent among William's critics was the Mayor, Alderman William Henry Dunn, who commented that 'dirty people make dirty houses, and he would not interfere with their pleasure in filth.'[11] The *Newcastle Chronicle*, however, was supportive in its editorial comment, urging 'the worthy Canon to stick to his guns' and commenting that

> strange to say Alderman Dunn does not admit the responsibility of the local authorities, although it is known the evil can be modified, if not cured, if the town council were to put into force the powers they possess. After what has been said the authority are morally bound to give some attention to it.[12]

Sadly, it seemed no such attention was likely to be forthcoming. These events however would turn out to be preliminary skirmishes in the long battle to tackle the housing crisis in Gateshead.

The lack of adequate housing in Gateshead and the apparent indifference of the council always remained an issue of particular concern to William. And despite his new role in Whitburn his concerns for the conditions of the poor in his old parish continued to preoccupy his thoughts. Shortly after he left Gateshead he became interested in a new house building scheme called Tenants Limited which had developed at the end of the nineteenth century. He had learnt about this from Co-operative activist Henry Aldridge, the man who had berated the miners at the Blyth Conference for their reluctance to put themselves forward for local elections. Tenants was a co-partnership building scheme originally pioneered by a small group of workmen in Ealing, London, under the guidance of a former builder, the MP Henry Vivian. The idea was that a group of houses were built by the members of the scheme, each tailored to the needs of the participants in terms of size and space, thus producing a mix of social groups. In

10. 'Topics by Tyne and Wear', BNA, *Newcastle Courant*, 15 July 1899.
11. F. W. D. Manders, *A History of Gateshead* (Gateshead Corporation, UK, 1973).
12. op cit., 'Topics by Tyne and Wear'.

addition there was an emphasis on the creation of a site which provided green areas and a pleasant community environment, and it was here, in particular, that Tenants Limited made common cause with the contemporary garden city movement developed according to the principles of Ebenezer Howard.[13] William became a great enthusiast, urging against the construction of rows of identical terraces which, he considered, created a socially uniform and ugly environment that reinforced societal divisions. People wanted more air, space, decent gardens, and other things that went to beautify home life, he said. Not for the first time he compared the exemplary care given to the accommodation of prize animals at the Royal Show, while thousands of human beings were living in Tyneside 'in conditions that the owners of these beautiful beasts would not tolerate for their animals.'[14] Again, however, he was the subject of heated criticism. It was a project that 'drifted away from individualism to collectivism. It savoured too much of socialism,' declared a Mr Edward Davis at a conference in Ashington.[15] It was that word again, employed as ever to provoke unease. However, in 1908 William persuaded the committee of the Aged Miners' Homes to lay out one part of a site at Middleton Moor along garden city lines. Finance for land purchase and house building was raised in part by any capital each person might be able to contribute, but largely from borrowing, while rents for completed houses were adjusted on a basis sufficient to pay all interest charges. Much of the capital was in fact raised from the Co-operative Society, who by this stage had considerable assets. The use of Co-operative funds to develop housing projects had been agreed at the Co-operative conference at Blyth in 1899 where William had argued persuasively that the question of housing was a 'religious question.' He agreed, he said, with Lord Shaftsbury that 'all hope of moral and social improvement

---

13. Ebenezer Howard, the founder of the garden city movement, proposed self-contained communities containing a mix of houses, industry and agriculture such that residents experienced the advantages of each.

14. WME, address at a Housing Conference in Newcastle. BNA, *Hartlepool Northern Daily Mail*, 20 July 1908.

15. 'Ashington Co-operative Conference,' BNA, *Morpeth Herald*, 17 November 1906.

was utterly vain without improvement in regard to housing . . . any idea of self-respect and decency and of the higher ideals of life when all were pigged together in a single room was well-nigh impossible.' And above all, he continued, 'the Co-operative movement is a working-class movement . . . working-class people are beginning to show that they did care and are beginning to stir and this is a very hopeful sign.' Henry Aldridge concurred. 'Dividend is not the end of Co-operation,' he said. 'It is a means of securing life in greater abundance and it is our duty to help those least able to help themselves.'[16]

In the early 1900s the garden city movement was just one of a number of new organisations which emphasised the importance of housing as an integral part of social reform. William was already in contact with a number of activists who belonged to this and other sympathetic organisations, such as Earl Grey who had helped him in the establishment of the Extension Scheme in the North East, as well as Henry Aldridge who was a founder member of the recently formed National Housing Reform Council. Various small housing developments were appearing across the country which espoused the principles of Garden Cities with model houses, community facilities and green space. Central to the idea was the co-operative nature of the enterprise, such that the value of the land and buildings remained in the community, which was thus the benefactor of any 'unearned increment'. With such settlements springing up around Birmingham, Manchester and Liverpool, William was naturally keen that Tyneside should not be left behind. In October 1906 the requisite committee was formed, this time under the chairmanship of Hugh Boyle, president of the Northumberland Miners' Association, with a view to building an exhibition of model cottages, showcasing different types of ideal houses for working people. William was appointed vice chairman with Henry Aldridge, as secretary. The following month a commitment was obtained from Newcastle Corporation to lease 16½ acres of land on the north side of the River

16. 'The Homes of Our Workers. Conference at Blyth,' BNA, *Shield Daily Gazette*, 20 June 1899.

Tyne at Walker, that 'blackened and disagreeable place', as formerly described by the *England and Wales Gazetteer*, and home to many eager recipients of William's lectures. It was agreed that the houses should be built from plans submitted in competition by architects according to particular specifications of size and price, to include architect's fees and builders' costs but not the cost of the land and roads. Not more than twelve houses were to be built on an acre of ground and back streets were to be dispensed with. There were four types of cottages, of varying sizes with different types of families in mind. In each category gold, silver and bronze medals were to be awarded. (For once, it seemed, William was willing to suspend his aversion to competition). The cottages, it was stated, should be built according to urban by-laws and wages paid in accordance with the 'fair contracts' clause of Newcastle City Council. A furniture and garden competition was also to be held. Drawing on the regrettable experience of recent housing construction at Letchworth garden city in Hertfordshire, the committee added a clause ensuring that the prices quoted were *bone fide*. 'Entry into the competition is conditional on the exhibitor agreeing, if called upon to do so, to sell the house to the Newcastle City Council at the stated price and to build twelve more cottages at that price.' The prices quoted by architects at Letchworth had not, it transpired, been entirely inclusive and as such were rather elastic!¹⁷

The opening of the exhibition was planned for the spring of 1907 but the enterprise was beset by a number of delays during the previous months. In particular there were problems with the construction of the sewerage system and arguments over responsibility for this. These were compounded by a depression in the building trade and the withdrawal of a number of nervous contractors worried about their financial position. And in March 1907 Hugh Boyle, chairman of the Exhibition Committee, died. William, however, immediately stepped in and took over, rising to the challenge with his usual dedication

---

17. 'The Week,' BNA, *Merthyr Express*, 7 October 1905.

and determination. Eventually all was resolved and on 23 June 1908 the North of England Cottage Exhibition was finally opened with considerable ceremony by the Lord Mayor of Newcastle who, as a mark of the importance of the event, 'wore his robes and chains of office and the sword and mace bearers were in attendance.' In his capacity as chairman, William presided over the opening ceremony, paying tribute to Mr Boyle and thanking all those involved. He was looking forward to much better town planning in the future he said. 'The committee desires flattery in the form of imitation.'[18] Throughout the following week several thousand people arrived to view the houses courtesy of special excursion trains laid on by the North Eastern Railway company with a connecting tram from central Newcastle. The Band of the Tramways Department played throughout each day as people joined conducted tours, enjoyed tea and cakes and watched the presentations of awards and bouquets. It was all a great success and even the Society publication *Queen* devoted some space to the event (sandwiched between the Horse Show at Olympia and 'Linen Sets for the Nursery').[19] William was clearly delighted with what had been achieved. There were, he said, eighty dwellings of different sizes in a convenient and healthy place for the working people of Tyneside. Another 120 were planned for the site. The exhibition was an admirable object lesson in laying out an estate and it came at a very opportune time, 'when we are likely to have greater powers given to municipalities in the direction of control over the development of suburban areas.'[20] This was a reference to the new Housing Bill currently progressing through the House of Commons. The Act of 1909 would prevent the building of 'back-to-back' houses and, significantly, require local authorities to introduce systems of town planning and construct houses to certain legal standards.

Many of the houses built during this optimistic period remain today, a testament to the garden city concept of urban living. Walkerville itself

18. 'The Model Cottage Exhibition at Walker,' BNA, *Shields Daily News*, 24 June 1908.
19. 'Model Cottage Exhibition at Walker,' *Queen*, 27 June 1908.
20. op cit., 'The Model Cottage Exhibition at Walker,' *Shield Daily News*.

An aerial view of modern Walkerville. (Courtesy of Historic England Archive.)

remains an attractive estate composed of a rich variety of private houses of differing sizes and designs. It is not immediately obvious that these houses were built for the Edwardian working classes. The large plots, which today are mostly built over with garages or extensions, provide evidence of the generous amount of garden space provided for these early twentieth-century inhabitants. From the air the trident shaped development, which spoke of an integrated community, is still obvious but much of the green space that surrounded it is gone and, on the ground, its roads are largely indistinguishable from the wider urban sprawl. Sadly, the communal co-operative element of many Garden Cities is also hard (although not impossible) to find in twenty-first-century Britain. And too many of these shrines to Ebenezer Howard's ideal now operate according to a form of competitive capitalism that would have disappointed William. The 'unearned increment', it seems, is difficult to suppress.[21]

---

21. In 2020, the average house price in Walkerville was reported to be just over £170,000.

Chapter Sixteen
TURNING BACK THE TIDE

In December 1902, amidst great controversy and much outrage, a new Education Act, commonly known as the Balfour Act, passed into law. It actually came into operation on 1 April 1903, an irony that was not lost on those who considered its contents to be an absurdity. The Act which abolished school boards and brought state education under the umbrella of county councils also granted voluntary schools (i.e. Anglican and Roman Catholic schools) access to ratepayers' money to pay their teachers, including religious teachers, and provide books and equipment. The Act was hailed a major triumph for a parliamentary faction known as the Church Party which had long campaigned against the growth of Board Schools and the lack of funding for Church schools which, they said, had amounted to the deliberate secularisation of education. By contrast religious non-conformists, political liberals and various radical groups were uniformly and vehemently opposed to the Act. Unlike many other members of the Church of England William was similarly opposed, joining various unsuccessful protest movements as the Bill made its way through Parliament during 1901. For him the enhancement of educational opportunity was the paramount concern and unlike many of his Anglican contemporaries he was essentially ecumenical in his thinking. On many occasions he stressed the importance of a variety of religious expression which he considered to be both inevitable and desirable, for it was not strict adherence to any one branch of Christianity that defined his faith, but rather what he saw as Christ's message of social justice and its practical application. It was a position that had enhanced his popularity amongst ordinary working people and enabled him to ward off accusations of Anglican bias as he struggled through fractious meetings of the Gateshead School Board. Now the new Act, intended to satisfy the competing demands of various faith leaders, seemed to have fanned the flames of religious strife once more. Rather than celebrating the provisions of the Act the various factions fought with renewed vigour for influence and control. Exactly what sort of religion should be taught and for how many hours/days each week? What was the distinction between Church teaching and Bible teaching? (None according to Anglicans and Roman Catholics, everything according to non-conformists.) Who should teach it? Could non-conformists teach in voluntary schools or (perish the thought) actually become head teachers? What should be the content of a morning assembly? Which hymns should be allowed and what sort of prayers? Every conceivable detail of potential strife rose to the surface to be aired in the febrile columns of both local and national newspapers.

In 1903 William, now a member of the Education Committee of the Durham County Council, made an attempt to mediate, raising his head above the parapet to propose a 'concordat', a document containing a series of compromises which he hoped might provide a basis for useful discussion. It offered the prospect of unfettered teaching of religion in denominational schools and the opportunity for members of the clergy to 'enter the provided (non-religious) schools one day each week specifically to teach children of their own denomination.'[1] Given that the county council also proposed to assist with repairs and maintenance of existing voluntary schools, not an official requirement of the Act, and despite the fact that many were in a neglected state, this might have seemed a reasonable compromise to a non-partisan observer. It was, however, immediately derided in an editorial of the *Church Times*. It seemed that nothing less than traditional Anglican church teaching taught throughout every school in the land would really do. The editor feared that the 'Radical leaders of Progressivism'

---

1. Letter from WME to the *Guardian*. 'The Proposed Concordat.' Reprinted in the *Newcastle Daily Chronicle*, 26 December 1903.

had been 'captured by the Hotspurs of Dissent' who were bent on creating a schism in the Anglican church.[2] Meanwhile non-conformists and secularists objected to any state funds being used to support denominational schools, especially those of the Roman Catholic church. No 'Rome on the rates' was the popular cry. The concordat was also largely disowned by Handley Moule, an evangelical Bishop who tended towards rather traditional views on religious education. He was happy to make common cause with William on some subjects, notably on the evil influence of alcohol (he too was an enthusiastic member of the Rechabites) but on his own admission he could not be described as 'radical' in his thinking. As Bishop of Durham he has been described as someone 'who excelled in pastoral ministry ... the epitome of kindness towards all' but 'he was not at home in political matters ... he was not a leader of people like Bishop Westcott ... some believe he was too quick to agree for the sake of peace.'[3] When it came to the concordat he felt that 'in their present form the proposals could not be entirely accepted' but conceded that they formed the basis for a conference on the subject after which he hoped that 'peace might be preserved in the county.'[4] Later that month at a meeting of clerics at Auckland Castle the concordat was resoundingly rejected. There was, it seems, no peace to be had.

The arguments surrounding religious teaching in schools are considered by many historians to be a major factor in the fall of the Conservative government in 1906. However, the Liberals, who won a landslide victory that year, fared little better on the religious education question, proposing three successive bills between 1906 and 1908, each an attempt to please all factions and all ultimately failing. The problematical relationship between religion and education would continue throughout the twentieth century and remains an equally

---

2. *Church Times*, 24 December 1903.

3. D. B. Calhoun, 'Bright Messenger of God: Bishop Handley Moule,' *Knowing and Doing* (CS Lewis Institute, spring 2012). Accessed via www.cslewisinstitute.org

4. 'The Proposed Religious Instruction Concordat,' BNA, *Hartlepool Daily Mail*, 28 December 1903.

contentious issue in the twenty-first. Far from moving towards any sort of concordat it seems to have gathered increasing complexity as the relatively straightforward divisions between different brands of the Christian faith have been joined by the new challenges of an ever increasing ethnic and cultural diversity. Today arguments swirl around issues such as the admission criteria for children of differing faiths, and the requirement for schools to teach different religious and non-religious beliefs within a wider, values and ethics-based curriculum. Many faith-based schools struggle with these dilemmas.[5] It is difficult to know where William would have stood on these questions. One suspects he might have joined today's 'Accord Coalition' an organisation composed of different religious groups, human rights activists and trade unions which campaigns for schools to follow 'an objective, fair and balanced syllabus for education about religious and non-religious beliefs.'[6] Certainly, with his progressive views and ecumenical leanings, he was often reluctant to fight the specifically Anglican corner, something that seems to have been widely known and accepted in both clerical circles and beyond. In December 1903 when the Bishop's conference rejected his concordat the *Durham County Advertiser* commented that 'the precious scheme rejected a fortnight ago was the joint production of Mr Samuel Storey,[7] Mr John Wilson and Canon Moore-Ede, a trio anything but calculated to inspire confidence in the breasts of Churchmen.'[8]

Meanwhile in 1904, following the resignation of the chairman of the Durham Education Committee, William was urged by several

5. In June 2020 the headteacher of every Roman Catholic school in Wales signed a letter expressing 'serious concern' about a proposal by the Education Department to change the nature of religious education 'towards a religion, values and ethics area of learning.' Under the proposal parents would have the right to demand religious education along the lines of that provided at non-faith schools. The Roman Catholic headteachers argued that the proposal 'failed to recognise the heritage and deep connection religious education has within schools of a religious character.' The 'i'. 6 June 2020.

6. The Accord Coalition for Inclusive Education. www.accordcoalition.org.uk

7. Samuel Storey was a Liberal member of the Durham County Council. He was also a publisher who founded the *Sunderland Echo*, a regional daily newspaper which was a mouthpiece for his radical political views. The newspaper still exists today.

8. 'Do You Know?' BNA, *Durham County Advertiser*, 11 December 1903.

Anglican members to put himself forward as a replacement. This, however, he declined, saying that he was a member of the Committee not as a churchman but as a citizen. He was there purely for the interests of education, having been sent there by the progressive miners of the area in which he lived. These were the miners of Marsden colliery. He had already been involved in a dispute with other members of the committee over the contentious issue of teachers' salaries. Teachers in Marsden, it seemed, were paid less than in some other, more affluent areas of the county. Were the miners' children not entitled to the same standard of education as other peoples' children he wanted to know. The position of chairman, he knew, would somewhat curtail his ability to speak out on Marsden's behalf, but he also added that he would, in any case, much prefer that someone who was 'not a churchman' should preside over the committee.[9] He would have sensed that his election was an attempt by Anglicans to maintain control over council policy, and he had no wish to embroil himself once more in the bitter religious feuds that he had experienced in Gateshead.

William had also broken ranks with his fellow churchmen a couple of years earlier, in November 1902, when he professed himself unconcerned about a particular proposed amendment to the Education Bill, the Kenyon-Slaney amendment. This proposed that teachers of religious instruction in voluntary schools should be appointed by school managers rather than the church. It provoked fury amongst many Anglican church leaders who saw it as a ploy to curb their influence over the form and content of religious education. Religious instruction, they argued, should only be given by Anglican clergy. At the height of the debate William found himself presiding at the laying of a foundation stone for the new Church of England school currently under construction in the village of Cleadon in his parish. It was the last school to be built under the auspices of the old School Board and he was obviously rather pleased that the school had managed to slip under the wire before the new Act came into operation. Addressing

---

9. 'Durham Education Committee: Election of Chairman,' BNA, *Sunderland Daily Echo and Shipping Gazette*, 24 November 1904.

the assembled onlookers, he commented that some people were of the opinion that they ought not to proceed with the scheme because the new Education Act might make great changes. He, however, saw no reason for delay, for it was imperative that their existing and plainly inadequate school was replaced, and the details of the financial position were such that only another £200 was required to complete the works. Clearly the people of Cleadon agreed, for with a considerable turn of speed they rallied round to raise the money and the school opened just seven months later, not only with a new building but also an additional teacher. For William it was the foundation of new improved educational facilities that was important, not necessarily the foundation of a specifically Church of England school. Aware of the controversy around the Kenyon-Slaney proposal he decided to address this head on. He saw no problem with it he said. Since a school like Cleadon would not necessarily contain only children from Anglican homes, he felt that 'it was only reasonable that laymen should have some voice and influence in supervising the religious instruction given in the school – especially when it happened to be the only school in the parish.'[10] Laymen, he said, had a great contribution to make and he felt that there was no reason for any concern.

If anything, it seemed, William viewed the religious issue as a distraction from what he saw as the primary purpose of the Education Committee, to ensure the best possible education for the ordinary people of the area. He was, however, hugely disappointed by the 1902 Act which seemed to him likely to undo many of the achievements of the previous thirty years. Two matters in particular caused him dismay. The first was the proposed abolition of higher grade schools replacing these with new designated secondary schools. He had been hugely proud of the higher grade schools in Gateshead which had provided free extended education for numerous bright children in the area, children who could never have dreamt of continuing their education beyond the age of fourteen. Ostensibly the Act had the intention of expanding

---

10. 'Canon Moore-Ede on the Education Bill,' BNA, *Sunderland Daily Echo and Shipping Gazette*, 17 November 1902.

secondary education by subsidising this on the rates but in practice, as William feared, the future development of secondary schools actually consisted of the development of schools which charged fees, modelled on the existing grammar school system, thus excluding most children of the working classes. And even the establishment of these schools was not mandatory. Rather the county councils were 'required to take such steps as seemed to them desirable to supply or aid the supply of education other than elementary.' It would have reminded him of the Housing Act which 'enabled' rather than 'required' the demolition of slums and the construction of better homes. His second concern was the replacement of small education boards, which he felt had intimate knowledge of their local areas, with large impersonal county councils, covering huge areas of administration. In the Durham County area there were 310 Voluntary Schools educating approximately 780,000 children and 185 Board Schools with around 58,000 pupils. The Durham County Council was an immense body of men, consisting of the Mayor, twenty-two aldermen and sixty-nine other members and in William's opinion there was no possibility of this unwieldy structure with its multifarious committees and subcommittees governing effectively. They would, he said, be making decisions affecting schools they had never visited, teachers they had never met and children of whom they had no knowledge. Moreover, the huge range of responsibilities now placed on the county councils would mean that education was likely to be relegated to a very minor concern.

Despite these misgivings William's enduring passion for the cause of education meant that he could not resist securing election to the county council and a place on the newly constituted Education Committee. Yet it was a frustrating time beset by bureaucratic wrangling, inevitably about religion, but also about the composition and administrative reach of various sub committees, about teachers' salaries and qualifications, and the right of children to attend schools outside their own areas. Effectively it meant that no new secondary schools, fee paying or otherwise, were established during his period of tenure. One small incident, however, nicely underlines his strong feelings of support for the underprivileged of the world. In July 1904 Alderman George Wraith placed on the agenda of the county council meeting a query about the appointment of Mr James Leonard, formerly a checkweighman at the local colliery, to a position as a district clerk.[11] Was it correct, he asked, that Mr Leonard's application had a number of mis-spellings, that his letter of application contained sentences with nouns but not verbs, besides other errors of punctuation and construction? Was it the case that Mr Leonard was preferred to a gentleman holding a university Degree and to numerous other gentlemen of education? Alderman Wraith considered that Mr Leonard was an illiterate person incapable of writing an ordinary letter in plain English. He considered that the appointment should be sent back for further consideration. William seems to have been stung by this apparent attempt to discredit a working man and immediately leapt to James Leonard's defence. There was an impression about, he said, that Mr Leonard had been appointed because he was one of the miner's men. He disclaimed this idea. The appointment committee, he said, had been attracted by Mr Leonard's personality. He might not have had a university education, but he had had the benefit of a practical education in administration, which was much more useful. In fact, there were only two mistakes in Mr Leonard's letter. Amid some laughter William added that he was not sure he could have done any better! Mr Leonard's appointment was subsequently confirmed by fifty votes to fifteen. Three years later the Committee met to discuss a rise in the salary of James Leonard. All expressed their high approval of his work, which had been extremely efficient. The recommendation to increase his annual salary from £150 to £175 per year was unanimously adopted.

---

11. In the mines where pay was determined by the weight of coal obtained, the checkweighman was a representative elected by the miners to check the weights recorded by the mine owner's weighman.

Chapter Seventeen
WORCESTER

On Tuesday morning 22 July 1908 William received a formal letter from the recently appointed Liberal Prime Minister, Herbert Asquith, asking him 'if he would consent to his name being presented to the King for the vacancy at Worcester.'[1] Announcing this to his congregation at Whitburn the following Sunday he professed that this was a great surprise to him. Whether or not this surprise was in fact genuine it is clear that he made up his mind very quickly to accept, informing the congregation that it was 'with great regret that he had to say that his work in that parish would soon draw to a close.'[2] His next words suggest that perhaps this regret was not total, on either side, for he recognised their forbearance while he had lived and worked among them because he knew they had not always seen eye to eye. They had not always approved of what he had done and said. What exactly he was referring to is unknown, but it was perhaps predictable that a radical progressive clergyman might present certain challenges to a deeply conservative and traditional village. And perhaps they had simply resented the amount of attention he had focussed on the people of Marsden.

The vacancy at Worcester was that of Dean of the Cathedral occasioned by the death of the previous incumbent Robert Forrest. There is little doubt that the choice of William as a replacement was a controversial one. According to the conservative leaning newspaper *The Globe* he was 'long considered an ardent radical

1. 'Canon Ede's Preferment,' BNA, *Hartlepool Northern Daily Mail*, 27 July 1908.
2. ibid.

whose appointment represented one more sign of the new political influences surrounding the Liberal government.'³ Certainly the decision to offer the post to William seems to have been made with remarkable speed, for Dean Forrest's funeral had taken place only twelve days earlier. Perhaps, however, the necessary discussions and recommendations had already taken place in anticipation of the Dean's death. These would probably have involved Charles Gore, the former Bishop of Worcester and one of the early founders of the Christian Socialist movement.⁴ Bishop Gore had recently left Worcester to form the new Diocese of Birmingham and knew William well. He was a strong advocate of Christian Socialist doctrine and would have been keen to promote this in Worcester. Meanwhile the current Bishop of Worcester, Huyshe Yeatman-Biggs, who confessed that William was 'unknown to me personally' seemed unlikely to be greatly sympathetic to progressive ideas or to involve himself unduly in the social problems of town life.⁵ He was once described as a 'convinced high churchman who had ideas of what should be the orderly system of the Church to which he expected his clergy to conform' and, with perhaps echoes of William Baylee, 'he depreciated practices that aroused controversy'. Somewhat tactfully the writer added that the Bishop 'found it difficult to recognise truth in unfamiliar forms.' He also, however

> thoroughly understood the difficulties of the country clergy and recognised the importance of their work. As the owner of considerable estates, his sympathies were with the landed gentry – the most valuable part of his Diocesan work was his care for the country parishes. With the social problems of the industrial parts of the diocese he was less at home.⁶

3. 'Dean of Worcester', BNA, *The Globe*, 24 July 1908.
4. Charles Gore, Bishop of Worcester, in office 1902–5; Bishop of Birmingham, in office 1905–11.
5. Huyshe Yeatman-Biggs, Bishop of Worcester, in office 1905–18; Bishop of Coventry, in office 1918–22.
6. 'A Long Episcopal Career,' BNA, *Coventry Standard*, 21–22 April 1922.

As things turned out, William's rapid appointment was followed by a rather long delayed installation. At the end of August, when the King had formally signalled his acceptance of the appointment, Bishop Yeatman-Biggs pointed out that a statute of the Cathedral required that the Dean must be a Doctor of Divinity. Regretfully he was obliged to decline the institution of Canon Moore-Ede, at least until this deficiency could be rectified. Despite his impressive performance at Cambridge, William's formal theological qualifications were of course rather limited. As so often, however, the difficulty was eventually surmounted by recourse to something called the 'Lambeth Degree', a device no doubt intended to deal with exactly this sort of problem. Essentially, (under the Ecclesiastical Licences Act of 1533) the Archbishop of Canterbury was able to award a higher Degree to a person who had served the church in a particularly distinguished way, without the usual requirement for an academic postgraduate thesis. Despite this inauspicious start therefore William, complete with his doctorate, was finally installed with the usual formalities as Dean of Worcester Cathedral on the afternoon of 30 October. Earlier that day he had also enjoyed a lunch at Worcester's Guildhall organised by John Stallard, the Mayor of Worcester, who had invited members of the Corporation, various representatives of the laity, several parochial clergy, and a number of 'Free Churchmen' all of whom wanted to meet the new Dean. No doubt fully aware of William's reputation the Mayor expressed the hope that he would 'unite with the Corporation and other bodies in the social work of the area.'[7] William, would have been greatly heartened by this and responded enthusiastically. He had always, he said, been closely identified with civic life. The union of civic and ecclesiastical authorities was, he felt, 'the true spirit of the times.'[8]

Meanwhile *The Times,* reporting on the day's events, seemed to feel that the appointment of a 'socialist' to one of the ancient Cathedrals of the English shires required some justification. Having pointed out that

7. 'New Dean of Worcester Installed,' BNA, *Yorkshire Post and Leeds Intelligencer*, 31 October 1908.
8. bid.

Canon Moore-Ede was 'well known for his interest in social questions and his zeal for the welfare of the working classes' the correspondent added that 'for his efforts as a social reformer he will find plenty of scope in a Diocese which includes Coventry and Dudley and not a little of the Black Country.'[9] William, it was assumed, would need to travel a little way out of the city to indulge his reformist zeal. No doubt the correspondent of the London-based *The Times* maintained a rather leafy, genteel view of Edwardian Worcester, a view which did not include, for example, Mr Henry Webb's chemical fertiliser factory, Hardy & Padmore's iron foundry and Hill & Evans Vinegar works, not to mention Fownes Gloves or Mr Henry Ward's chrome tanning works at Barbourne. These were just some of the larger industrial enterprises situated within a stone's throw of the city centre. The forest of tall smoking chimneys which marked the positions of the numerous steam engines that drove these factories and many more like them seem to have been airbrushed out of the popular imaginings of early twentieth-century Worcester. For in reality this was a smoky, rather grim industrial city employing thousands of poor workers often in miserable hazardous conditions. William would barely need to step outside the immediate precincts of the Cathedral to encounter the Royal Worcester Porcelain factory, occupying land leased to the owners by the Church itself.

The slums of Worcester covered a smaller geographical area than those on Tyneside and the houses were of a different character, but the lives of their inhabitants were essentially the same. Close to the Cathedral in an area called Birdport there were large numbers of centuries old, decaying half-timbered houses, formerly occupied by the middle-classes of earlier times, which by the early twentieth century had turned into squalid tenements teeming with poor families. Here numbers of ragged children played in the streets and along the river quays, while in Edward Webb's horsehair carpet factory nearby the women began work each day at 6 a.m.

9. A comment by *The Times*, reported in *Shields Daily News*, 24 July 1908.

and emerged two hours later in their clogs and shawls to eat their breakfast before returning to work to complete their twelve-hour shift. Tellingly one woman recalled that 'on Sundays it was a pleasant sight to see the gentry coming out of the Cathedral. The dresses were beautiful and much envied by the workers.'[10] Meanwhile on the eastern side of the city just outside the boundary of the former city walls was an area known as the Blockhouse. Here there were rows of cheap back-to-back houses built in the mid nineteenth century to accommodate the large numbers of incomers who flocked to the city to work in the numerous developing factories. Groups of twelve houses were situated around an enclosed court, sharing one toilet and one wash house. Undoubtedly William would find plenty to occupy him in the Black Country, but he would also find many of the same problems in Worcester that had occupied him in Gateshead.

Perhaps understandably it was some time before William began to raise his head significantly above Worcester's social parapet. He had after all taken on a new, highly responsible role in a completely unfamiliar environment. As head of the Cathedral Chapter, the body which essentially governed the everyday workings of the Cathedral, he had a significant range of administrative and ecclesiastical duties. He had also been required to take on the official residence of the Dean, a picturesque historic house adjacent to the Cathedral set in large gardens which sloped gently down to the River Severn. This was the Old Palace, so named on account of it being one of the former residences of the Bishop who by now confined himself to his other official home, Hartlebury Castle, a few miles outside the city. Bishop Yeatman-Biggs, reputedly to be the richest Bishop in England, was perhaps one of the few men capable of meeting the financial demands of Hartlebury Castle. His predecessor Charles Gore had refused to live there because of the expense and there was some difficulty in recruiting subsequent Bishops to Worcester

---

10. B. Gwilliam, *Old Worcester: People and Places*. (Halfshire Books, Bromsgrove, 1993).

when faced with the prospect of maintaining the castle.[11] William, meanwhile, also struggled with the demands of the Old Palace. As an enthusiastic student of history he would have been impressed by the long list of significant events and royal visits associated with the ancient building, not to mention an apparently unique painting of a certain Dr Thomas, a seventeenth-century Dean, later Bishop of Worcester, which graced the wall of the Great Hall. He would have been less enamoured, however, of the cost of the upkeep of the Palace with its cavernous rooms, endless repairs and the need for a large contingent of servants to keep it all running. During his tenure as Dean he would make several attempts to persuade the church authorities to dispense with or at least re-allocate the building and replace it with a small modern Deanery. In 1917, for example, when the question of Hartlebury Castle was again raised he suggested the removal of the Bishop to the Old Palace as an appropriate option. His efforts to abandon the old building, however, were to no avail and he was destined to remain there until his retirement in 1934.[12]

In 1908 William was hardly in need of such a large house. Of all the children that had filled the Rectory in Gateshead only one now remained under his roof and this would be a temporary arrangement. His eldest son William Edward, a medical practitioner, had spent some time living and working at Toynbee Hall, the social reformist settlement house in East London which provided a range of educational, social and health facilities for the poor.[13] In 1906 he had married and subsequently would set up a medical practice in the village of Cradley a few miles outside Worcester. In the meantime, however, he was living at the Deanery with his wife, Beatrice, and their young child.

---

11. Bishop Gore lived in Worcester, first at a house on the Tewkesbury Road which subsequently became the Loch Ryan Hotel and later in Lansdowne Crescent, where his former residence is now known as the Bishop's House.

12. In recent years the Old Palace has housed Diocesan offices.

13. Toynbee Hall was a university-affiliated community settlement set up in 1884 by Henrietta and Samuel Barnett in memory of their friend Arnold Toynbee. It provided educational and social services to the local community.

Interestingly it seemed to be medicine rather than the Church which fuelled the ambitions of most of William's children, departing from the prevailing trend of the period, for the sons of clergy to follow in their father's footsteps. Three of his sons and his elder daughter Laetitia all became medical doctors and his younger stepdaughter Mary became a hospital nurse. His remaining son Stuart became an engineer, travelling the world to pursue his profession, and his younger daughter Elizabeth who married another engineer, Henry Rivers-Moore, would similarly spend time abroad, in her case in South Africa. Only William's elder stepdaughter Eleanor might be said to have followed a more conventional path in that she married a clergyman, although the clergyman in question, John Elliotson-Symes, was far from a conventional choice. A radical socialist and a devoted follower of Frederick Maurice the Reverend Elliotson-Symes was also a founder member of a Christian Socialist organisation called the Guild of St Matthew which gained considerable, if rather brief prominence at the end of the nineteenth century. The prime mover in the establishment of the Guild was the Reverend Stuart Headlam whose extreme socialist views had led to his dismissal from various curacies during the 1870s and '80s. William shared many of Stuart Headlam's views on the causes of poverty and the path to reform, but not perhaps his preference for a return to high Anglican forms of worship – or his tendency to attach himself to controversial causes which alienated many in the middle classes. He was, for example, a great supporter of theatres and music halls and various other much maligned forms of artistic expression. He campaigned vigorously on behalf of Oscar Wilde imprisoned in 1895 for homosexuality, and also for the abolition of the House of Lords, to name but a few contentious issues of the time. By the early 1880s he had effectively been exiled from the Church of England and reduced to taking part in church services only when friendly clergy were willing to invite him. Stepdaughter Eleanor and her husband, however, were clearly devoted supporters and it was probably Eleanor who persuaded William to allow the Reverend Headlam to take part in their marriage ceremony in 1885. William was probably aware that he was sailing quite close to the ecclesiastical wind, especially when their wedding that year was described in the *Newcastle Courant* as 'so characteristic of the Rector.' Perhaps, however, the newspaper was simply referring to the somewhat unusual guest list for the reception. After the wedding it was reported 'three hundred poor residents of St Mary's were entertained at breakfast in the Town Hall.'[14]

By 1908, therefore, nearly all of William's children had flown the nest and he was largely free of family responsibilities. As an Honorary Canon of Durham Cathedral he would have been familiar with the workings of the Chapter, the body of Canons which oversaw the everyday organisation of a Cathedral and its services, but Worcester, and more particularly Worcestershire, must have seemed a very different environment to that he knew so well on Tyneside. During his first twelve months he seems to have focussed on acquainting himself not only with the complex workings of the Cathedral itself but also with the city, its people and its surroundings. He and Eleanor attended and hosted garden parties, lunches, dinners (non-alcoholic of course) and bazaars in aid of good causes. They met the local gentry, of whom, he observed, there were many more than in Tyneside, and the local aristocracy of which Worcestershire could also be said to have more than its fair share. Some of the more prominent in local affairs included Earl Beauchamp of Madresfield Court, the Earl of Coventry of Croome Park, Viscount Cobham of Hagley Hall, and Sir Harry and Lady Georgina Vernon of Hanbury Hall. The Viscount and the Vernons, he observed, would be significant allies in the promotion of temperance in the area. He attended the Annual Speech Day at the Kings School attached to the Cathedral where, he was informed, his office meant that he was required to be a School Governor, and he took the opportunity to talk at length to the staff and boys about his views on education. More widely, however, he also took an active part in a national campaign to reform the Poor Law following the Poor Law Commission report of 1909 which highlighted the need for at

---

14. 'Fashionable Wedding,' BNA, *Newcastle Courant*, 2 January 1885.

least one of the measures he had long advocated, the introduction of a universal old age pension. The measure, when it came, was rather more limited than he had hoped for, but it was start and did at least establish the principle of income support in old age. In July 1910 he accompanied Charles Gore to London as part of a clergy deputation to the Prime Minister, led by the Archbishop of Canterbury, to appeal for immediate and wholescale reform of Poor Law legislation.[15] And the following month he spoke at a conference of the Fabian Society on the causes and prevention of destitution.[16]

By the end of the year, however, he was beginning to resume more of the local activities which had filled his time on Tyneside, for his overriding ethos remained one of practical involvement in the local community of which he was a part. He accepted an invitation to become a vice president of the Worcestershire Wayfarers' Relief Society which aimed to provide assistance to the unemployed in order to prevent them resorting either to a life 'on the road' or in the workhouse. In addition to the provision of food and shelter the society established a labour bureau which identified available employment around the immediate area to which men could apply. Similarly, he became a vice president of the Worcestershire branch of the Discharged Prisoners Aid Society which provided food, clothing, shelter and assistance with employment for those leaving gaol who had no obvious means of support. He was also a member of the committee formed by Lady Georgina Vernon to develop district nursing in the county and a founder member of the group which raised funds for the establishment of Worcestershire's Open Air School for delicate children which opened in Malvern in 1914.[17] Meetings and speaking engagements again began to crowd his diary notably those of the local

---

15. Archbishop Randall Thomas Davidson, in office 1903-1928

16. The Fabian Society had been founded in 1884 by Beatrice and Sydney Webb and played a major role in the founding of the British Labour Party. As a socialist organisation committed to non-violent political action to advance social reform its aims were very much in tune with those of William.

17. This was originally known as the Mount School. It is now the site of an Outdoor Activity Centre for children.

branch of the CETS and the Birmingham branch of the IOR, where he gave regular talks on his favourite topic of temperance promotion. In nearby Leamington Spa he was delighted to be invited to dedicate their first temperance cafe, the Milverton Coffee-House, where he was introduced as 'someone who has been at the birth of more coffee taverns than any other clergyman in the Kingdom.'[18] He also involved himself in the work of the recently formed Digbeth Institute in Birmingham, a recreational and educational centre in an area of extreme poverty and deprivation. The Institute had been founded by an old friend, John Jowett, congregational minister of nearby Carrs Lane Church and William both admired his work and relished the opportunity for ecumenical cooperation.[19]

Back in Worcestershire meanwhile he found some unexpected common ground with the Bishop in the form of a mission to those involved in hop picking, an agricultural practice prominent in Worcestershire. Huyshe Yeatman-Biggs might have been less than comfortable in the city slums and alleys but William, it seems, was equally ill at ease in the countryside. At the opening of a new church in the beautiful rural village of Colwall on the edge of the Malvern Hills he was asked to say something about the need for an attached 'Institute' which was intended to provide recreational and educational activities for the local population. Was a church not enough people asked? Rather tactlessly he said that charming as the village seemed he 'imagined it was rather dull, particularly in the winter, and men might have recreations that exposed them to temptation.'[20] William was basically a townsman, energised by the bustle of urban life and industry, a factor which had tended to draw him away from his congregation in Whitburn and towards the miners of Marsden. Now,

18. 'At the Sign of the "Welcome". Milverton Coffee-House,' BNA, *Leamington Spa Courier*, 11 October 1912.

19. The church at Carrs Lane, Birmingham, is now a partnership, created in 2011, between the United Reformed (formerly Congregational) Church and the Methodist Central Mission. It is a progressive church and a conference centre with a continuing concern for social justice and dialogue between people of different faiths.

20. 'Opening of the New Church at Colwall,' BNA, *Herefordshire Times*, 2 April 1910.

it seemed, he had much to learn about rural Worcestershire and it was only with the Bishop's help that was able to launch the Hop Pickers Mission and Tea Tents in the country parishes around the county. Hop pickers were not strictly rural workers, but they were, temporarily at least, working in a rural environment, arriving in their hundreds each year to pick the hops of Worcestershire. Funds were raised from the local gentry and tents were erected in the fields where tea and refreshments were served during the day and talks and entertainments on Christian themes (and particularly temperance themes) were provided in the evenings. Donated clothes were also sold at much reduced prices, for these workers were largely from poor areas of industrial towns. 'Goin hoppin' was for them and their children a working holiday in the countryside. From William's point of view of course there was a certain irony in the fact that he was attempting to extract 'the pledge' from workers whose occupation was an integral part of the brewing industry.

Chapter Eighteen
FOR THE MANY NOT THE FEW

It was not long before William's regular sermons in the Cathedral with their uncompromising Christian Socialist message were beginning to attract attention. Some of those emerging from the building in their pomp and finery, observed by the women in clogs and shawls, may have been rather more chastened than the onlookers realised. William's sermons took slightly different forms as he tailored them to his various audiences, but the message was essentially the same. The Church, William told the congregation on a typical Sunday morning, was prone to consider Christianity as consisting of attending church services, of being present at Communion and attending devotions both public and private. But if the Church really wished to save souls it must endeavour to save society. As he had told the people of Sunderland in a final sermon there, 'it was putting the cart before the horse to preach the gospel to starving men and women.'[1] The principle which should underly such a society, he emphasised, was 'brotherhood, a mutual helpfulness between all concerned in industry. Justice demands that in every industry the welfare of the workers and not the profits of the employers should be the first consideration.' We should not, he added with an uncanny reminder of more recent British politics, 'tolerate a system in which the few would benefit at the expense of the many.'[2] In the North East William had frequently demonstrated his

---

1. WME, farewell address at St Thomas' Church, Sunderland, BNA, *Newcastle Daily Chronicle*, 26 October 1908.

2. A political slogan of the British Labour Party during the election of 2019 was 'For the many, not the few'.

practical commitment to these principles. Now he asked the people of Worcester 'to contrast on the one hand the luxury of the idle rich with the revelation of degradation and misery, wretchedness and hopelessness in which millions of families lived, as shown in the recent report of the Poor Law Commission.[3] How could they reconcile these two things to their idea of Christian brotherhood? They should insist that every child should have the fullest opportunity for mental and moral development – and not plead the cost of the rates as a reason for not doing so. And as regards housing they should endeavour to secure for others the advantages they enjoyed themselves. There was, he said, 'a terrible slackness and indifference on the part of Churchmen in relation to such things . . . an indifference shown to the policy of corporations – a feeling that they could not soil their fingers with those dirty local politics.'[4] Those prone to argue that the Church should not involve itself in politics were, it seems, to be given no quarter. In what the correspondent of the *Leamington Spa Courier* described as 'a passage of surpassing vigour' he informed his audience that 'there is no Heaven up there for those who do not try and do something to make Heaven down here.'[5]

A similar message was delivered to a congregation in Putney on Mayoral Sunday in 1910. A perhaps little-known fact about the Diocese of Worcester, probably unknown to William himself before he arrived there, was its historical connection with the church of St Mary's, Putney. This had apparently originated in the sixteenth century when Henry VIII carried out one of his 'land exchanges' in an attempt to boost the contents of the Royal coffers. In exchange for various lands in Worcestershire the Dean and Chapter of Worcester had apparently received, willingly or otherwise, the advowson of the

---

3. For content and appraisal of this report see Kathleen Woodroofe, 'The Royal Commission on Poor Laws, 1905–09', *International Review of Social History*, vol. 22, no. 2 (Cambridge University Press, 1977). Accessed via www.cambridge.org/core

4. 'Dean of Worcester on Social Problems. Sermon at the Cathedral,' BNA, *Western Daily Press*, 2 March 1910.

5. 'The Church Militant. Sermon by the Dean of Worcester at the Festival of St Michael and All Angels, St Mary's Church, Warwick,' BNA, *Leamington Spa Courier*, 4 October 1912.

Rectory of Wimbledon with its two chapels, Putney and Mortlake, Essentially, this meant that the selection of the priests there and the payment of part of their stipends became the responsibility of Worcester, an arrangement that appears to have lasted until the mid eighteenth century. At some point Worcester seems to have divested itself of this relationship, at least in terms of its financial obligations, but the traditional and historical ties remained. As a result, on an extremely chilly Sunday morning in early January 1910 William found himself processing along an icy road alongside the Mayor, aldermen and councillors of the borough of Wandsworth in a municipal cortege that wound itself through the streets of Putney to St Mary's Church. It would have been a miserable experience with probably few onlookers prepared to brave the weather to watch a group of elderly men in ceremonial robes struggling through the snow. The church, when they arrived, was unlikely to have been particularly warm, although it would have been full, for the congregation on Mayoral Sunday was composed largely of invited guests. In these uncomfortable and unpromising circumstances William could perhaps have been forgiven for delivering what was probably expected, a short uncontroversial sermon, the necessary prelude to a good lunch in the Town Hall. Instead, however, he delivered a hard-hitting address, one that encapsulated all his beliefs about the role of those endowed with power and influence in society. He began, as was customary, with a Biblical text, on this occasion a verse from St Paul's Epistle to the Hebrews: 'As Moses was admonished of God when he was about to make the tabernacle. See, saith He, that thou make of all things according to the pattern shewed to thee on the Mount.'[6] This was, William pronounced, an allegory about the need for effective action to achieve the loftiest ideals, which in turn should be 'inspired by communion with God.' It was essentially Maurice's Christian Socialism, the social action that had its primary origins in divine inspiration rather than the evolutionary processes of Darwin or the economic laws of Alfred Marshall.

6. Hebrews 8:5, King James Bible.

We cannot build noble cities without noble ideals or make our own life worth anything without noble ideals. What is a civic ideal? An increase in the rateable value? If the rateable value is rising and especially if it is increasing more rapidly than the population it shows that the wealth of the town is growing. This is true but the poet has said 'Ill fares the land to hastening ills a prey, where wealth accumulates and men decay.'

Suppose you take a foreigner and show him not the chief streets of big towns (Birmingham, London, Liverpool, Manchester and Wandsworth) but show him back streets and lanes, the slums, and say this is what Englishmen have made of town life ... the dull monotony of the miles of dingy streets, all exactly alike, those dirty evil smelling courts and slums. How is it by our united efforts with all our skill and all our powers of organisation we have arrived at such a result? What ideal went into the making of it. Everybody is busy making money, making the most out of the land he possesses and the making of man is forgotten. We have a Town Planning Bill which gives us greater powers but how shall we draw that plan? We need definite ideas, clear principles, which we recognise as essential to the true development of town life. What principles? Here is one that comes from God to Moses on the Mount. All things whatsoever ye would that men would do unto you, do you even so unto them.

Education is entrusted to the Corporation. Your aim should be to secure for all of the children of the Municipality such advantages of education and mental development as you desire for your own children.

You wish for your families fresh air and healthy homes. It should be your aim to secure these things for all your fellow townsmen. Are the death rates recorded by the Medical Officer of Health double that in some parts of the Municipality than in others and similarly ill-health rates? Certain ideals must spring from this knowledge even if it cannot be done overnight.

Christians must be enthusiastic. There can be no advance unless Christians endure hardship rebuke and disappointment as they try to fashion things that are after the likeness of the pattern shown to us on the Mount. But belief in the Divine character of Christ's teaching gives enthusiasm to endure the drudgery of inconvenient meetings, weary committees of working the heavy machinery by which the city is slowly improved and to go and take up some neglected duty, some unnoticed work and persist without praise or profit.[7]

William concluded,

> For some men the object is wealth, but if men are to make much of their lives they must have higher ideals than moneymaking or even professional success. Ideals must be more than petty ideas, they must be deep convictions. Only those whose lives and ideals bear the stamp of Divinity live the truest lives.

His choice of John Wesley as an example was perhaps a curious one for a steadfastly Anglican congregation but he made it anyway. 'He died worth only two suits of clothes and a Bible,' he informed them.[8]

John Wesley and other prominent non-conformists were, it seemed, always prone to feature strongly in William's teaching. In the spring of 1909, he had reverted to familiar territory by proposing a series of Sunday afternoon meetings for men to be held during Lent. There was some disquiet about these amongst the city clergy, ostensibly because they would be held within the Cathedral which apparently was not permitted during Lent, but more probably, because of suspicions about their form and content. In February they called a meeting with William where he was asked to respond to a number of probing questions about his intentions which, he said, were 'to explore issues of social and theological interest, dealing also with Biblical and moral difficulties and including an opportunity for asking questions.'[9] He reassured them that the meetings would also consist of hymns and prayers and would not interfere with Bible classes or with any project relating to the formation of branches of the Church of England

---

7. WME, sermon at St Mary's Church, Putney. 'Civic Visit to St Mary's Church,' BNA, *Wandsworth Borough News*, 28 January 1910.

8. ibid.

9. WCL scrapbooks, 9 February 1909.

Men's Society (CEMS), apparently a matter of particular concern.[10] The meetings were finally agreed to, provided they took place in the adjacent College Hall and not in the Cathedral itself. The incident underlines the degree of suspicion surrounding William when he arrived in Worcester and for some these suspicions would have been confirmed when he delivered lectures on two of his favourite topics, 'What is Christianity and what is heresy' and 'The use and abuse of dogma'. These were followed later in the year by a further series entitled 'Some religious leaders and what they have taught us', which predictably included John Wesley, George Fox, Martin Luther, Cardinal Newman, Edward Pusey and finally Frederick Maurice and Charles Kingsley. Following each lecture participants were invited to submit questions to him in writing 'relating to religious difficulties or objections of any kind' which he promised to answer in full.[11] William's need to move rapidly into an educative role was, it seems, irrepressible.

In terms of wider non-religious education, however, William found a different situation to that he had encountered in the North East. Typically he secured a place on the County Education Committee but here he was a minor player with much less influence than he had been able to exercise in either Gateshead or Durham. And there was much less of an appetite for University Extension in the area, either amongst the local education authorities or the workers themselves. William's response was to affiliate his lectures to an organisation which was already well established in the area, the Workers' Educational Association (WEA), founded by Albert Mansbridge and his wife, Frances, in 1903. They had been particularly concerned about the elitist element which seemed to have crept into much adult education, including the University Extension Scheme. Increasingly, they felt, this appealed largely to middle-class students, something that William himself had long feared and fought against. Forming an alliance with a group of lecturers from the University of Oxford, Albert and

10. The Church of England Men's Society, established in 1899 by Archbishop Frederick Temple to provide a social meeting place for men, with an emphasis on Christian Education.
11. op cit., WCL scrapbooks.

Frances had established the Association for the Higher Education of Working Men which, famously on the advice of Frances's mother, was changed in 1905 to the non-sexist Workers' Educational Association. William became an enthusiastic supporter of the Worcester branch providing evening lectures on industrial history and economics and organising a variety of educational visits to places such as Barbourne Waterworks, Hartlebury Common and Worcester Electricity Works.

William's choice of 'religious leaders' in his lecture series, with its strong representation of non-conformists, would have provoked a certain amount of unease in Cathedral circles. In his sermons he frequently cautioned against what he called 'pharasaical pride that disparaged other bodies of Christians, differently constituted.'[12] He would meet this difficulty head on in May 1911 when arrangements were in progress for a special service in Worcester Cathedral to mark Coronation Day. As part of the celebrations, it was proposed that the Mayor, who that year was a non-conformist called Emanuel Thomas, would lead a procession of prominent citizens through the streets to the Cathedral. However, on hearing that his Wesleyan chaplain would not be allowed to read the lesson during the service (non-conformist ministers were by Cathedral statute not afforded this privilege) the Mayor refused to play any part in the proceedings. As head of the Chapter it fell to William to adjudicate on the matter. Suspecting that his sympathies probably lay entirely with the Mayor, a number of city clergy would have been watching the outcome of this dispute with interest. Fortunately, he was able to diffuse the row on two counts. The Coronation service, he noted, was not a statutory service in the normal sense and was thus an occasion when the usual custom might be departed from, especially as 'the Cathedral had a distinctly national character.' He hoped, he said, that 'all citizens, irrespective of differences of politics and denomination will meet in our grand old Cathedral and unitedly offer prayer for God's blessing on the King

---

12. op cit., 'Dean of Worcester on Social Problems: Sermon at the Cathedral,' 2 March 1910.

and his Kingdom.'[13] More to the specific point, however, he noted that the form of service issued by the Archbishop of Canterbury did not, in fact, include a lesson at all.[14] Hence 'the special point of contention falls to the ground,' and he hoped, therefore, that this might 'heal the breach that has been occasioned.'[15] On this occasion, it seemed, William managed to dodge the problem, but the incident underlines the storms that could envelop the unwary in a church wedded to religious protocol and exceptionalism. There would be other occasions in the future when he would have to confront such issues. And the Bishop of Hereford, it seems, was not so lucky.[16] Having decided that the service should include the administration of the sacraments he had also invited non-conformists to attend, laying himself open to the possibility that they might choose to partake of something reserved exclusively for confirmed Anglicans. This provoked a strong letter of complaint from Lord Halifax to the Archbishop of Canterbury.[17] 'If the Bishop is allowed to thus openly set at nought the law of the whole Catholic church,' raged the noble Lord, 'it will expose the Church of England to the imputation of faithlessness to the sacred charge committed to her trust.'[18]

13. 'The Mayor and Cathedral Chapter,' BNA, *Worcester Journal*, 13 May 1911.
14. Archbishop Randall Thomas Davidson, in office 1903–28.
15. 'The Mayor and Cathedral Chapter,' BNA, *Worcester Journal*, 13 May 1911.
16. John Percival, Bishop of Hereford, in office 1895–1917
17. Lord Halifax was president of the English Church Union which campaigned for reunification with the Roman Catholic Church.
18. 'Protest Against Invitation to Non-Conformists,' BNA, *Birmingham Daily Gazette*, 12 May 1911. Archbishop of Canterbury, Randall Thomas Davidson, in office 1903–28.

Chapter Nineteen
CRADLEY HEATH

The Edwardian years immediately preceding the First World War were not, as often popularly depicted, just a time of balmy summers and garden parties, when wealthy people in large hats moved effortlessly between the major events of 'the season'. For large sections of the population this supposedly blissful calm before the storm was in reality a period of increasingly violent industrial unrest. When, in 1908, however, the correspondent of *The Times* mentioned the Black Country as a potential hunting ground for enthusiastic social reformers he could not have predicted the events that would take place there just two years later in a place called Cradley Heath. There are two places bearing the name of Cradley in the English Midlands. One is a rural village, situated a few miles south of Worcester on the western side of the Malvern Hills. This Cradley lies just over the county border with Herefordshire in one of today's designated Areas of Outstanding Natural Beauty. It has a lovely Norman church approached through a sixteenth-century lychgate, and a timbered village hall. It was here that William's eldest son, William Edward, would set up his medical practice. The other Cradley is a settlement on the banks of the River Stour, nearly thirty miles north of Worcester, close to the town of Dudley which, despite its distance from the city, lies within the Diocese of Worcester. This is part of the district known as the Black Country, so called because of the layer of soot and grime which for many years covered the area. For the Black Country was once considered to be the most industrialised place in England with its coal mines, coking ovens, iron foundries, glass factories and brickworks. Since his arrival in Worcestershire William had in fact been quietly acquainting himself with the local industries of the county. The *Western Mail* which seemed to follow his career quite closely reported that, since he had become Dean, he had made a special study of 'Black Country Life', socially and economically. In his travels around the diocese he would almost certainly have come across one particular area of Cradley called Cradley Heath. In former rural times the villagers had grazed their animals here but now it was the site of an industry called chainmaking. On this blighted heath several hundred women worked at forges in outhouses attached to their cramped insanitary cottages, hammering out the chain links for twelve hours a day, six days a week. Most of these women were also wives and mothers, their small children lying beside them in cots or playing around their feet in the midst of the smoke and dust. When they were slightly older the children would operate the bellows for the forge, working 'like a squirrel in a cage or a criminal on a treadmill' as the writer Francis Brett Young graphically described it.[1] It was unlikely that these children benefited from much in the way of formal education.

Chainmaking was undoubtedly one of the worst examples of what had become known as sweated labour. For not only were the working conditions appalling but the pay was meagre. The women were paid piece rates, depending on the amount of chain they produced from the iron rods delivered to them by middle-men (known as foggers) who in turn were paid by companies to which they supplied the chain. Unsurprisingly much of the money earned stayed in the pockets of the foggers. It was an exploitative system, repeated in many other industries where the poor were paid a pittance for huge amounts of labour, the very opposite of the kind of co-operative industrial arrangements that William and other Christian Socialists strove to promote. A few years earlier in 1906, William had visited the Sweated Trades Exhibition in London organised by the *Daily News* which had thrown a spotlight on the conditions and pay of these

---

1. F. Brett-Young *Far Forest* (Heinemann Ltd, London, 1936). See also Sherard, *The White Slaves of England*.

workers. The exhibition had led to the foundation of a pressure group known as the Anti-Sweating League led by a number of union organisers including the women's campaigner Mary MacArthur. This in turn resulted in the first Trades Board Act passed by the Liberal government in 1909 which established regulatory bodies to designate minimum wages in specified trades. Chainmaking was one of the first to be considered and in March 1910 the board designated a minimum wage of 2½*d* per hour to replace the piecework system.[2] Although a pitifully small amount this did at least establish the principle of a basic minimum which exceeded what they currently earned. Establishing the reality on the ground, however, was to prove more difficult. Predictably the foggers chose to ignore the new ruling and many forced their workers to sign contracts opting out of the minimum wage. Those women who refused were denied work, essentially a recipe for starvation. In September 1910, however, much to the surprise of many, not least the foggers and the iron masters, the women of Cradley Heath decided to insist on their legal rights and launched one of the most significant industrial actions in labour history. More than six hundred of the women came out on strike. Against this background William had no hesitation in throwing his support behind the cause.

The chainmakers were galvanised into action by the charismatic union leader, Mary MacArthur, who organised the strike and expertly mobilised the media to publicise the conditions of the workers and the injustices they suffered. She attracted huge support from all sections of society, including some prominent clergy. The strike lasted ten weeks and fundraising to support the women during this period was crucial to its success. This was an area where William could bring his influence to bear and he set about writing numerous appeal letters to newspapers across the country and acting as a collection point for funds. Typical of these was his letter to the *Coventry Evening Telegraph* where he referred to the vehement expressions of

2. In pre-decimal currency there were 12*d* (pence) in one shilling. One shilling was the equivalent of 5p (pence) in decimal currency.

pity and indignation he had heard expressed at the Sweated Trades Exhibition. 'Now is the time to show the value of such expressions in a practical fashion,' he urged, 'by sending financial help to the sweated workers of Cradley.'[3] The strike had gained the support of the Trades Union Congress, he said, but two thirds of the women were non-unionists and they could not hold out unless they could be assured of four shillings a week.

On the afternoon of 12 September William visited Cradley Heath and gave a rousing speech to a crowd of about two thousand people who had assembled at the Empire Theatre to express their support for the women. The previous Saturday Mary MacArthur had made a flying visit there on her way to a labour congress in Sheffield and had told the delighted crowd that so far £1,500 had been raised, £500 more than expected. It was she who invited William to visit Cradley and speak to the women and their supporters. On the twelfth, the vicar of Cradley, the Reverend Walker, chaired the meeting, urging the women to hold firm and to 'stick to the union, for then the union will stick to you.' William who reportedly, 'received a very hearty reception' began by saying that he came bearing a letter of support and a donation of £5 from Bishop Yeatman-Biggs, something that provoked an initial surprised silence followed by an outbreak of loud applause.[4] William went on to say that 'possibly someone would ask the question why a clergyman should interfere or interest himself in a trade dispute.' He went on to describe his own work in Gateshead, his duty as a Christian and as Dean of the Cathedral of the diocese of which Cradley was a part. No true patriot, he said, could be proud of the conditions of labour in Cradley Heath. The women were fighting the battle of underpaid women workers in all parts of the country. If they failed to make a success of the new Trades Boards Act the efforts to check the evils of sweating elsewhere would be

---

3. WME, 'Chain Workers' Strike. Dean of Worcester's Appeal for Workers,' BNA, *Coventry Evening Telegraph*, 8 September 1910.

4. 'The Chain Trade Dispute. The Bishop of Worcester's Subscription,' BNA, *Birmingham Daily Gazette*, 13 September 1910.

discredited.[5] With hindsight it is fair to say that William's words were no exaggeration. Today the chainmakers' strike is regarded as a highly significant turning point in labour history, underpinning the validity of the Trades Boards and paving the way for what became known as the living wage.

The strike came to an end on 19 October when the last of the foggers and their iron masters gave way to the women's demands. There began a long period of improvement in both the pay and working conditions of the chainmaking industry. If the crowd were indeed surprised by

Strikers and supporters marching through Cradley Heath to the Empire Theatre in 1910. (Courtesy of the Black Country Living Museum.)

William's 'interference' they were even more so by that of the Bishop. His letter expressed regret at being unable to visit Cradley Heath that day. In truth he was probably relieved not to do so, for this was of course a Bishop of whom it had been said 'his tastes were those of a country gentleman, with the industrial parts of the diocese he was not

---

5. William continued to contribute personally to a number of similar campaigns following the end of the Chainmakers' Strike. For example, he is listed amongst those donating one guinea to the relief of women in the holloware industry, makers of tin boxes and other containers. BNA, *Manchester Daily Citizen*, 21 November 1912.

at home.' However, in his enclosed letter he told them that he rejoiced that the chainmakers were being well-supported in their determination to avail themselves of the full provisions of the Trades Board Act. He wished them success in the splendid efforts they were making to improve their position and was hoping a report would eventually reach him that the result of their movement was satisfactory.[6] It was an unexpected endorsement, widely reported in the press as far away as Tyneside, and no doubt bearing the mark of William's influence on this deeply conservative Bishop. It brought cheers from the crowd but provoked some wrath in more conservative circles. Some typical views were expressed by a Mr Thomas McBean as he presided over the Annual Dinner of the 'Pride of Sinton Green Lodge of Shepherds'.[7] He depreciated very strongly clergymen interfering in industrial matters. Some of their remarks were absolutely scandalous, he said. And as for the Dean, 'if he wished to mix himself up in industrial questions let him give up his Deanery and go and join Ben Tillett and Tom Mann.'[8] These remarks were greeted with loud applause. An anonymous correspondent to the *Tewkesbury Register* was equally unimpressed following a sermon William had delivered in the abbey. Discussion of 'funny stuff' such as labour unrest, strikes and lockouts might be appropriate to the backbenches of the House of Commons, he said, but it was a misuse of the pulpit of our ancient abbey church.[9] *The Western Mail*, however, took a rather different view.

> Some people might regard the Dean as rather dangerous because of the strong line he has taken on social and industrial questions, but he is really one of the most cool-headed of men and pursues his ideals with a

---

6. 'Women Chainmakers. Sympathy and Cheque,' BNA, *Sunderland Daily Echo and Shipping Gazette*, 13 September 1910.

7. A benefits club based in the Worcestershire village of Sinton Green.

8. 'Dean of Worcester Taken to Task,' BNA, *Birmingham Daily Gazette*, 10 July 1912. Ben Tillett and Tom Mann were renowned union leaders who led the famous London Dock Strike of 1886 when 130,000 went on strike, bringing the Port of London to a standstill.

9. 'Letter to the Editor: The Dean of Worcester and Labour Unrest,' BNA, *The Tewkesbury Register*, 28 September 1912.

quietness and moderation of tone which wins him many victories over individual doubters.[10]

Shortly after the end of the strike at Cradley Heath, as labour activists celebrated, William himself was struck by a very personal tragedy, for on 25 October Eleanor died suddenly at the Deanery. Her death was not entirely unexpected for she was suffering from diabetes, a largely untreatable disease in the early twentieth century, and she had been struggling with ill health for some time. It had been noted in diocesan circles that she had largely disappeared from the round of social events which featured as part of her husband's position as Dean and had ceased to take any active part in the life of the Cathedral. William, however, would probably have been unprepared for the sudden, dramatic worsening of her condition at the beginning of October. Her doctors, however, including her own son, would have recognised that the end was near. Eleanor had left a large group of friends on Tyneside and had, according to the local newspapers, become a popular figure in Worcester during her early months there. She had been William's wife for over thirty-six years, contributing to his work and sharing his passion for social justice. As a mother of eight she had a particular affinity with the problems of women and children, not least because of her own personal tragedies, a stillbirth and the loss of two children in early infancy, and she had quietly and efficiently pursued her own projects as well as supporting those of her husband. Her death would have left a huge gap in his life. She was buried a few days later in a simple grave within the Cathedral cloisters following a small family funeral, and William was forced to return to life without his helpmate. It is perhaps fortunate that he still had the company of his son and daughter-in-law, together with their small son, two-year-old Oswald, to fill the rooms of the Deanery which must have seemed even more cavernous than before. It was not until well after Christmas that he began to look beyond anything other

10. 'An Ardent Social Reformer,' BNA, *Western Mail*, 9 September 1910.

than his formal duties in the Cathedral and even then, it seemed, he was increasingly feeling unwell. He struggled on until the summer of 1911 but on 25 July it was announced that he had gone into a nursing home in London for surgical treatment. The nature of his illness is unreported but, although the surgery was apparently successful, he clearly required an extended convalescence. In early August he went to stay with his son William Edward, who had by then moved out of the Deanery, and did not return to Worcester until the beginning of September. It had been a very difficult time. Usually so full of energy and activity he was obviously both physically and emotionally debilitated. Things were, however, about to change.

During his early years in Worcester William made frequent visits to the North East, in part to receive testimonials and gifts at the invitation of organisations with which he had been associated, but probably also because he found it difficult to break the ties which bound him so strongly to the area. Although he was no longer treasurer of the Aged Miners' Homes Association he remained on their committee and regularly attended their meetings. He also maintained a strong interest in the Walker Homes, attending conferences to discuss the extension of their activities and collaboration with other housing organisations. Usually on his visits to the North he was invited to preach at various clubs or in local churches, events that attracted a fair amount of coverage in local newspapers. It was probably during one of these visits that he renewed his friendship with the family of a local medical practitioner called Robert Wilson who had been on the staff of the Gateshead Dispensary, another initiative supported by St Mary's Church. In 1887 William had conducted the marriage ceremony of Robert's daughter Ellen. In 1892 Robert's other daughter, Sarah, had married Hugh Salvin Pattinson, Newcastle's public analyst, a metallurgist and industrial chemist who also worked in the business founded by his more famous uncle Hugh Lee Pattinson.[11] Sarah, however, had been widowed in 1904 when Hugh Salvin Pattinson

---

11. Hugh Lee Pattinson perfected a process for extracting silver from lead (subsequently known as pattinisation).

had died suddenly. She knew William from old, having grown up in Gateshead where she had attended some of his extension lectures during the 1880s. William may also have known Hugh since he had studied at Newcastle's College of Physical Science during William's tenure there as professor of history. Interestingly the Pattinson family were Quakers who came from Alston, later setting up their business in Newcastle. There was, it seems, much to link William and Sarah and certainly they would have found a great deal to talk about. With echoes of William's somewhat hasty formation of a relationship with Eleanor so soon after her husband's death he now seems to have made another rapid matrimonial decision. Just fifteen months after Eleanor's death and shortly after he himself had emerged from an extended period of convalescence, it was formally announced in the *Worcester Journal* that a marriage had been arranged between the Dean and Mrs Pattinson. As with William's first marriage there was no fuss and the minimum of publicity. The couple were married quietly in Tynemouth on New Year's Day 1912.

Chapter Twenty
UNDER THE WIDELY BLOWING BANNER

Sarah was by all accounts a strong minded and determined woman. She was also a prominent member of the suffrage movement. Women in Britain had been agitating for female suffrage ever since the Reform Act of 1832 but by the beginning of the twentieth century they had still only secured the right to vote in local elections for county and borough councils. In 1897 campaigner Millicent Fawcett had set up the National Union of Women's Suffrage Societies (NUWSS) which favoured peaceful protests such as petitions and formal deputations to Members of Parliament. By the turn of the century, however, many women and their male supporters were becoming frustrated by a conspicuous lack of progress. In 1902, for example, 37,000 Lancashire mill workers had signed a petition which was politely received, but largely ignored. The result was the birth of a much more militant movement spearheaded by a new organisation, the Women's Social and Political Union (WSPU) led by Emmeline Pankhurst. In addition to the industrial strife that repeatedly beset the nation during the pre-war period, therefore, another form of unrest was rapidly coming to the boil. During the next few years under the motto 'Deeds Not Words' the suffragettes, as they became known, launched a series of increasingly violent demonstrations and protests. The story is well known with its tales of imprisonment, force feeding, martyrdom and self-sacrifice. Meanwhile the NUWSS steadfastly continued its peaceful campaign of processions, rallies, deputations and petitions.

William was a natural supporter of women's enfranchisement,

for within the context of restrictive early twentieth century society and his own Victorian upbringing it is fair to say that he was progressively feminist in his thinking. Where middle-class women were concerned his emphasis tended to be on responsibilities rather than rights, on numerous occasions urging them to reject the role of 'social butterfly' and general ornament and to do something useful with their lives. For William the emancipation of women was first and foremost a religious question. Both in word and in actions, he maintained, Christ had upheld the absolute equality of men and women. Nowhere in the New Testament, he said, would they find one gospel for women and another for men. Nowhere in Christ's utterances did he express the common male opinion that there was one code of morals for men and another for women. William elaborated relentlessly on this theme in his sermons, discussing the details of Christ's life and work and relating this to the practicalities of women's lives. He was, by all accounts, a highly accomplished preacher and orator and he brought all his talents to bear on this issue, just as he had done before on the problems of poverty and injustice. He said on many occasions that he considered that the Church had an absolute duty to help and inspire the suffrage campaign. Eleanor's views on this question are unrecorded, but in his new partner Sarah he undoubtedly found an uncompromising supporter of the cause. Sarah had been an ardent suffragist for twenty-five years and on arrival in Worcester it was not long before she became president of the recently formed local branch of the NUWSS.

At the end of October 1911 William agreed to address a meeting of the WSPU to be held a few weeks later in nearby Stourbridge. This highly active branch of the organisation was looking forward to hosting Emmeline Pankhurst herself as the speaker in January and it was perhaps a measure of the importance attached to William's support that he had also been recruited to speak. The campaign had reached a high point in mid 1911, for the previous June on the eve of the Coronation over forty thousand women, dressed in white and singing 'The March of the Women' had processed from Westminster to the Albert Hall.[1] With impressive theatrical flair they were led on horseback by prominent campaigners Charlotte Despard and Margery Bryce, the latter dressed rather strikingly as Joan of Arc! The march was composed of women from twenty-eight different suffrage societies representing everything from different professions and different groups of workers to different countries of the Empire. Numerous representatives of the Church of England's Society, the Church League for Women's Suffrage (CLWS) were also present including several clergymen. William, busy with the forthcoming processional arrangements for Coronation Day in Worcester, not least the smoothing of ruffled non-conformist feathers, would probably have been there too if he'd been able. This, however, was probably the last time that all these different groups would come together as a unified force to support the cause.

In 1911 hopes were high that Parliament would proceed with the third reading of the Conciliation Bill, which would give voting rights to women who owned property, a first step towards universal female suffrage. Against all expectations, however, Asquith introduced instead the Manhood Suffrage Bill which gave all men, regardless of property ownership, the right to vote. Meanwhile the Conciliation Bill was subsequently defeated in Parliament. The fury unleashed by this resulted in an increasingly violent suffrage campaign which split the supporters into two distinct camps, those like the WSPU led by Emmeline Pankhurst who now considered that violent action was entirely justified, and those like the NUWSS who maintained a commitment to peaceful protest.

William was due to speak at the Stourbridge event on the 2 December. Unaccountably and at very short notice he sent a message to say he was unable to attend. His place was taken by Lady Adele Meyer, a prominent social reformer who was highly active in the East End of London. William would have admired her work but would not have agreed with her conclusions that evening. According to the *County*

---

1. The official anthem of the suffrage campaign, composed by Ethyl Smyth and Cicely Hamilton. It contains the line 'wide blows our banner and hope is waking'.

Express (which began with a typical observation of the time that she was 'wearing an evening dress of dark blue velvet and a chain of lovely pearls') she spoke for over two hours and urged that women should now take extreme measures. Nothing had come of forty years of peaceful agitation she said. The suffragettes had done all the dignified things it was possible to do, and now the militant section were going to be a nuisance to Mr Asquith. In fact, they had already become rather more than a nuisance.[2] The campaign of window smashing which would soon escalate into more serious acts of violence had already begun, and there had been numerous arrests at demonstrations up and down the country. It was most unusual for William to let people down, particularly at the last minute and without good reason, and there seems little doubt that he had decided he could no longer support the activities of the WSPU. Instead, in April 1912, he threw his support behind the non-violent NUWSS and set about speaking at numerous events where he relentlessly promoted the religious and moral aspects of the question.

William's stance was part of a steadfast rejection of any form of violent action. During his time in Gateshead he had belonged to something called the Peace Society. It was a small organisation that attracted only a handful of participants to its meetings and rarely got much of a mention in the newspapers. In the nationalistic times of the Boer War doctrines of peace were difficult to promote. It is clear, however, that William had held pacifist views for a long time, again perhaps a legacy of his time in Alston when he had observed at close quarters the attitudes and behaviour of the Quakers. And Sarah's first husband, described in his obituary as a 'kindly and gentle man', came from a Quaker family. These pacifist tendencies came into sharp focus during the suffrage campaign when both William and Sarah found themselves at odds with the Church-based CLWS of which they were both members. In January 1914 William attended a meeting of the organisation's council in London where the question

---

2. 'In Support of Christian Suffrage: the Militant Movement Explained,' BNA, *County Express*, 2 December 1911.

of violent militancy, which by then had escalated into arson attacks and bombings, was discussed. He was dismayed at the resolution which emerged from this discussion, namely that 'CLWS members should refrain from expressing their personal opinion on methods of propaganda unless specifically questioned and, in that case, should make it clear that the League expresses no opinion as to such methods.' William always disparaged what he saw as an attempt to face both ways in an argument simultaneously, to use the art of language to create an impression of neutrality on what was essentially a matter of principle. This, he considered, was a prime example. It declined to say that the present actions of the militants are wrong, disloyal to the head of the Church and false to His teaching, he said. He further observed that:

> When the CLWS was first formed the actions of the suffragettes were merely obstructive (if exasperating and unwise) but now they have become dangerously destructive to life and property. A society which calls itself a Church League [he went on] and which deliberately refuses to express an opinion on a grave moral question and declines to say the present methods of militancy are not in accord with the spirit and teaching of Jesus Christ, is not true to the principles of the Church. It is condoning doing evil that good may come, which is wrong in principle, and also forgets that God's will can only be done in God's way.[3]

This was William at his most determined, his absolute conviction of the tenets of his faith and his complete refusal to compromise. Nothing less than a resolution unequivocally condemning militancy would do. In this, it must be said, he was supported by a number of ordinary parish clergy, including his sister's husband the Reverend Thomas Lawrence, vicar of St Andrew the Great in Cambridge, who wrote to the secretary of the CLWS, the Reverend Claude Hinscliffe, saying 'it passes my comprehension how a Church Society can condone such acts as bomb-throwing and arson, interruptions of services and

---

3. 'No Condemnation of Violence; the Dean of Worcester Resigns,' BNA, *Church League for Women's Suffrage*, 6 March 1914.

destruction of churches, and I, for one, can take no part in such a terrible responsibility.'[4] The Reverend Hinscliffe, a founder member and hitherto devoted supporter of the League replied in terms that William would have considered unacceptably equivocal. 'The upholding or condemnation of methods,' he said 'never entered into our scheme.'[5] In retrospect, however, this seems to have been a last attempt by Claude Hinscliffe to reconcile competing opinions and allay his own misgivings about it all, for shortly afterwards he also resigned from the League.

William and those who supported him failed in their bid to change the mind of the CLWS. Returning to Worcester he announced his intention to resign from the League and was followed by Sarah, his great friends Sub-Dean Canon James Wilson and his wife Georgina, Bishop Yeatman-Biggs, and most of the other members of the local branch.[6] Effectively, the Worcester branch of the CLWS was dissolved. More widely the CLWS lost members nationwide as the dispute divided opinion across the country. Subsequently William and Sarah directed their energies first towards supporting the non-violent secular organisation, the NUWSS, of which Sarah became president of the Worcester branch, and second to the formation of yet another local organisation, the non-militant Worcester Society for the Extension of the Franchise to Women. This in turn was affiliated to the National Council for Adult Suffrage of which William became a council member. The events in Worcester, however, had brought to a head the age-old question of whether violence might ever be justified in support of a seemingly just cause, a question that continued to divide the suffrage campaign. Later that year of course this question would be raised again in more immediately serious circumstances with the declaration of war, something that would cause William considerable soul searching.

William and Sarah continued their involvement with the suffrage campaign throughout and beyond the First World War. Increasingly

4. ibid.
5. ibid.
6. Canon James Wilson was Sub-Dean of Worcester, 1905–26.

the campaign majored on the contribution of women to the war effort as a justification for their right to vote. However, it was also a campaign that shifted its base towards the demand for universal suffrage for all men and women, not just those in possession of property. As William pointed out to the local suffrage society in 1916 the support for men's suffrage did not represent the abandonment of the women's campaign. Rather the demand for suffrage for *all* adults would also include *all* women. Alongside fellow campaigners such as the Bishops of Hereford and Lincoln he put his name to a series of multi-authored letters directed at Prime Minister Herbert Asquith during that year. Universal suffrage for all adults would not come until 1928 although a significant step forward was made in 1918 when, under Liberal Prime Minister David Lloyd George, married women over the age of thirty (and all men over the age of twenty-one) were granted the vote. William and Sarah made their own peace with the CLWS after the war when it changed its name to the League of the Church Militant (LCM) and shifted its focus to include the campaign for the ordination of women as well as universal suffrage. Despite its name the LCM was a non-violent organisation which existed until 1930 when it changed its name once more to the somewhat cumbersome 'Anglican Group for the Ordination of Women in the Historic Ministry'. William served as a vice president of the LCM until 1930 and both he and Sarah were active members.

Chapter Twenty-One
THE VINDICATION OF RIGHTEOUSNESS

William's reputation was always one of conciliator and peacemaker and certainly at different times in his life he worked tirelessly to promote this aspect of the Christian message. However, his adherence to pacifism as an uncompromising tenet of his faith came under intense and ultimately intolerable strain during the war. Those who have researched the views and attitudes of Anglican clergy during this period have suggested that initially the majority were extremely uneasy about the prospect of armed conflict. However, reports of German atrocities which circulated during the early months of the war, notably those associated with the invasion of Belgium, resulted in a considerable hardening of attitudes. Increasingly Britain was conceived as conducting something akin to a moral crusade against Germany. According to historian, Albert Marrin, by the end of 1915 it was difficult to find a single ordained clergyman, 'apart from a handful of Christian Socialists' who did not support the war.[1] Given the lead provided by some senior clergy this is perhaps unsurprising for it was made clear from the outset that the duty of the clergy, at least on the Home Front, was first to maintain morale and second to remind young men of their moral duty to enlist. The Archbishop of York delivered a sermon late in 1914 when he insisted that 'there can be no peace until this German spirit has been crushed' and he appealed to 'friends of peace to be supporter of our war.'[2] 'Force when coupled

---

1. A. Marrin, *The Last Crusade: The Church of England in the First World War* (Duke University Press, Durham, 1974).

2. Archbishop of York, Cosmo Gordon Lang, in office 1909–28

with moral authority,' he argued rather curiously was 'a little like love'.[3] A few months later the Archbishop of Canterbury said that he did not entertain any doubt that 'our nation could not, without sacrificing principles of honour and justice more dear than life itself, have stood aside and looked idly on the present world conflict.'[4] More extremely the Bishop of London, one of the most vehement supporters of the war, who was subsequently made a Knight Commander of the Victorian Order for his services to recruitment, called for the men of England to 'band in a great crusade – we cannot deny it – to kill Germans, not for the sake of killing them but to save the world. I look upon it as a war for purity. I look upon everyone who dies in it as a martyr.'[5] Even Charles Gore expressed support for the conflict, referring to it as a 'moral crusade'. It was, he said, 'the duty of the nation ... to go to war, and it was the duty of the Church to organise its spiritual weapons to help the nation.'[6]

Similar sentiments were expressed by one of William's greatest friends, the Reverend Geoffrey Studdert Kennedy, better known as 'Woodbine Willie'. Writing in his parish magazine in 1914 Geoffrey said 'I cannot say too strongly that I believe every able-bodied man ought to volunteer for service anywhere. There ought to be no shirking of that duty.'[7] Geoffrey had arrived in Worcester in the summer of 1914 as vicar of St Paul's Blockhouse. A much loved and respected figure he had worked tirelessly on behalf of the poor and he and William were in many ways kindred spirits. In 1915, however, Geoffrey went to France as an army chaplain convinced of the justice of the cause. Rather than remaining behind the lines and fulfilling the designated role of funeral director and condolence letter writer, he was renowned for going up to the Front Line with the troops, directly sharing their

---

3. Quoted by K. C. Fielden in 'The Church of England in the First World War' (Master's Thesis, East Tennessee State University, 2005). https://dc.etsu.edu/etd/1080/.

4. ibid, Fielden. Archbishop of Canterbury, Randall Thomas Davidson, in office 1903–28.

5. ibid, Fielden. Bishop of London, Arthur Winnington-Ingram, in office 1901-1939

6. *Oxford Diocesan Magazine*, October 1914.

7. M. Grundy, *A Fiery Glow in the Darkness: Woodbine Willie: Padre & Poet*, (Osborne Books, Worcester, 1997).

experiences – and famously supplying them with the comforts of the ubiquitous Woodbine cigarettes. The attitudes of many of the army chaplains however changed during the war as they struggled with the carnage and suffering, and also with the expectations of the commanding officers who often saw the clergyman's role as stiffening the resolve and reinforcing the necessary level of aggression amongst the troops. Major-General Sir William Thwaites, for example, reputedly informed his fellow officers 'I told them that I wanted a bloodthirsty sermon next Sunday and would not have any texts from the New Testament.'[8] Geoffrey survived the war and returned to Worcester, although he died a few years later after contracting influenza. In the years immediately after the war he became increasingly famous both as a preacher and a poet as he attempted to make sense of the war both for himself and others in a world overwhelmed with grief and loss. He confessed that at the beginning of the war he had believed it would ultimately bring about a benefit to mankind, 'that a better order was coming to the ordinary man,' but he had now come to realise that it was not through war that this order could be brought about. 'There are no fruits of victory,' he said, 'no such thing as victory in modern war. War is a universal disaster . . . a sin in a million forms.'[9] As William said of his friend, 'He went to war as a holy crusade which by victory would vindicate righteousness, but he returned hating the wickedness and folly of war . . . he became an apostle for peace.'[10]

Perhaps, however, William was describing his own sentiments as much as those of Geoffrey Studdert Kennedy, for he too had undergone a change of heart during the war. William had long been 'an apostle for peace' and in the years before 1914 he had delivered a number of speeches across the country in which he urged Christians to act as peacemakers in the world 'to use our influence to strengthen our demand for settling differences between nations by an appeal

---

8. op cit., Marrin.
9. op cit., Grundy
10. ibid.

to justice and equality.[11] In May 1911 he even took the opportunity to carry this message to US President Taft when he went with the Quaker MP Joseph Allen Baker and Baptist minister, John Clifford to the International Peace Congress held that year at Lake Mohonk a renowned beauty spot in New York State.[12] Having given an address to the conference, William recalled, 'I explained to him the movement to unite all churches for the furtherance of international peace.' President Taft, who enjoyed a reputation for peaceful arbitration in matters of dispute, reportedly 'expressed his cordial interest in the affair.'[13] Greatly encouraged by the events at Mohonk William returned home and joined with a small group of like-minded clergy to form the Church Peace League whose stated aim was

> to keep prominently before the Church of England the duty of combating the war spirit as contrary to the spirit of Christianity, and by working for the adoption of arbitration and conciliation in the place of war and for other peaceful means of settling international disputes.[14]

In this venture he was joined by two of his more colourful friends whose reputations may well have detracted somewhat from the League's success. Canon John Horsley of Southwark Cathedral was involved in a variety of laudable projects to improve the conditions of the poor in London but also kept a menagerie of animals in his back garden which included a small tribe of monkeys and a guinea pig employed in a rolling cage to cut the grass in his lawn! Meanwhile, the Reverend Arthur Waldron, vicar of Brixton and self-proclaimed Vicar of London's Palace of Varieties, was a writer and producer of controversial plays

---

11. Opening of the Africa and the East Exhibition at Bingley Hall, Birmingham. Dean of Worcester on 'Removal of National Barriers,' BNA, *Birmingham Daily Gazette*, 23 June 1910.

12. Mahatma Gandhi attributed the foundation of his non-violent method of passive resistance to John Clifford.

13. 'Arbitration for War. American Peace Conference: The Anglo-Saxon Example,' BNA, *Daily Telegraph and Courier*, 25 May 1911; 'Mr Taft and the Dean of Worcester,' BNA, *Birmingham Mail*, 1 June 1911.

14. 'Church Peace League,' BNA, *Gloucester Citizen*, 29 January 1912.

such as 'Should a Woman Tell?' a morality tale on the subject of adultery. His attachment to standard Christian doctrine was always somewhat tenuous and he finally resigned from his post in 1915 after saying that he did not believe in the resurrection. He subsequently went to France and worked for the Red Cross during the war. In 1912, however, both these somewhat controversial characters joined William in establishing the Peace League, helping him to organise a series of lectures on the subject and the distribution of promotional literature.

By this time it was clear to William and many others that the drums of war were beginning to roll. As the competitive expenditure on armaments at home and abroad grew rapidly he continued to hope and believe that armed conflict could be avoided and that the Church could and should play a significant part in this. While antagonism towards Germany grew he preached at a number of meetings designed to raise funds for the Anglo-German Friendship Society and gave a powerful address at the British National Peace Congress in London where he urged the Church to do more to raise the intellectual and moral conscience of the nation. Throughout this period he toured the country tirelessly, repeating his uncompromising message, which was endlessly reported in the local and national newspapers. 'Christians have allowed their consciences to go to sleep,' he said.

> War is absolutely antagonistic to Christian principles. If in England and Germany they had behind them the consciences of the great mass of Christians there would be created such an atmosphere that distrust would disappear and the two nations would lead the way in international accord.[15]

Moreover, he added, organised labour had done more for the brotherhood of man and had been more faithful to the idea than organised Christianity ever had. If they wanted peace, he said, they must take the trouble to prepare for peace. William's comments

15. 'The Peace Movement. Dean of Worcester,' BNA, *Shields Daily Gazette*, 24 April 1911.

about organised labour were not without substance. In August 1914 his old friend and ally Thomas Burt in his capacity as president of the International Arbitration League (formerly the Workmen's Peace Association) sent a resolution to the Prime Minister urging the government to maintain a position of absolute neutrality. It was, he said 'a policy which is alike essential to our interests at home and abroad and to the influence of Great Britain on the side of conciliation and peace.'[16] Thomas had been president of the League for over thirty years and by 1914 enjoyed enormous respect and support amongst large numbers of workers across the country, not least the miners. Similarly, the executive committee of the London Trades Council (a labour organisation that united London's trade unions) pointed to the prospect of 'the ruin and starvation of great masses of the people' if the government did not 'keep the country out of the quarrels of Eastern Europe, in which we have no concern.'[17]

On the eve of the outbreak of war, on 1 August 1914, William attended a meeting in Constance, Germany, where an ecumenical Christian organisation, the World Alliance for Promoting International Friendship Through the Churches, was formed, holding its inaugural meeting on that day with its stated aim of promoting peace, disarmament, arms control and conscientious objection. Recalling this meeting after the war William said that those who attended it would never forget how Englishmen, Frenchmen, Germans, Bulgarians, Italians and Americans met together to pray for peace and, as they prayed, they heard the rumblings of the first troop trains of the German mobilisation as they passed close by. Neither would he forget the scorn with which the stationmaster used the expression 'Peace Delegates!' as they stood on the railway platform preparing to return home the next day. They had a feeling of feebleness, he said, as they stood there, comparing themselves with the power and force of the soldiers who were being mobilised. And yet, he said, he clung on to the belief that

---

16. 'Powerful Pleas for Peace. Masses Threatened with Hunger,' BNA, *Manchester Daily Citizen*, 3 August 1914.

17. ibid.

God often chose the weak to fight the mighty.[18] Despite everything, the Alliance continued to function during the war. In Britain William assisted with the production and distribution of its publication called *Goodwill* which discussed the Christian response to the conflict and urged the Churches to

> make the Divine power felt throughout the whole human race such that it obtained universal influence over the actions of whole communities and nations ... to bring about good and friendly relations between nations, so that along the path of peaceful civilisation they may reach that universal goodwill which Christianity has taught mankind to aspire after.[19]

Given this background it is perhaps surprising that in the early months of the conflict William ceased to be one of the 'handful of Christian Socialists' who opposed the war. It is difficult to reconcile this with many of his earlier statements about the incompatibility between Christianity and armed conflict and the reasons behind his change of heart can only be a matter of conjecture. Like many well-read reformists in Britain he had long viewed Germany as a beacon of civilisation, admiring its science and literature and in particular its social organisation. And during the years before the war he had been a staunch supporter of the Anglo-German Friendship Society. Perhaps it was these very factors that engendered a reaction of shock and disappointment at what took place in 1914. Like so many people, it seems, he was strongly influenced by the invasion of Belgium in August that year and the reported atrocities that accompanied this. And two months later the 2nd Worcester Regiment suffered huge losses when they heroically drove back a much larger German force at Gheluvelt in Ypres, Belgium, successfully preventing the Germans reaching the channel ports. In Worcester the news was received with a mixture

---

18. 'Lessons from the Great War: Dean of Worcester's Coventry Address,' BNA, *Coventry Herald*, 29 May 1920.
19. 'International Friendship and the Churches,' BNA, *Uxbridge and West Drayton Gazette*, 28 July 1916.

of almost unbearable grief and fierce pride, reinforcing the growing patriotism and antagonism towards Germany. At this stage William seems to have given up all hope that conciliation could prevail and considered that the only course was to pursue the defeat of Germany. In August 1915 he attended a 'Common Hall' in Worcester Guildhall, a traditional gathering where citizens met to express their opinions on matters of current concern. At the conclusion of the discussion the Lord Lieutenant, the Earl of Coventry, moved a resolution recording 'inflexible determination to continue the struggle for the maintenance of the ideals of liberty and justice which are the common and sacred cause of the allies.'[20] In response William said that he never thought he would ever live to support a resolution for the continuance of war, but he was convinced that there was no other honourable alternative than to declare war and he was now convinced more than ever 'that they must go on and on' because he would rather die than live under German rule. Amidst loud applause he offered fulsome praise for the fleet and the army, declaring that they had much to thank God for and should look forward in hope for the long hard struggle ahead. William Bund, leader of the county council fully endorsed these sentiments. He did not believe that there was a single man, woman or child in the country who would not be heartily in support of the resolution. He felt sure that Germany would not be able to retain Belgium, 'because she attempted to build up her rule on murder supported by the sword, which never prospers.'[21]

It is clear that by 1915 William's pacifist views had given way to a strong feeling that this was 'a just war' and that right was on the British side. Preaching in the Cathedral in November 1915 he was clearly horrified at recent events pointing to the massacre at Louvain, the terrorism in other parts of Belgium, the sinking of the *Lusitania* and the execution of Nurse Edith Cavell. He was vehement in his criticism of the German people. This nation he had so long admired and whose virtues he had so recently extolled he now described as

20. 'Common Hall at Worcester,' BNA, *Birmingham Daily Gazette*, 5 August 1915.
21. ibid.

'docile and obedient, submissive to a ruling class that appeals to might as the supreme power and was ruthless and destructive to the higher qualities of the soul.'[22] A year later as an increasing number of British ships fell victim to that fearsome new German weapon, the submarine, he wrote a fierce article in England's biggest selling Sunday newspaper, the *Weekly Dispatch* in which he urged that at the end of the war, should Britain be victorious, the Germans should be forced to hand over one of their own ships for every British one they had destroyed. William, of course, was deeply attached to ships and to the Royal Navy and the wanton destruction of what he considered to be both beautiful in shape and form and heroic in terms of its manpower grieved him very greatly.[23]

Despite his support for the war, however, William never seemed to have lost his abiding respect for those who stuck fast to their pacifist principles. Following the introduction of conscription in January 1916 he grew increasingly concerned about the unsympathetic treatment of conscientious objectors by the authorities. He could not, he said, see anything wrong with such men conducting work of national importance, rather than being subject to imprisonment and harsh treatment. And in May that year he added his name to a list of signatories, which included prominent Anglicans, non-conformist churchmen and Quakers, to a widely published letter asking for an enquiry into the way tribunals were conducted. Many such hearings, it said, had denied the right to exemption from military service on the grounds of conscience and others had failed to recognise any genuine conviction that was based on moral rather than religious grounds. One magistrate, it was claimed, had stated that he could not deal with 'questions of conscience.' He was simply there 'to stop the rot.'[24] As Christians, the letter urged,

---

22. 'The Dean's Address,' BNA, *Evesham Standard & West Midlands Observer*, 6 November 1915.
23. 'Must Take Ship for Ship,' BNA, *Weekly Dispatch*, 11 November 1916.
24. 'Tribunals and the Conscientious Objector,' BNA, *The Scotsman*, 24 May 1916.

let us remember what grievous harm has been done to the cause of religion by persecution and intolerance, we cannot persecute those who disagree with us, for opinions conscientiously held, without cheapening our own conscience, coarsening public morality and destroying the foundations of all freedom.[25]

It was an unpopular stance in 1916 when so many were losing their loved ones to the war and it is doubtful whether it made any significant difference to the treatment of 'conchies' who were variously scorned, imprisoned and subject to months of hard labour. However, William's support for them perhaps emanated from his own internal moral struggle as he confronted the dilemma posed by the war. In the years after 1918 he would renew his dedication to pacifism and work for peace and reconciliation with a new determination that took him beyond his own country and into the international sphere.

William continued his active involvement with the Alliance throughout the war and beyond, even travelling to Berne in Switzerland to chair one of its meetings in August 1915. The organisation seemed to offer him a way to reconcile his fundamental pacifism with the reality of a conflict that he felt unable to unequivocally condemn. And it gave him a vision of hope for the future. In December 1917 as the war entered its final stages the Alliance held a conference in London where the delegates discussed the idea of a League of Nations, recently proposed by President Woodrow Wilson in the United States. William urged the inclusion of Germany in such an organisation. 'If Germany is left out,' he said, 'we shall have this same state of things all over again. We must look forward to sitting side by side with Germans some day in working out a better state of things in relation to international politics.'[26] It was the view of the conciliator, the position he had so often adopted before the war in Tyneside. He would reiterate this view in a number of addresses he delivered in the months that followed the

25. ibid.
26. 'Can We Destroy the German Army?' BNA, *Newcastle Daily Chronicle*, 15 December 1917.

end of the war, frequently in the face of aggressive opposition. In one section of the population, however, he had increasing support. Shortly after the armistice had been signed in November 1918, he attended a crowded international meeting in London, convened by Lord Parmoor MP, an Anglican who had steadfastly opposed the war and supported the rights of conscientious objectors.[27] The stated aim of the meeting was the creation of 'a Universal Christian Conscience in the face of the problems of international reconstruction.' Opening the meeting Lord Parmoor pointed to 'the danger of denying that Christian ethics have any place in international law.' To loud applause he asked for co-operation between all the Churches and urged that there was 'a need to bring to the front and keep to the front that Christ taught all alike, peace, goodwill, charity, mercy and forgiveness.'[28] It would have been music to William's ears.

---

27. Lord Parmoor, otherwise known as Charles Cripps, was initially a Conservative MP but later joined the Labour Party. After the war he rose to prominence as the British representative on the Council of the League of Nations.

28. 'A Universal Christian Conscience,' BNA, *Newcastle Journal*, 4 December 1918.

Chapter Twenty-Two
TWOPENNY DINNERS

By the spring of 1917 the increasingly successful German U-boat campaign against British ships had turned what had been lingering worries about food supplies into a full-scale emergency. The government response was twofold, a call for people to turn over every conceivable patch of ground to the cultivation of fruit and vegetables and the establishment of food centres where people could obtain cheap nutritious meals at low cost. William, always a practical man, responded to both these initiatives with typical enthusiasm. Although the county of Worcestershire was, and remains, predominantly rural in character Worcester itself contained a high density of both housing and industry. When the city council surveyed the city with a view to maximising food production, they concluded that there was only one large piece of land available for cultivation, namely the 100-acre racecourse. Unfortunately, this area was (and remains) subject to regular flooding and considered unsuitable for anything other than the intermittent grazing of cattle. They turned instead, therefore, to small plots of land such as peoples' gardens which together comprised about a dozen acres. One such was the Cathedral Green which initially looked unpromising material. Described as 'about two thirds of an acre of greensward' it had recently been laid bare by the ravages of a gale which had blown down a score of two-hundred-year-old elms. This sad event no doubt made it easier for William to raise support from the Cathedral Chapter for his idea of turning the greensward into a vegetable plot. The task, which fell to the boys of the King's School during their Christmas holidays, was by no means an easy one. The ground, already in its unyielding winter state, had apparently remained undisturbed since the middle of the eighteenth century. With considerable fortitude, however, the boys 'did their bit' and laboured through the winter weather to dig up the stubborn roots of the ill-fated elms. And in the spring the new crops were sown. The Old Palace, meanwhile, had a large garden and William had no hesitation in offering the lower half at the back of the house for cultivation. In peacetime summers this beautiful area had offered Deanery guests lovely sweeping views over the river and beyond. By early spring, however, the lawns and herbaceous borders had been replaced by rows of potato plants. In September 1918 William presided at the opening ceremony of the Worcester Produce Exhibition where he said that the various 'allotments' in the town were providing food for over one thousand families.

Alongside all this digging and planting the government was also considering various options for controlling the distribution of food. One idea which took hold was that of the national restaurant, later termed the 'communal kitchen'. Large scale use of these would, it was argued, help the government to maintain control over the amount of food consumed and reduce the amount of waste which seemed to result when individual households bought their own food supplies and cooked their own meals. It would also provide a means of feeding the mounting numbers of poverty-stricken families whose breadwinners had either disappeared on the battlefield or simply lost their jobs. The government, however, was keen to play down this aspect fearing that the association with poverty would discourage people from taking advantage of what was on offer. These establishments, they emphasised, were not the same as the already ubiquitous 'soup kitchens' for the poor, largely run by the Salvation Army, but places where everyone could obtain appetising and good quality food and help the war effort in the process. The term 'communal kitchen' was intended to reinforce this image.[1] It was also

---

[1]. Lord Rhondda who oversaw the organisation of the scheme preferred the term 'National Kitchen' fearing the radical communistic overtones of 'communal'. He urged a change of name but, in reality, most towns who set up kitchens seem to have continued referring to them as 'communal'.

emphasised that communal kitchens were not intended as charitable enterprises. Although the initial set up costs could be subsidised by a Treasury grant, they should, it was stipulated, be run as financially viable concerns. In reality, some were run by local businessmen, some by local factories and many by local authorities. Ultimately thousands of these kitchens, in different forms ranging from fully functioning restaurants to small kiosks, opened across the country during the war.

Given that the very first kitchen was opened by Queen Mary in London on 21 May 1917, Worcester seems to have been remarkably speedy in setting up their own scheme, perhaps because in the person of their Cathedral Dean they had their own readymade expertise to hand. In the middle of April that year the Mayor, Arthur Carlton, convened a meeting of the already established City Food Economy Committee where it was agreed they should ask for a grant of £100 from the War Relief Fund to set up a kitchen and that William should prepare a report on 'the cookery question because of his unique experience in this direction.'[2] Casting his mind back to his Penny Dinners of thirty years before, he was, it seems, able to put together an organisational structure and a viable business plan with remarkable speed. Worcester's communal kitchen opened just six weeks later, taking over the rooms of the Cookery College in Bank Street where a few alterations were made to the rooms and two additional cookers installed. A paid cook was engaged and a large number of voluntary helpers were recruited such that twenty-eight were available each day working on a rota system. On 23 May the Mayor with due ceremony declared the communal kitchen open. He considered, he said, that it was just as important that they (presumably the council) should see that people were provided with proper food as clean water. The intention was to supply two hundred meals per day. William followed with an address to the 'small knot' of people who had already assembled outside. He was careful to emphasise the government line. The kitchen was not a charitable institution, he said. The public were asked to pay for the

---

2. 'Food Economy Campaign at Worcester,' BNA, *Birmingham Daily Post*, 19 April 1917.

food, a sum that would cover the cost.³ Drawing on his experiences in Gateshead he would, no doubt, have calculated this with great care. The food would be sold in portions at a charge of 2d per portion. Thus all citizens could obtain well-cooked meals at reasonable prices. Certainly the menu he described was considerably different from the traditional soup and bread offered to the poor and destitute. The menu options for that day, for example, were savoury hot pot and dumplings, baked liver, chocolate mould and rice pudding with jam. Later in the week there would be scotch stew, treacle pudding, beef stew and fish pie. There was also barley kernel pudding, a popular alternative to rice pudding which offered William a golden opportunity to remind people of the need to preserve stocks of barley by drinking less alcohol. 'Anyone who drinks two pints of beer a day is really consuming double rations of bread,' he declared. It was quite possible, he said, that the nation might be driven to choose between beer and bread and he hoped for the sake of existence people would choose bread!⁴ In one sense the Worcester kitchen did bear some resemblance to the model of a charitable soup kitchen in that there was no facility for eating on the premises. Essentially this was a 'take away'. People were required to bring their own bowls and basins to carry the food home. With perfect timing, as William underlined this point, one small girl dropped the basin she was clutching and it smashed to pieces on the ground. The Mayor, it was reported, immediately stepped forward, put his hand in his pocket and gave her the money to buy another!⁵

William's concerns always tended towards the needs of children and on the 10 January 1918 a further communal kitchen was opened under the auspices of the Food Economy Committee. This was set up in the Mission Room at Barnards Green in nearby Malvern and on that day it was reported that eighty children were provided with twopenny dinners. In mid September 1918 as the end of the war

3. 'Meals at 2*d* a Portion'. BNA, *Birmingham Daily Post*, 23 May 1917.
4. 'Bread or Beer,' BNA, *Birmingham Daily Post*, 23 May 1917.
5. 'First World War Centenary: 1914–1918.' Worcestershire World War 100. 18 May 1917–24 February 1918. www.ww1worcestershire.co.uk

approached William presented a report to the Committee which showed that the communal kitchens were working well and their finances were sound. At that point two more kitchens were planned for Worcester, in Mealcheapen Street and at St Clements church, and new cooks had been appointed. However, given the proximity of the Armistice which took place a month later, it is unclear how long these kitchens continued to operate. Ultimately they were a victim of their own success for during 1919 they began to encounter considerable opposition from the commercial catering trade and government support was gradually withdrawn. By the end of that year most across the country had closed. However the idea lived on, to be resurrected some twenty years later when the nation once more found itself at war.

Despite his preoccupations with food William of course had considerable responsibilities at the Cathedral. Whatever his private thoughts about the war he took very seriously the role of the Church in maintaining morale amongst an increasingly grief stricken and traumatised civilian population. He was renowned as an inspirational preacher and his ability to uplift and comfort the congregation in equal measure was invaluable in a time of national crisis. Inevitably as time went on he was forced to draw on his own personal experience of loss and that of his friends and colleagues when he spoke about the war. By the spring of 1916 his close friend, Sub-Dean Canon James Wilson, had lost two of his four sons to the war and Bishop Yeatman-Biggs's nephew Harry would die in Palestine in November 1917. A month later William's own nephew Ernest, son of his brother James, was killed when a German shell penetrated the engine room of his ship HMS *Pellew* on escort duty in the North Sea. He was, said William, 'a keen young officer in the Royal Navy, the most modest and single-minded young man I ever knew.'[6] Despite these cruel personal griefs however William and Canon Wilson, with other members of the Chapter, kept the Cathedral running to its

---

6. WCL scrapbooks, 22nd September 1914.

familiar, comforting timetable of regular services punctuated by memorial services and national days of prayer as the occasion demanded. William's programme of Sunday afternoon lectures continued with a variety of guest speakers and with the help of Sarah, local volunteers were organised into the provision of supplies to be sent to the troops, which included everything from books to knitted gloves and balaclavas. The balaclavas had been specifically requested by his nephew in a letter he sent to William back in 1914. William and Sarah had laughed when Ernest added 'please don't let anyone make pyjamas – sailors don't know what to do with them!'[7] Fund raising for charity, always a significant part of Cathedral activities, was now turned towards organisations concerned specifically with the war effort such as St John's Ambulance and an English military hospital at Arc-en-Barrois in France managed by Madeleine Bromley-Martin, the daughter of Worcestershire's deputy Lord Lieutenant. Although it proved impossible to hold the usual Three Choirs Festival, of which William was a dedicated supporter, music maintained its central role in the life of the Cathedral.[8] The choir, diminished in numbers but not in resolve, continued to sing, not

Memorial window in Worcester Cathedral cloisters to William Moore-Ede's nephew, Ernest Ede. (Courtesy of Chris Guy, Worcester Cathedral.)

7. WCL scrapbooks. Letter from Ernest Ede to Reverend Moore-Ede. 12 September 1914.

8. The Three Choirs Festival is a long established annual musical festival. The venue rotates between the three neighbouring counties of Herefordshire, Worcestershire and Gloucestershire.

only in the building itself but also in hospitals for wounded soldiers where they performed every Sunday afternoon. On one occasion wounded soldiers were brought to the Cathedral to listen to a recital of Handel's oratorio *Samson*. Special concerts were performed frequently to raise money for the Red Cross and also as memorials for those who had died. In December 1915, for example, there was a performance of *Mozart's Requiem* and in March 1917 Sir Edward Elgar, who in happier times had played a central role in the festival, conducted a special performance of his recently completed work 'For the Fallen' which he had dedicated 'to the memory of our glorious men, with a special thought for the Worcesters.'[9]

William and Canon Wilson also organised special events in the city designed to raise the spirits of local people. Some of these had a specific focus such as the annual CETS fete in May 1915 when William addressed one thousand children in the Cathedral after which they marched in procession to the County Cricket Ground to take part in various sports and of course tea. The temperance movement had received a considerable boost during the war with the imposition of various legal restrictions on the sale and consumption of alcohol.[10] These were supported by the King who pledged to abstain for the duration of the war, and the minister of munitions, David Lloyd George, who did not, despite famously declaring that 'drink is doing us more damage in the war than all the German submarines put together.' Meanwhile in July of the same year William and Canon Wilson joined with local parish congregations to organise a Missionary Festival that included a large pageant, and a procession through the streets of Worcester culminating with a service at the Cathedral. Later that year they established 'study circles' where people met together to explore Christian literature, faith and prayer, an idea William had brought back from the conference in Berne, part of the Alliance's

---

9. The third part of a three-part work *The Spirit of England* based on the poems of Laurence Binyon written in 1914. The complete work was first performed in Birmingham on 4th October 1917.

10. Restrictions were brought in as part of the Defence of the Realm Act, 1914.

proposed National Mission of Repentance and Hope. And in May 1917 they worked with the city authorities to set up an Empire Day celebration for eight thousand local children held in the Cathedral and at the local Pitchcroft racecourse. Presumably the cattle were removed for the day!

William obviously kept extremely busy during the war, but despite this typically practical response he also seems to have sought personal solace in the pursuit of one of his abiding interests, that of history. Since his arrival in Worcester he had come to love the beautiful old building with its witness to many previous generations of the faithful. He was fascinated by the various memorials and historical stonework that adorned the Cathedral and in 1910 had launched a fund-raising campaign to pay for a replacement copy of the crumbling statue of King Edgar which sat above the gatehouse of the Cathedral's Edgar Tower.[11] A number of smaller terracotta figures designed to illustrate the four great epochs of the See of Worcester were also added to fill the previously empty niches surrounding the King. William personally contributed £20 to the figure of Bishop Bosel, the first Bishop of Worcester, which was largely paid for by the Chapter. More controversially, in 1914, he had spearheaded a campaign to commemorate the popular Worcester born authoress, Mrs Henry Wood, with a marble wall plaque placed in the Cathedral nave. Mrs Wood had set many of the scenes of her numerous novels in and around the Cathedral precincts, notably immortalising the gatekeeper of the tower in her novel *The Channings*. William was a great admirer of her books and was also well aware that she brought large numbers of visitors into the building, all keen to know where this and that had actually happened. 'Where was the inkpot thrown?' people would ask as he showed them round the cloisters. Some people in higher literary circles were disparaging about Mrs Wood's literary talents. The editor of the *Pall Mall Gazette* was

---

11. The Edgar Tower was originally the main gate to what was once the Royal Castle and Priory and for many centuries it was known as St Mary's Gatehouse. It was renamed the Edgar Tower in the late nineteenth century to reflect the presence of a stone figure of King Edgar (crowned in 973) above the gate.

particularly snooty. 'With so much that is first rate in literature to claim our attention and reprove our neglect,' he opined 'is it really desirable to start a posthumous cult of unmistakably minor novelists? Is it not kinder to let the aberrations of popular taste be forgotten when they have happily passed away?'[12] William was undeterred. If anyone wanted to learn about ordinary life in Victorian Worcester, he said, they need look no further than Mrs Wood's books. During the war William set about researching the origin of other memorials and the lives of the people they represented. He would no doubt have been helped by Canon James Wilson who also filled the role of Cathedral librarian. The two men were close like-minded friends whose mutual support throughout the war would have been invaluable to both. The result of William's research was a series of articles published in *Berrows Worcester Journal*. These were widely circulated, not least among the troops in France, many of whom wrote to William telling him how much they looked forward to the arrival of 'each story of old times.' After the war the articles were collected into a book, published at Easter 1925.[13] In a rare public admission of his own mental struggles William said that he had undertaken the project as a way of diverting his attention from the anxieties of the war. He dedicated the book to Sarah to whom he said he was indebted, for it was she who had encouraged him to persevere with the task.

12. 'Notes of the Day,' BNA, *Pall Mall Gazette*, 11 April 1914.
13. W. Moore-Ede, *The Cathedral Church of Christ and the Blessed Virgin Mary, of Worcester: Its Monuments and Their Stories*. (Phillips & Probert, Worcester, 1925).

Chapter Twenty-Three
A GARDEN SUBURB AND GHELUVELT PARK

William's enthusiasm for the garden city movement had been undiminished by his move to Worcester. In fact his early encounter with the district of Blockhouse had only served to strengthen his conviction that decent housing was an essential element of any programme of social reform. Early in 1910 he had announced his intention to pursue the idea of building some new houses in Worcester along the lines of the Walkerville project in Newcastle. Quite recently he had heard about a similar project in nearby Hereford. The Hereford garden city scheme was initiated by the current Deputy Mayor, Frederick Bulmer, joint founder with his brother Percy of Hereford's major industry Bulmer's Cider Company. In September that year, therefore, William and a group of other enthusiasts had taken a train ride to Hereford to meet Mr Bulmer and his workers who conducted them on a tour of inspection of the houses (currently twenty-three in number) and invited them to take tea with the tenants. Under the terms of the town council lease, it seemed, the Bulmers had now secured permission to build a further thirty-four houses on the site and an application had been made through the local loans board for an advance of £6,000 at 3½ per cent interest. Thus inspired William gathered together a number of interested and influential parties which included Earl Beauchamp, Lord Cobham and some enthusiastic members of the Cathedral Chapter and together they formed the Worcester Housing Scheme.

In some ways the financial model of the Worcester scheme was similar to that employed in Walkerville, (Co-operative Tenants Ltd) rather than that in Hereford which relied entirely on the benevolence of a major employer. Inevitably, however, some seed funding was required. In Walker this had been provided by the Co-operative Society but in Worcester it came from a combination of local aristocracy and clergy. As ever William was suspicious of the motives of wealthy industrialists and the degree of control they might wish to exert in future years. More particularly of course he could not condone the source of Frederick Bulmer's income despite the fact that in many respects the two men were rather similar. Fred, the son of the Rector of nearby Credenhill, had formed his progressive liberal views at King's College, Cambridge in the early 1880s. He considered that some form of intervention was essential to help the poor of England and advocated the minimum wage, medical aid, the founding of schools, as well as the building of houses. He was not, however, prepared to condemn the capitalist system itself or to embrace its replacement with a co-operative economic model. 'The capitalist,' he said, 'must be judged by the use he makes of his money and the amount he spends on himself.'[1]

It would be another four years, in April 1914, before the first few houses of the 'Worcester Garden Suburb' would be opened. Much of the intervening time had been spent in pursuing a prolonged and ultimately unsuccessful attempt to acquire a site at Battenhall a leafy area close to the Cathedral. The current residents of Battenhall, however, were not enamoured of the idea of less genteel people living nearby and mounted a spirited and prolonged challenge to the scheme. In the end, therefore, another site of eleven acres was found just off Tolladine Road, 'not so accessible or pleasant in approach from the city,' declared Lord Cobham at the opening ceremony, 'but having the advantage of lying on much higher ground and being near the railway.'[2] He was fulsome in his praise for William who he said 'could be fairly considered to be the father of the project who has worked zealously

---

1. E. F. Bulmer Trust. www.efbulmer.co.uk. In 1938 E. F. Bulmer used a tenth of his personal wealth to found the E. F. Bulmer Benevolent Fund providing help for former employees of the company who were suffering from hardship. The fund continues to operate today.

2. 'Garden City at Worcester,' BNA, *Evening Dispatch*, 18 April 1914

to carry it out.'³ Both Lord Cobham and Earl Beauchamp were now substantial shareholders in the Tenants Limited Company. A year later fourteen more houses had been added, despite the fact that the country was now at war and obviously had other pressing concerns. In the circumstances, remarked Lord Beauchamp, the continuation of the scheme was a great leap of faith but it was essential that the future development of Worcester was not left to haphazard plans but was laid out properly with houses that were pleasant, convenient and

Part of Worcester's 'Garden City' development, opened in 1915, pictured in 2021.

economical. These houses were of varying sizes, each with a garden, with rents between 3/9d to 5/6d. They were built on three sides of a lawned square which was formally named Earl Grey Square after William's old friend, Earl Grey, who came to Worcester to perform the official opening. In the presence of a prestigious guest list which included the Mayor and Mayoress, the high sheriff of Worcestershire,

3. ibid.

Sir Henry Urwick and George Cadbury, he ceremoniously unlocked the door of the central house with a golden key.[4] Rather poignantly William announced that unfortunately the architect of the houses, Mr Vernon Rowe, could not be present as he had 'left for the Front.'[5]

Mr Rowe, however, had left a message for William. He asked that one of the houses in Earl Grey Square should be earmarked for an incapacitated disabled soldier. It was a request that would set in motion another scheme, to build a group of houses specifically for the purpose, something that was very much in tune with a wider national movement which developed after the war. As with the communal kitchens, however, Worcester seems to have been quite well ahead in its thinking for by December 1916 the requisite committee, led by the Mayor, Arthur Carlton, had been set up and an appeal for funds launched. The committee was a much-expanded version of the group that had delivered the houses in Earl Grey Square and now included a number of military men such as General Sir George Higginson, Colonel of the Worcester Regiment, and also a local MP Stanley Baldwin. Funds flowed in rapidly with small and large donations, fetes and garden parties were held and individuals promised goods and services.[6] Mr and Mrs Colville-Stewart of Tomatoland in Malvern promised to provide and equip one bungalow, the pharmacists of the city undertook to provide free of charge all the necessary drugs and medicines for the residents of the houses, and Mr Henry Tarrant, a lime manufacturer of nearby Broughton Hackett, promised five tons of lime for the construction work.[7] In November 1918, just before Armistice Day, the Mayor announced that the fund now stood at £6,000 and that he had just received a further cheque for £50, together with

---

4. Sir Henry Urwick was chairman of Malvern Town Council and a keen supporter of the garden city movement. George Cadbury, with his brother Richard, developed the factory village of Bournville in Birmingham, based on the principles of good housing at affordable rents set in a leafy environment.

5. Vernon Rowe survived the war and returned to his architectural practice in 1919.

6. William's wife, Sarah, gave £100

7. Tomatoland was a large area of glasshouses in Malvern which produced tomatoes (known as 'Malvomas'), cucumbers and lettuces.

commitments from the Worcester Foresters to provide one bungalow and from the workers 'at a certain factory' to provide four more.

The homes were to be built in the grounds of Barbourne College, a former school which had been purchased by the council in January 1918 and had been used for the billeting of soldiers during the war. By September a detailed plan had been drawn up for twelve houses and a surrounding recreational area which, it was agreed, would be renamed Gheluvelt Park in honour of the Worcester regiment

Houses for disabled ex-servicemen in Gheluvelt Memorial Park, Worcester, opened in 1920, pictured in 2021.

which had fought so bravely in Gheluvelt, Ypres, in the early days of the war. The foundation stone was laid by Field Marshall Sir William Robertson on 16 January 1919 and eighteen months later the houses were complete and ready for occupation. They were officially opened by General Lord Rawlinson on 13 July 1920. A memorial arch was constructed at the entrance to the park in 1924 and in the years that followed the area was developed to include trees and grassy areas, a children's playground with a paddling pool, tennis courts, a putting green and a miniature railway. A pond was also constructed with a small island, on which stands a bandstand reached by an ornamental bridge, and in 1925 a tea house, gifted by Richard Cadbury, was installed. More recently a renovated Victorian Pumping Station was converted into an Environment Centre, a model of sustainable energy. Gheluvelt remains a very popular venue today and importantly continues to provide a powerful reminder for successive generations of the fallen of the Great War. Its most recent addition is a circular memorial of steel panels, constructed in 2010, each recalling a military engagement of the war involving a Worcester regiment.

William played a full part in the committee that brought Gheluvelt into being. Not only was this a very practical response which honoured the living as well as the dead, but he also had a strong belief in the significance of remembrance. One of the problems which had arisen during the war was the increasing number of requests from individual families to place a memorial to their lost loved one in the Cathedral. In 1917 William had been forced to rule that no more such memorials would be allowed until after the war when, he promised, consideration would be given to a 'collective memorial'. When the war came to an end he was determined to make good on this promise. His first opportunity came on the 7 June 1919 when he accepted into the safe keeping of the Cathedral Chapter a memorial to the men of the county who had served. In a moving ceremony, one hundred surviving troops formed a guard of honour as a banner given by 'the ladies of Worcestershire', commemorating the men of the 2nd and 3rd Worcestershire Regiments who went out to France in 1914, was carried in procession from the Guildhall to the Cathedral. It was reverentially placed in a carved oak cabinet which also contained the names of 1,300 men inscribed on vellum. In his acceptance speech William said that the memorial would be placed in the north aisle near the door of the Cathedral 'so that all who enter may have access to it and read the names of the brave men who by their courage and constancy played so great a part in checking the first onrush of the invading hosts, most of whom gave their lives to save England and the cause of liberty.'[8] His subsequent address based on a verse from Psalm 118 'It was the Lord's doing and it was marvellous in our eyes' was unequivocally patriotic, tending to confirm his support for the war and his conviction that he ascribed the victory of the allies to God's providence.[9] No doubt on such a day he could express no other sentiments but perhaps by now he had, in any case, made his own personal peace with a form of pacifism that embraced the concept of justifiable violence in an honourable cause. The cabinet remains in the north aisle today alongside what is now St George's military chapel.[10]

There would soon be further memorials to the dead of the war both inside and outside the Cathedral but these had to wait for a few months while William recovered from an uncharacteristic bout of ill-health. By the time the Gheluvelt foundation stone was safely laid at the beginning of 1919 he had been feeling increasingly unwell. He was now seventy years old and had worked tirelessly during the last few years. Like so many others he would have been feeling physically and emotionally weary at the end of the war. Far from experiencing a period of respite, however, his responsibilities at the Cathedral had temporarily increased for September 1918 brought the culmination of a diocesan project that had been in progress since 1914. This was the official creation of the reconstituted diocese of Coventry.[11] It was an enterprise initiated and led by Huyshe Yeatman-Biggs and on the successful completion of the project, it was natural that he would become the new Bishop of Coventry. His departure from Worcester in early November meant that, pending the appointment of a replacement,

8. '2nd and 3rd Worcesters Memorial Banner Placed in Cathedral.' BNA, *Evesham Standard & West Midlands Observer*, 7 June 1919.

9. ibid.

10. St George's Chapel was created and formally consecrated as a military chapel many years later on Armistice Day 1936.

11. Since 1836 Coventry had been part of the See of Worcester. The decision in 1918 to create a new diocese of Coventry was a response to the huge rise in population in the area. Similarly, the Birmingham diocese, also formerly part of Worcester, had been created in 1905 with Charles Gore as its first Bishop.

William found himself appointed 'guardian of spiritualties' the result apparently of a ruling made by Pope Boniface in favour of the prior of Worcester in 1268. Essentially it meant that the Dean was required to carry out most of the Bishop's duties of office. This 'privilege' as the *Birmingham Mail* called it lasted until the beginning of March 1919 when the Reverend Ernest Pearce was finally enthroned as Bishop of Worcester.[12] (The usual difficulties associated with the expense of Hartlebury Castle had, no doubt, created a delay). The nature of William's health problems was unstated, but at the beginning of June, shortly after the memorial ceremony in the Cathedral, it was reported that he had left Worcester for a stay in a London nursing home. While there he again underwent surgery and Sarah reported a fortnight later that he was making satisfactory progress. He returned to the Old Palace at the beginning of July and made what was described as a 'semi-public appearance' to open a fête for the YWCA where his three young grandsons were manning the flower stall. 'He was dressed in a grey lounge suit rather than his official apron and gaiters,' reported the *Worcester Echo*. 'It was good to hear his genial voice again but his face bore the traces of his recent illness.'[13] In fact William did not take up his official duties again until the middle of September, spending the intervening period recuperating in North Wales. For someone normally so energetic this long absence and his failure to appear at any of the various peace celebrations which took place around that time bears testimony to his frailty that summer. By the autumn, however, his old enthusiasm was returning. The Dean is now fully recovered the *Worcester Echo* reported enthusiastically and will preach on Sunday 14 September.[14]

William's first appointment had in fact been the previous Thursday when he had attended a meeting to discuss the erection of a county war memorial. The discussion on the form and position of this memorial would prove to be both heated and protracted. Fortunately William

12. Ernest Pearce, Bishop of Worcester, in office 1919–30.
13. WCL scrapbooks, 4 July 1919.
14. WCL scrapbooks, 4 September 1919.

seems to have fully recovered his long practised ability to weather these sort of committee meetings, and to negotiate something approaching his own preferred outcome. Eventually, to please everyone, it was agreed that the memorial should take several forms, a cross on the Cathedral Green, the writing of a history of the Worcestershire regiment, the distribution of relief grants to ex-servicemen and finally a stained-glass window in the Cathedral. The window, the first of these to be completed, was unveiled by General Sir George Higginson on Armistice Day 1921. The design, which had been selected from four submissions, bore the distinct hallmark of William's influence, for it was the work of his old friend from the Gateshead Stained-Glass company, Christian Socialist artist, James Eadie-Reid. In the centre of the window is the figure of Christ on the Cross representing the Supreme Sacrifice. It is flanked by two angels representing on one side a cup of pain and suffering and on the other a crown of life representing the triumph of victory over death. Significantly, however, below these sacred representations are several figures of all too human men and women struggling in the heat of battle. It was a typical response to the commission from Eadie-Reid, as were several other smaller memorials completed earlier at William's instigation. These were the simpler, but equally beautiful, decorated windows placed in the Cathedral cloisters, some recording the time and place of death of an individual young man and others the names of six former members of the choir, twenty-three bellringers and eighty-two previous pupils of the Kings School. Before the war William had played a prominent role in the organisation of the Three Choirs Festival. He was also president of the Worcestershire and District Association of Change Ringers, a position he would continue to hold until 1932, and he was an active school governor. As such he would have known all these men personally and felt their deaths very keenly.

A year after the unveiling of Eadie-Reid's memorial window, the series of formal commemorations in and around the Cathedral were at last completed when, on Armistice Day 1922, several hundred people gathered to see Lord Coventry unveiling the Memorial Cross on Cathedral Green. Some had argued that the Cross was a rather too modest affair compared with the more elaborate and impressively triumphalist South African War Memorial that already graced the Green. Countering this, however, Lord Coventry stressed that a decision had been made to devote the largest share of the money raised to a relief fund to meet the needs of the bereaved and the disabled, rather than spending it all on the memorial itself. It was a pointed reminder of changing times and changing priorities – and one no doubt William would have thoroughly approved of.

Chapter Twenty-Four
THE DEAN'S COWSHEDS

Despite the determined optimism that accompanied the opening of Earl Grey Square in 1915 the war seemed to have put an end to any further expansion of the garden city movement in Worcester. However, the housing crisis in the city had worsened during the war with thousands of residents now living in slums, some of which still had no mains water or sewerage. In 1918 the country as a whole was facing an acute shortage of building materials and labour, making it difficult for private developers to build houses at prices people could afford to buy or rent. The government response, framed in the ambitious Housing Act of 1919, was its famous promise to build within three years 500,000 'homes fit for heroes'.[1] Although in earlier years a few local authorities had built small numbers of council houses this was the first time that a government had issued a direct mandate to local councils to provide housing at affordable rents for working people.[2] Under the Act every local authority was required, within three months, to submit a proposal for a new housing scheme. Land purchase was to be financed by the issuing of bonds at good rates of return and the Treasury would back approved schemes, namely those that met certain criteria, with a grant of £150 towards the construction cost of each house. Encouragingly the committee which drew up

---

1. A popular misquote of the Prime Minister's words 'to make Britain a country fit for heroes to live in'.
2. The first 'council houses' in the sense of houses built and owned by a local authority were built in Liverpool in 1869.

these criteria, led by the architect and Liberal MP Tudor Walters, was much inspired and informed by the principles of the garden city movement such that the recommendation was for low density cottage type houses, with front and back gardens, arranged around green spaces. Each house should contain three bedrooms large enough to contain two beds, a living room, a kitchen, bathroom and a separate lavatory. Like many other local authorities, however, Worcester City Council were completely unused to any involvement in house building and the hastily convened housing committee struggled to meet the requirements of the Act.

William, however, was immediately interested in the proposal. He had, so it was reported, chided the council on numerous occasions about its slowness in tackling the housing problem. Casting his mind back to Walkerville and the Aged Miners' Homes he decided to embark on an experiment. Unlike his earlier projects in the North East, however, his object this time was not to embark on the establishment of a co-operative housing scheme but simply to demonstrate to the council that perfectly adequate houses could be built very quickly and cheaply, for no more than £500 each. In the first instance he planned to build two bungalows, each consisting of a large living room, a kitchen, three bedrooms and a bathroom. Most importantly these houses could then be let at an economical rent which was within the range of the average wage earner. 'I may burn my fingers,' he acknowledged, 'but I'm going to have a try.'[3]

William enlisted the support of a local building firm, Phelps & Johnson, to build his houses. The site, in Lansdowne Road, Worcester, was currently owned by Mr Phelps's foreman, a Mr Henshaw, who used it for an allotment. Both men were enthusiastic supporters of the scheme, as was Major Vernon Rowe, now happily returned from the war and employed as the county architect. Between them they designed and built two houses in five months, at a cost not exceeding the proposed £500. Constructed of brick with stone

3. 'Dean's Housing Plan. An Interesting Experiment in Worcester,' BNA, *Birmingham Daily Gazette*, 8 December 1919.

window frames these were attractive cottages which, according to the *Birmingham Gazette*,

> were models of compactness and good taste, an object lesson as to what can be done with the use of ordinary materials arranged with a view to economy. The three bedrooms were airy and light, the living room windows faced south with plenty of sunshine, the bathroom was fitted with a bath and wash basin and there was an adjoining lavatory, kitchen, gas heated boiler providing hot water, a gas stove, coal house and storage space in the loft.[4]

The houses were formally opened with the obligatory silver key at a ceremony on 13 May 1920 attended by Charles Milward the current, High Sheriff of Worcestershire, and the chairman of Worcester's Health Committee, Dr Walpole Simmonds. William acknowledged that criticism had come from a number of quarters.

> People said what on earth was I doing bothering myself with house building – surely its his duty to preach the gospel they said. But I believe preaching without practice is not of much value. One saw a great need to provide adequate housing for the people of the country and of Worcester. So I thought it right, despite slow progress through the difficulty of raising money, to see if a house could be built for a much smaller sum than was generally quoted. I believe that this is the house for the future. We should give up two or three-story houses. There is enough ground to build ten or twelve to an acre and no stairs to erect. The houses are labour saving and do not need luxury, given the difficulties of obtaining service. People who looked at them liked them.[5]

Charles Milward, owner of Milward's Needle Manufacturers

4. 'A Housing Dean. Venture to Provide an Object Lesson in Building,' BNA, *Birmingham Daily Gazette*, 12 May 1920.
5. 'The Dean's Bungalows. Opening Ceremony at Worcester,' BNA, *Worcester Echo*, 14 May 1920.

in Redditch, which employed several hundred people and reputedly supplied the world with eight million needles per week, felt that the Dean should be congratulated. He said,

> Members of the clergy were not usually practical businessmen, they were inclined to gloss over practical difficulties, but the Dean was one who combined practical sagacity and common sense with that special knowledge which was his as a member of the profession to which he belonged. He had not set out to make money, he was not a bloated capitalist, he had set out to provide an example that others might follow – to show that houses might be built at a cost which meant they could be let out at an economic rent.[6]

From one of the most successful businessmen in the county this was high praise.

William referred more than once to the good co-operation that existed between the architect, the builder and the workmen who frequently, he said, had offered useful suggestions to improve the mode of construction as the project progressed. Sadly, however, his famed ability to foster co-operation from those who might now be termed 'stakeholders' seems to have foundered when it came to the city housing committee. Some of the most scathing criticism of his scheme came from this direction. One committee member suggested that the houses had probably been 'jerry built' in order to keep costs down. William rejected this. The proof, he said, was Mr Phelps's reputation and the fact that he had agreed to build two more, slightly larger, for no more than £550 despite the fact that wages had risen.[7] Another member of the committee, local solicitor Arrowsmith Maund, referred disparagingly to the bungalows as 'the Dean's cowsheds.' William retorted that he thought the citizens of Worcester would be better pleased if the council put up a few more cowsheds. In part

6. ibid.
7. Mr Phelps was one half of the well-known Worcestershire firm of Phelps & Johnson, highly regarded builders in the county.

the council's attitude may be explained by the fact that while praise was heaped on William from far and wide the housing committee was equally assailed by criticism, accused of ineptitude and delay. 'The Dean has already ordered two more bungalows,' declared the *Birmingham Gazette*. 'They are in great demand. In the meantime the city council who contemplates the provision of one thousand houses have not yet laid the foundation stone of one!'[8] The *Shields Daily News*, always an enthusiastic follower of William's activities, asked why local authorities wasted millions on housing schemes when it was possible to erect houses as good or better by adopting a more economical model. 'The Dean's results have been arrived at by wise planning and careful specification and at much lower costs than the contracts made by the public authorities throughout the country,' the editor wrote.[9] A Mr Thomas Skinner from Sevenoaks in Kent summed up what seemed to be the general view with the curt observation 'Councils talk, parsons talk, people talk. We should be better served if they did what the Dean of Worcester is doing – building houses for the working classes.'[10]

Worcester's housing committee, however, were disinclined to take Mr Skinner's advice. As William's houses moved towards completion the committee dithered over vague plans to build about five hundred houses and worried whether they would be able to meet the costs. Given the requirement to provide details of a housing scheme within three months they were a long way behind schedule. A few days before the opening ceremony in Lansdowne Road the chairman of the committee had received a somewhat threatening letter from the Ministry of Health whose officials had already compiled a report on the state of housing in the city. They had concluded that 1,046 new houses were currently required. The Ministry, the letter said, was prepared to accept five hundred houses, to be built by the end of 1920, but also called

8. 'A Dean's Bungalows. Lead Given to Housing at Worcester,' BNA, *Birmingham Daily Gazette*, 7 May 1920.
9. 'Dean as Builder. Lesson in Economy for the Government,' BNA, *Shields Daily News*, 29 December 1920.
10. 'Thomas Skinner,' BNA, *Sevenoaks Chronicle & Kentish Advertiser*, 19 December 1919.

attention to the Ministry's power to 'declare Worcester in default of the legislation in which event financial assistance would not be available.'[11] Amidst the resultant panic and flurry of activity the city council invited tenders for the large scale construction of houses and by July had accepted a proposal by the Birmingham construction company of Thomas Rowbotham & Son to build 357 on a site in the Northwick area of the city. Mr Rowbotham was quite used to ambitious projects, although admittedly small cottages were not exactly his usual line of work. He is best known for his construction of the central buildings of the University of Birmingham including its iconic clock tower 'Old Joe', then reputed to be the tallest structure in Europe, as well as Worcester's innovative hydro-electric power station at nearby Powick.[12] Mr Rowbotham drove a hard bargain, proposing to build the houses at a cost of £1,200 per house. One committee member, Richard Fairbairn, objected vociferously moving an amendment that the council should confine the contract to 112 houses at present, for they could not afford to build so many at that figure. The cost would be in the region of £420,000. On a recent fact finding visit to Newbury they had seen houses built for £800 each. 'What did we visit Newbury for – to see the races?' he demanded to know.[13] Moreover the Dean could build houses for £500 pounds each and the difference between this figure and that of the proposed contract was too big to be ignored. Coventry Council was greatly interested in the Dean's scheme, Mr Fairburn concluded, and considered that Worcester Council was writing specifications for palatial houses which attracted tenders they could not afford. Mr Arrowsmith Maund, who was by now describing William's houses as 'dog kennels', was unimpressed. Mr Rowbotham had made it clear that the contract was for 357 houses or none. At present the council

11. 'Worcester Housing. Ministry's Hint to Get a Move On,' BNA, *Birmingham Daily Gazette*, 6 May 1920.

12. Aston Webb, the architect of the University of Birmingham buildings, modelled the central square and main buildings on St Mark's Square in Venice.

13. 'Worcester Housing: Council to Build by Direct Labour,' BNA, *Cheltenham Chronicle*, 10 July 1920; 'Worcester to Build 357 Houses. Contract with Birmingham Builder Sealed,' BNA, *Birmingham Daily Gazette*, 7 July 1920.

had only £25,000 but they had reason to be believe that the rest of the money would be forthcoming. Mr Fairbairn's amendment was rejected and the contract was signed.

There was a political undercurrent to these exchanges of which William may or may not have been aware. The city council had long been the scene of continuous in-fighting between its Conservative and Liberal members. Relations between the two parties had always been tense but became particularly acrimonious after 1906 when the Liberals, led by Earl Beauchamp, accused the Conservatives of corruption in the Parliamentary Election of that year. The Royal Commission set up to investigate the case found the Conservatives guilty of the bribery of a number of electors (with either drink or money) and the election was declared null and void. The city was without an MP and its citizens disenfranchised for a period of two years. The Conservatives considered that the Liberals had been motivated by malice and personal gain (they had high expectations of winning the election that year) and had destroyed the reputation of the city in the process. Many Conservative councillors, notably Arrowsmith Maund, maintained a deep personal animosity towards Liberals in general, and towards several of William's friends and supporters in particular. These included Earl Beauchamp, Lord Cobham, and Richard Fairbairn.

Ultimately William achieved the construction of two more bungalows as well as the installation of electric heating and lighting in one of the houses that formed the garden city scheme. This was intended to demonstrate that, contrary to popular opinion, at current prices electricity was much less expensive than coal and could provide for three adults the needs for daily cooking, heating, lighting and hot water. He suggested that the council should consider this when building new houses. He also built an experimental wooden house modelled on one recently exhibited at the Ideal Home Exhibition in London. Wooden houses were much less expensive to build than brick and were already under construction in Birmingham. The Standard Housing Company had offered to build one hundred such houses for Worcester in six months. However, William found that any plans or suggestions he submitted to the housing committee were summarily rejected and without the wherewithal to acquire land he was unable to pursue the scheme any further. As the construction of the second pair of bungalows progressed he put to the council one last proposition. If they would hand over to him one acre of land which they had purchased, or one of their existing building sites he would endeavour to put up ten houses immediately. The Committee however was obstructive, offering, as William described it, some land which was not yet purchased and other plots that were let for allotments and would not be free for some months. Meanwhile a reporter on the Worcester Herald aired a suspicion that William had been denied the opportunity to build on the site that he had requested (Park Avenue) because it was adjacent to larger and more luxurious houses whose residents would object. William himself was clearly angry, writing to the housing committee that he 'failed to comprehend their actions.'

He said:

> Houses are sorely needed. Dissatisfaction and irritation are growing in consequence of the absence of houses and threatens to become dangerous. I offered to help the Committee by building houses without throwing any burden on the ratepayers or affecting your appeal for housing bonds. I have men ready and willing to build. I even offered to take a portion of the allotment land and make my own arrangements with the allotment cultivators so as to start building at once. Thereupon the housing committee imposes impossible conditions that they must know I cannot possibly accept. I can only conclude that the housing committee do not really want houses built.[14]

William appears to have given up the fight at this point. It is not entirely clear how many houses were eventually built in Northwick during the early 1920s, or how the council coped with the debt it inevitably incurred. However, two years later, in July 1923, it was

---

14. 'Dean of Worcester and Housing Committee. Complaint of Obstacles Against Building,' BNA, *Gloucestershire Journal*, 26 June 1920.

announced that the rents of the houses built on the Northwick site were to be reduced by a shilling in most cases and in the case of the larger houses by 1s.6d. The housing committee stated that the rents currently being charged were more than could be paid by many for whom the houses were built. Many people who had originally applied for a house had therefore given up their chance when their turn came because they could not afford the rent. In 1925 it was reported in the *Birmingham Gazette* that 'Worcester Corporation cannot overtake the housing needs of the city. They cannot prevail on the overworked local builders to tender for the 170 houses they wish to build. And even for those 170 there are already more than 700 applicants.'[15] The reporter went on to describe how two years previously, in February 1923, some disused cells in the local gaol had been converted into tenements. However, several of the sixteen families housed there had recently been subject to an eviction order since apparently even these rents were beyond their means. Meanwhile William's group of cowsheds (alias dog kennels) remain occupied today, standing on Lansdowne Road looking sturdy and attractive, a testament perhaps to what might have been. And perhaps the nicest tribute to William's efforts came in a speech from the Bishop of Worcester, Ernest Pearce, on the occasion of William's eightieth birthday. 'I never see a ganglion of new council houses without saying to myself, I wonder what price the Dean would have built these for?'[16]

Exactly one hundred years after the first of William's houses were opened in 1920, a committee was formed by the Archbishops of Canterbury and York to discuss the ever-worsening housing crisis in England. A report by the National Housing Federation in 2020 had concluded that 'around eight million people in the country were living in overcrowded, unaffordable or unsuitable housing.'[17] Similarly

15. 'Rents of Corporation Houses at Worcester,' BNA, *Gloucester Citizen*, 5 July 1923.
16. 'Octogenarian Dean. Bishop of Worcester's Tribute,' BNA, *Gloucestershire Citizen*, 4 October 1929.
17. People in Housing Need. Report by the National Housing Federation. (which represents approximately 800 housing associations across England). 15 September 2020. www.housing.org.uk

the most recent English Housing Survey (2020) had shown that 4.3 million homes did not meet the minimum requirements defined by the goverment's Decent Homes Standard in 2018.[18] It was clear that the sources of this problem were both longstanding and multi-faceted. As journalist Vicky Spratt noted in 2021, we seem to have completely forgotten the Tudor Walters Report of 1918 and the Housing Act that followed, with its recommendations for garden suburbs with well-proportioned houses. Moreover, the pandemic of 2020–21 has

One of the Dean's cottages (aptly named 'Deanscote') in Worcester, built in 1920, pictured in 2021.

shown us once more that bad housing accentuates health problems and increases vulnerability to infectious disease.[19] The solutions to this problem now promise to be complex, involving input from many different parties. As one of the major landowners in the country, however, the Church of England was willing to concede that potentially they

18. The English Housing Survey is a continuous national survey commissioned by the Ministry of Housing, Communities and Local Government.
19. Vicky Spratt, 'Have We Forgotten that Good Housing is Key to Public Health?' report in the *i* newspaper, 27 March 2021.

had a significant role to play.[20] In response, therefore, the Archbishops established their 'Commission on Housing, Church and Community' which in February 2021 produced a major report, putting forward a series of solutions involving not only the Church with its extensive land holdings, but also the goverment and numerous other stakeholders. Several aspects of this report have distinct echoes of the words and aspirations of William Moore-Ede and his fellow enthusiasts a century earlier. The forms of expression may be different but the meaning is essentially the same, for the emphasis throughout is on building not just good houses, but better communities. Good houses, the report argues, should be environmentally sustainable, they should provide safe places to live, places where people feel mentally, physically and emotionally secure. They should provide stability in the sense that people need not constantly fear eviction and disruption to their lives, and they should enable a sociable and satisfying community life. There are references to 'practical theology', a full acknowledgement that engagement with practical social issues such as housing are fully in harmony with the teaching of Jesus Christ. And at the very centre of the recommendations is the heartfelt plea that different parts of society must work together if the problem is ever to be solved.

> The Church's primary loyalty is to the City of God, not the City of this World. Its purpose is focussed on the two great calls of the Church – to worship the God of Jesus in the power of the Spirit and to bear witness, in both actions and words, to that God, and the difference that faith in this God makes to human life and our understanding of the world. That does not mean that the church has no interest in the 'messy business' of this world, such as the building of communities and the buying or renting of homes. In fact, it is precisely in such a context that the Church is called to bear witness – in particular times and places, and especially in the most deprived neighbourhoods and among those living in poverty. This report picks up where others have gone before, examining how that

---

20. The Church of England holds approximately 200,000 acres of land and a large number of historical and other buildings.

tradition can be revitalised today and become a mainstream part of the Church of England's mission.

If the housing crisis is to be solved it will need all of us – central and local government, landowners, developers, landlords, homeowners, and housing associations, as well as the Church – to play our part. It is the poorest and most marginalised amongst us who are suffering the burden of our housing crisis, and that will only change if we take collective responsibility and action . . . our prayer is that (the report) will be a catalyst towards the creation of homes and communities that enable all of us to live well and flourish together in ways that reflect God's good will for us in Jesus Christ.

Coming Home, 21 February 2021.[21]

William Moore-Ede would have said 'Amen' to all of that.

---

21. *Coming Home. Tackling the Housing Crisis Together*. The Commission of the Archbishops of Canterbury and York on Housing, Church and Community. February 2021. www.archbishopofcanterbury.org

Chapter Twenty-Five
AN APOSTLE FOR PEACE

In the years immediately after the war William was called upon to deliver the address at successive dedications and unveiling of memorials to the dead. In these early days of raw grief he rarely departed from the script of a just war, emphasising the honourable sacrifice of the fallen in a noble cause. Faced with the overwhelming need to provide comfort to the bereaved, he could perhaps do no other. Yet there were hints of his unease, particularly when on occasions he referred to the enduring commitments of the Quakers, frequently alluding to their 'plainness and simplicity' and their 'undoubted spirituality'. In 1931, a full thirteen years after the Armistice, he attended a ceremony where he gave full expression to the change that had taken place in his thinking since the end of the war and the extent to which he had now resolved the conflict that had haunted him since he had essentially abandoned his pacifist stance in 1915. The ceremony in question was the unveiling of the Peace Memorial erected in Stevens Park, Quarry Bank, a short distance from Cradley Heath where, twenty-one years earlier, he had stood alongside Mary MacArthur and addressed the rally in support of the women chainmakers. Much had changed in the intervening years. The women's victory in 1910 would go down in the nation's history as the forerunner of the right to a living wage, but for the women of Cradley Heath other unrelated changes were already underway as they fought for their rights. In the early years of the twentieth century nearly 50 per cent of the chainmakers had been women. Women made the lighter chain used predominantly for agricultural purposes such as harnesses. Soon, however, iron would give way to electrically welded steel and the traditional way of making chain would be replaced by a process that was both quicker and required fewer workers. By the early 1930s only about 10 per cent of the workers making chain in Cradley Heath were women. But the people there had not forgotten the support of the Dean and the Bishop of Worcester in 1910. When the time came to unveil their memorial to their lost loved ones it was to William they turned as the person to perform the ceremony.

There was, in fact, already a memorial to the fallen in Quarry Bank, tucked away in the local parish church. But the people of the area had long felt that it was not sufficiently accessible to them, particularly on Remembrance Sunday when large numbers wanted to attend the service. They wanted their own memorial, outside in the open air, where all faiths and none could come at will to pay their respects. It was a sentiment that Ernest Stevens, a local industrialist, understood well. Stevens, a highly successful manufacturer of pots and pans, made the popular 'Judge' holloware in his factory in Cradley Heath. In 1921 he had gifted land to the local authority for the creation of Stevens Park and now, ten years later, he had decided to pay for a memorial to be placed there. Designed by the sculptor George Wade it is a striking monument, of which the centrepiece is a bronze statue of Christ, raising his hand in the traditional gesture of blessing. The figure is set on a pedestal in front of a Portland stone wall on which are inscribed the names of the 147 men of the area who died in the Great War.[1] Most significantly, however, as William was keen to point out, this was not a 'war memorial' but a 'peace memorial.' The years that had passed since 1918 had perhaps softened any triumphalist tone that might sometimes have touched the design of earlier monuments. On the pedestal bearing Christ's figure are inscribed the words 'My Peace I Give Unto You' and on the other side of the memorial, the words 'Nation shall not lift up sword against nation. Neither shall they learn war anymore.' William considered it a huge honour to be asked

---

1. The names of fifty men who died in the Second World War were added after 1945.

to perform the unveiling ceremony that day. As he told the assembled crowd he considered it to be one of the finest memorials that had been erected since the war, for while it commemorated those who had fallen in the war 'it also turned our thoughts away from war, with all its hatred and its cruelty and slaughter, into the way of peace, along which Christ was pleading with us to walk.'[2] The moving address he gave that day was probably his clearest exposition of his own personal change of heart about the war, and the peace testimony that by now he had given so often. Paying fitting tribute to the men whose names were inscribed on the wall he said,

> You who loved them, the fathers, brothers and sons of many of you standing here today, are glad to think that for years to come the people of Quarry Bank will honour the memory of those you loved, who sacrificed their lives for what they believed to be the call of duty . . . But many of the men who left Quarry Bank looked forward to the war that would end war. And yet that was not God's way, to cure war by war. God's purposes can only be achieved in God's way.[3]

There were distinct echoes here of the comments he made when confronted by the violence of the suffragettes in 1914. Between then and now, in the face of the appalling atrocities of the war, it seemed that this ideal had deserted him, but now it had returned. 'Men bred war as long as men's hearts were filled with hatred and malice and bitterness and suspicion,' he said. 'They believed that force was the only power that really governed the world, that peace was but an interval between wars. But peace did not drop down from heaven without any effort on our part.' Inviting the gathering to look at the inscriptions on the memorial he drew attention to what he considered to be one of the 'eternal verities, He hath made of one blood all the nations.' 'Remember that,' he urged his listeners. 'We are all brethren, all God's

2. WME, address at the dedication ceremony, Quarry Bank Peace Memorial on 24 October 1931. BNA, *Dudley Chronicle*, 5 November 1931.
3. ibid.

children, none superior to another, remember that and act upon it and there will be harmony and peace. Forget it or ignore it and there will be strife and conflict.'[4]

William's address that day was born of a long personal journey of reflection and reappraisal which had begun in 1919 as he began to look to the future and the need to heal the legacy of animosity and ill-will left by the war, 'to bind up the wounds of war and re-create an international spirit of organisation.'[5] For inspiration and encouragement he turned first to the emergent League of Nations, becoming a member of its local Worcestershire branch but more particularly to the organisation he had helped to found in 1914, the World Alliance for Promoting International Friendship Through the Churches. Despite his 'feeble feeling' as he stood on the railway platform in Constance in 1914, he had been heartened by the fact that since the beginning of the war over six thousand people in Britain alone had joined the Alliance. In 1919 he attended the first of its post war annual conferences at The Hague, returning with a renewed enthusiasm and commitment to the cause of peace and the prevention of future conflict. He felt very strongly that the Church had a unique role to play in this but could only do so if it healed its own divisions and made it her special mission to foster strong ties between its various branches, both within and between nations.

The Peace Memorial in Stevens Park, Quarry bank, unveiled by William Moore-Ede in 1931. Courtesy of Graham Beckley, Black Country Society.

4. ibid.
5. ibid.

In May 1920 he gave a passionate address to a Labour Party gathering at the Empire Theatre in Coventry where he spelled out his vision for a new peaceful world and how that might be achieved. He began by giving vent to his great disappointment that nearly two years after the Armistice there were few signs of the building of 'the new Jerusalem' which people had looked forward to. He drew comparisons between the churches and organised labour both of which, he argued, had failed to apply the three great words emphasised by Christ, justice, brotherhood and love. They must first seek justice, he said. Then and only then would other things which men desired – peace and happiness – be added to them. There could be no stable order, he maintained, no prosperity in any social system which was not founded upon justice. The second word, 'brotherhood', was of course something that had permeated William's thinking from his first sermons in Gateshead. 'If the war has taught us anything,' he said, 'there is no hope of justice, happiness, freedom and the stability of peace in this world unless nations recognised each other as belonging to one great family having common interests and learning to live together in mutual forbearance and co-operation.' Initially, he conceded, the governments of the world had understood this and had set up the League of Nations. But soon, he continued, 'selfishness reasserted itself and politicians seem to have forgotten what the war had made them see. Christians, however, should not forget.' And on the third great word, that of love, he was particularly eloquent, and notably critical of those in positions of power. 'Society is not, and never has been, built upon the destructive principle of every man for himself', he said. 'Rather it has been built up by people working together for the common ends by mutual helpfulness, sympathy and co-operation.' 'Every section of the Christian Church believes that,' he continued, 'but John Bull does not.[6] The House of Commons as a body does not. Statesmen do not. And it is because there is no such belief that they have made such a ghastly mess of the peace.' Yet the Church was in no way absolved of responsibility. 'Why

---

6. John Bull, a national personification of England and the English character often used in cartoons and political satires, depicting a stout, jolly, prosperous middle-aged man.

have the churches not convinced so-called Christian countries of the truth of the principle of love?' he asked. 'Because they have not stood shoulder to shoulder in upholding that principle and have not spoken with a united voice.' It was a direct statement of his own ecumenical principles and his belief that the strength and influence of the churches in this most crucial of matters depended on their mutual adherence to these three basic principles, justice, brotherhood and love. The need for such action was urgent, he concluded, and the times were ripe. 'Militarism has had its opportunity to govern the world and we have all seen the result. There can be no permanent peace at home or abroad until nations are convinced that the principles for which Christ stands are eternal principles.'[7]

William seems to have been entirely justified in emphasising that these were propitious times for the promotion of peace. The ethical stance of the Alliance was much in tune with the current zeitgeist with large numbers of people joining pacifist organisations. During the 1920s peace marches and rallies were regular features in many towns and cities, second only to the labour demonstrations and hunger marches that signalled the mass unemployment that beset the land. William himself put a huge amount of energy into the promotion of the peace gospel and, despite his advancing years, embarked on a dizzying round of conferences and meetings, both at home and abroad, repeating the substance of his Coventry address many times both in secular and religious settings. In 1921 the Peace Society, to which he had long been a member, held its Centenary Celebrations. Years before in Gateshead he had struggled through sparsely attended meetings in draughty church halls but now he found himself speaking at a number of major events. One such was held in Worcester's Guildhall on the 6 June that year attended by the American and Austrian Ambassadors, a Belgian senator and a group of local MPs. It was chaired by the staunch pacifist and supporter of conscientious objectors, Lord Parmoor. As a devout

---

7. WME, 'Lessons from the Great War. Dean of Worcester's Coventry Address,' BNA, *Coventry Herald*, 29 May 1920.

Anglican he had repeatedly emphasised the dangers of denying Christian ethics in international law and now, newly installed as the British representative on the council of the League of Nations, he had an ideal platform from which to propound his views. Following the meeting in Worcester he and William took a train to London where in the evening Lord Parmoor presided over a mass meeting in Westminster's Central Hall where the speakers included Dean Inge of St Paul's Cathedral, more MPs and numerous delegates from America, Australia and several continental countries.[8] In October the Peace Society held another major meeting, this time in London's Caxton Hall, on the subject of economic recovery. With many eminent delegates from a range of countries present there were addresses on the Russian famine, reduction of armaments, world depression and, from William himself, religion and world peace. This was followed by a mass demonstration on disarmament at Central Hall again addressed by Lord Parmoor, as well as by Ramsey MacDonald, current leader of the Labour Party and a prominent critic of the war.

Between these two meetings, in September 1921, William and Sarah joined a group of twenty British delegates to attend a meeting in Prague of the World Brotherhood Organisation, founded in 1919 'to exemplify the principles of brotherhood as taught by Jesus and to make them dominant in all life.' It was just one of the organisations founded during the heady days immediately after the war, when the time seemed right to achieve a new world order based on peace and justice. The organisation included among its officers representatives from all over the world, including the staunch and uncompromising pacifist, John Clifford, who had accompanied William to the Peace Congress in the United States in 1911. Following the conference in Prague, William and Sarah took the opportunity to visit Vienna on their way home, staying with lawyer Dr Gustav Scheu and his wife, Helene Scheu-Riesz, prominent members of Austria's Social Democratic movement, known as Red Vienna, which emerged after

---

8. William Ralph Inge, Dean of St Paul's 1911–34.

the war.⁹ The house was a renowned gathering place for Quakers, pacifists and suffragists as well as advocates of social welfare and radical housing ideas such as the garden city movement. It was described by one visitor as 'the intellectual and spiritual centre of left-leaning intellectuals and artists.'¹⁰ William was much inspired by the people he met there and two years later would invite the Scheus to stay at the Old Palace where they gave a series of lectures in the Vaulted Hall. William considered that Vienna was the most beautiful city he had seen in Europe, but also the saddest. 'If one looked behind the scenes without being content to walk the principal streets,' he said, 'you would realise the sufferings of the people many of whom are in a state of semi starvation kept alive by soup kitchens.' It was an experience he recounted the following February when he addressed the Soho Men's Movement in Birmingham which claimed proudly to be 'one of the biggest assemblages of men to be found anywhere in the country on a Sunday afternoon.' Suitably impressed William took the opportunity once more to emphasis his 'three great principles', focussing for this audience particularly on 'brotherhood', which he described as 'a spiritual kinship, embracing affection, sympathy and mutual helpfulness.'¹¹

Later in 1922 William travelled to Europe again, attending a meeting of the Christian Socialist Congress in Strasbourg, followed by a meeting of the French Protestant Brotherhood. Back in London in May he relayed the proceedings of these meetings to the Congregational Union gathered in their memorial hall. And in August that year he set off once more, this time to Copenhagen for another meeting of the World Alliance, accompanied by two strong supporters, Hubert Burge, the recently appointed Bishop of Oxford, and his close friend the Reverend

---

9. Helene Scheu-Riesz was a translator and worked to supply Austrian schools with new, more progressive literature after the war. She later founded the children's book company 'Sesame Books'.

10. For a description and discussion of the movement see Veronika Duma and Hanna Lichtenberger, (Translated by Loren Balhorn) 'Remembering Red Vienna'. www.jacobinmag.com

11. 'Dean of Worcester on Brotherhood,' BNA, *The Standard*, 25 Feb 1922.

John Jowett, minister of Carrs Lane Church in Birmingham.[12] Here there where discussions covering the rights of minorities, concerns about lack of progress in disarmament and the nature of action for reconciliation and reconstruction. Resolutions were duly passed and formally conveyed to the League of Nations. By any standards this meeting was an impressive demonstration of co-operative endeavour for two hundred delegates were present from twenty-five countries, representing ten Christian denominations including, they were keen to emphasise, several dignitaries of the Greek Orthodox Church. Regret was expressed, however, about the only 'outsider' being the Church of Rome, which, remarked the chairman, 'was according to their usual policy of non co-operation with other churches.'[13] Meanwhile back in England the following month a meeting was held at Ripon College, Cuddesdon where a British Council of the World Alliance was launched, presided over by Hubert Burge with William and John Jowett as its vice presidents.[14] Plans were made for education in schools and colleges, preparation of tracts and pamphlets, arrangements for public meeting, supplies of information to the religious press and, importantly, devotional prayer meetings.

---

12. Hubert Burge, Bishop of Oxford in office 1919–25.

13. 'International Friendship. World Alliance Conference at Copenhagen,' BNA, *The Scotsman*, 15 August 1922.

14. Ripon College was a training college for Anglican clergy.

Chapter Twenty-Six
BLACK FRIDAY AND WHITE COAL

In December 1922, William's long history of involvement in labour issues resulted in another invitation, this time to a Peace Conference in The Hague organised by the International Federation of Trade Unions. It was by all accounts a lively event which provided a foretaste of a debate which would continue throughout the 1920s concerning the relative merits of communism, as practised by the leaders of postwar Russia, and socialism, as advocated by the British Labour Party and others in continental Europe. The appearance of a clergyman on the platform was apparently somewhat alien to continental trade unionists, but most were willing to concede the importance of 'brotherhood, fraternity and goodwill' whatever system they embraced. Matters discussed included the necessity of education in the principles of peace, public control over armaments and the admission of Germany into the League of Nations. There should be no extension of the occupation of German territory they agreed 'nor any partition of that country that tended to stir up mischief and hate.'[1] A group of Russian Bolshevists, however, appeared to be intent on just that. They were particularly incensed at William's presence, denouncing the committee for inviting a member of 'the bourgeoisie' to the conference. Prominent among them was Karl Radek, leader of the Soviet Communist Party, who described William as 'an old English gentleman steeped in petroleum.'[2]

1. 'Dean's Peace Deal,' BNA, *Birmingham Daily Gazette*, 13 December 1922; 'Labour Views on World Problems. Russian Protest at Hague Peace Congress,' BNA, *Dundee Courier*, 13 December 1922.

2. 'Radek and the Dean of Worcester,' BNA, *Gloucester Journal*, 23 December 1922.

It was an ill-informed judgement that nevertheless must have stung as William recalled his long years of effort on behalf of industrial workers. Even now he closely followed the current miner's struggle, writing letters of support to the newspapers, as they attempted to resist wage reductions following the return of the industry from government to private hands at the end of the war.

In April that year his old friend and colleague Thomas Burt had died in Newcastle, no doubt bringing back many memories of his time in the North East and the days when they had worked together on Bishop Westcott's Conciliation Boards. Thomas, who formally retired from politics at the end of 1914, had been ill for some time with ever worsening respiratory problems, the legacy no doubt of his years as a miner. During the war he had stayed with William and Sarah for several weeks in Worcester, the two men enjoying gentle strolls along the banks of the River Severn together, no doubt reminiscing about past struggles and discussing present ones. Ever since William's letter about Mary Jane in 1882, Thomas had been a thread that had woven itself through his life, connecting him irresistibly to working people, even after he himself had ascended the ranks of the clerical hierarchy and begun to mix rather more regularly with the higher echelons of county society. On Tyneside Thomas was now a greatly respected figure and William would have read in the newspapers that his funeral was one of the largest gatherings ever seen in Newcastle with all sections of the community represented. He himself, however, had been unable to attend, prevented by the obligation as a senior member of the clergy to attend the funeral of Huyshe Yeatman-Biggs, Bishop of Coventry, who had died the same week and whose funeral was held on the same day. It must have grieved William considerably and the suggestion that he had become a 'bourgeois old English gentleman' perhaps hit a raw nerve. To his surprise, however, the accusation provoked an avalanche of support for him in the hall. As he recounted the incident later he noted that the Bolshevists appeared to stand alone in their 'extreme and violently expressed utterances' on a number of issues and that 'the great mass of sober and sensible trade unionists are seriously undertaking peace propaganda.'³ It was clearly something that encouraged him greatly. His adherence to conciliation and co-operation rather than a struggle for dominance and power had always been something on which he and Thomas had unreservedly agreed. It underpinned his view of how industrial relations should be conducted as the only means to achieve peace and social justice.

On May Day 1923, a date synonymous with Labour Day, William travelled to Leeds and preached to a packed congregation of working men and women in the parish church. Referring to the conference in The Hague he described the 'Bolshevik philosophy' as one which focussed on personal material gain and the raising of production for the use of themselves and their fellows. 'But that was not the trade union way,' he said.

> A better standard of living was undoubtedly desirable but Labour could neither get this nor keep it unless men rose to a higher ideal of life, were more imbued with the spirit of brotherhood, and with the desire to serve. Our social conditions are of our own making, they are what they are because of what we are.⁴

Meanwhile the round of meetings, conferences and demonstrations continued. In January 1923 the French sent sixty thousand troops into the Ruhr region of Germany and took control of parts of German industry in an attempt to extract unpaid reparation payments agreed at the Treaty of Versailles after the war. The German government had refused to pay on the grounds that their country was bankrupt and could not afford it. In February William joined a demonstration against the occupation organised by the Peace Society at Westminster's Central Hall. In front of a rowdy and unsympathetic audience he spoke of his regret at the action of France and urged the government

---

3. 'Peace Conference at The Hague. Described by the Dean of Worcester,' BNA, *Bury Free Press*, 6 January 1923 (reprinted from the *Worcester Echo*)

4. 'The Aristocracy of Labour. Ideals that Form the Only Basis of Industrial Peace,' BNA, *Yorkshire Evening Post*, 30 April 1923.

to use its influence to end the military occupation which hindered the establishment of world peace. In September he attended the Church Congress, held that year in his old hometown of Plymouth, and spoke passionately about the dangers of nationalism and the need for 'moral unity'. The following January found him in Lille, France, at a specially convened Alliance meeting of delegates from Great Britain, France and Belgium to discuss growing concerns about 'misunderstandings' between these countries and how they might influence their respective governments to foster international friendship. William's use of publicity was growing ever more sophisticated, giving details to the press of his sermons and public addresses at scores of venues that ranged from the Sunday morning service at Brockmoor parish church in rural Worcestershire to one of the largest Alliance conferences in Stockholm in June 1925. In November 1926 he made full use of some recent technology, the amplifier, to conduct a specially organised Peace Service, broadcast at Birmingham Railway Station. And in 1928 he took part in an innovative 'Exchange of Pulpits' exercise in Birmingham organised by the Alliance. This had begun tentatively two years earlier with a small number of churches and chapels taking part but by 1928 there were sixty-one participants. William himself preached at Hamstead Road Baptist Church on the chosen theme that year of 'International Peace.'

The conference in Sweden in 1925 was recounted in an extensive two-part article he wrote for the national press, and which was reproduced by local papers across the country.[5] For the visit to Sweden had given him very significant pause for thought. Following the conference he had taken the opportunity to enjoy a few days of sightseeing, travelling from Stockholm to Gothenburg along the Gotha Canal. What he encountered there forced him to radically reassess his views on the problems that currently beset the British coal industry. As he returned to England in June that year large parts of the nation's workforce were in turmoil. Central to the problem were

5. WME, to Stockholm for International Friendship and Christian Unity. BNA, *Boston Guardian*, part 1: 19 September 1925; part 2: 24 September 1925.

the workers that had always been closest to his heart, the coal miners. The government had taken over control of the mines during the war and under their administration wages, safety and hours of work had improved considerably. The miners had hoped that this situation would continue after the war, in the form of full nationalisation. Instead, however, in 1921, the industry had been returned to private ownership, immediately resulting in longer working hours and significantly reduced pay. The mine owners argued that coal production was going through a significant downturn and they could not afford the generous terms that had been on offer when coal had been essential to the war effort. The industry had lost many of its old markets during the war and there was now a much lower demand for coal. In response the miners called a strike in 1921, but had been forced to abandon this when, on the morning it was due to begin, other unions withdrew their promised support. It was a notorious betrayal, ever after referred to as 'Black Friday'. In subsequent years unrest continued to simmer amongst the miners, coming to a head in 1925 when the mine owners announced further cuts in wages and an extra hour to the working day. By now, as the economic depression deepened, many other industrial workers were experiencing similar effects on their wages and employment conditions and this time other major unions were fully prepared to join the miners in a threatened strike. Throughout 1925 a series of protracted and ultimately unsuccessful rounds of negotiations took place between the government, the miners and the mine owners, culminating in the General Strike of 1926.

William had spent many hours in the company of miners, and was hugely admiring of their skill and fortitude, not to mention their dedicated approach to educational advancement. In 1921 his support for their position had been unequivocal. The management of mines under individual ownership was completely unsatisfactory, he said, and they were quite right to endeavour to change that position. When he returned from Sweden, however, he felt compelled to confront them with a stark truth that he had now discovered, that coal was no longer king. It is being dethroned, he said, by water generated power and by oil. For everywhere in Sweden he had seen the conversion of waterfalls into electric power stations, the production of what they called 'white coal'. He had found the scale of power production quite breathtaking, describing the enormous force of hundreds of tons of water driving the turbines night and day, generating power which supplied all of southern Sweden and was even carried under the water of the Sound to run the lights, the factories and the trams of Copenhagen.[6] He sympathised with the British miners' desire to have employment at the old wage rates, he said. Nationalisation of the mines might be desirable, but it cannot make people who have cheap white coal want to buy our black coal. A similar process was taking place in Norway, in Italy, in the South of France and in Spain and they must face the facts that less and less coal would be needed in the future and fewer men would be employed in the mines. The real problem that must now be faced was how to minimise the hardship in a declining industry, a problem that confrontation and strikes, as advocated by some current miners' leaders, would only intensify.

William took to the newspaper columns in the North East to urge the miners to desist from strike action. Strikes never helped anyone, he said, echoing the often-expressed sentiments of Thomas Burt. The miners, however, were in no mood to listen to the advice of a pacifist clergymen. Many preferred the combative approach of one of their current militant leaders, Arthur J. Cook, who famously campaigned under the slogan 'Not a Penny off the Pay. Not a Minute on the Day'. 'I believe in strikes,' he said, 'they are the only weapon.'[7] The strike went ahead in May 1926, but it was a short-lived and acrimonious affair marked by attacks on buses and trams carrying people to work. There were violent clashes between the strikers and the police such that the army was deployed to help restore order. In Northumberland a group of miners from Cramlington Pit removed a section of the

---

6. The Sound, also known as the Øresund Strait, which runs between southern Sweden and Copenhagen, is now crossed by a bridge which opened in 1999.

7. A. J. Cook, *The Nine Days. The Story of the General Strike told by the Miner's Secretary.* (Co-operative Printing Society, 1926). www.wikisource.org

railway line in an attempt to stop the movement of coal, an action that resulted in the derailment of the *Flying Scotsman* carrying over five hundred passengers. Fortunately, only one person was injured but the government sent tanks and armoured cars to the area. Nine miners were subsequently arrested and sentenced to periods of penal servitude. After only nine days, however, the government issued a warning to the strikers that would prove pivotal in bringing it to a rapid end. It was pointed out that the strike was not protected by the Trade Dispute Act of 1906 meaning that the strikers involved would have been liable for 'the intention to breach their contracts of employment'.[8] In the midst of a severe depression where every job was precious this was a frightening prospect. On the stated understanding that no worker would be victimised for their decision to join the strike a growing number began to drift back to work. The miners held out for longer than most, but no concessions were gained from the mine owners. By November that year most men were back in the mines under the same conditions as before, while others had joined the ranks of the long term unemployed. What promised to be one of the largest demonstrations in the country's history had, it seems, achieved nothing.

In 1928 William attended the Durham Miners' Gala, as he always did, and as usual he accepted an invitation to speak. His message, delivered to a bitter and demoralised audience was the same as always, a rejection of force, a call for conciliation and compromise and a joining together to reconstruct the industry into something more viable for these new and difficult times. He wanted to provide a vision of hope, a possible way out of the mire in which they now found themselves. It was perhaps a measure of the affection and esteem in which he was held that he was listened to quietly and with respect, even by those who would have found little comfort in what he had to say.

Back in Worcester, meanwhile, he continued his promotion of peace. Despite his earlier disappointment with the League of Nations, he seems to have maintained a belief in its ultimate role as a

8. ibid.

force for good, remaining an active member of the local branch and becoming its chairman from the mid 1920s. In 1930 he organised an essay competition for children across the city and the county on the subject of 'The League, its Aims, Achievements and Hopes'. Over three hundred children took part, the first prize going to thirteen-year-old Frank Field from Badsey Council School. With pride and considerable composure for one so young Frank read his essay to a number of distinguished guests assembled at the Cathedral and then received his award, a book and a handsome certificate designed by a Miss Greaves of Worcester School of Art. William, who had acted as judge of the essays, praised their excellent standard and went on to urge the children to 'seek for what is right and just by methods of reason and conference – not only in international affairs – but in all other matters and difficulties in life and deal with them in the spirit of the League of Nations.' The League, he said was dedicated to God, who was the God of Love, which meant that they believed that the world was not ruled by force, but by a mightier force, the power of love, and that it was by the extension of love, and the spirit of love, that the human race would go on to higher and nobler conditions.[9] Sadly neither young Frank nor William could have known that a few years later Britain would once more find itself at war with Germany. William did not live to see this crushing defeat for his pacifist hopes and it will never be known how he would have responded to the aggressive threat posed by Nazi Germany. Neither is it known how Frank fared in the Second World War, but in September 1939 the British government immediately introduced the National Service Act which imposed conscription on all men between the ages of eighteen and forty-one. That year Frank would have been twenty-two years old.

---

9. 'League of Nations. Success of County Essay Scheme,' BNA, *Evesham Standard & West Midlands Observer,* 12 July 1930.

Chapter Twenty-Seven
HOME TERRITORY

William, it seemed, thrived on hard work and seemingly frenetic activity well into his advanced years. His energy was such that, far from struggling with the demands made upon him, he was animated by a desire to be involved in multiple projects and quite incapable of letting issues of concern pass him by. During the 1920s and early 1930s, for example, he not only continued his support of temperance organisations but extended his critical gaze to the subject of gambling, travelling the country to lecture on the evils of such activities and making headlines when he criticised the introduction of National Savings Investment Bonds on the grounds that they involved a form of lottery. Equally controversially, he refused to take part in lotteries at church bazaars and on one occasion declined to bid at an auction for a bottle of Bass beer, reputedly brewed by King Edward in 1902. The beer eventually raised £46.16s, but William got his own reward in the form of press coverage. His only desire, he said, was to smash the bottle. Needless to say, no such events were allowed to darken the doors of Cathedral premises. Invariably, as he talked to secular societies and preached his sermons in numerous parish churches, he linked the subjects of drunkenness and gambling to one of his other great passions, the prevention of the abusive treatment of children. He had continued to support the NSPCC since his Gateshead days and in Worcester he served as chairman of the local branch. He had numerous tales to tell of the poverty and neglect parents visited on their children when in the grip of the twin vices of alcohol and gambling, provoking shock and sympathy from his audience, and raising considerable funds for the NSPCC in the process.

William also channelled his concern for the welfare of children into various efforts to improve the open spaces available for them to play, often using the trappings of his job to good advantage. Clerical appointments invariably came with long established traditional obligations and one such was an interest in the administration and provision of pastoral care for almshouses. In Gateshead the Rectorship had encompassed the role of master of King James' Hospital and in Worcester the Dean was similarly the master of St Oswald's Hospital, a group of almshouses in the city centre.[1] Sometime during his early years in the city he had, it seems, noted the potential of some unused land attached to St Oswald's which he felt could be put to good use on behalf of the city's children. Whether or not the land was gifted or rented is unclear, but it was soon employed as an extra playing field for the adjoining grammar school and a running track for the city's pioneering residential school for the blind, Worcester College. The college had strong links with the Cathedral and William, as a member of the school's governing body, was well aware that the current headmaster was particularly keen to introduce more sports facilities for the children.

In 1919 amidst the deprivations of the post war period William felt more strongly than ever that children confined to a crowded urban environment needed opportunities for outdoor activities in a safe place. That year, therefore, the council was able to purchase some land from the Church with the intention of developing an extension to a small green space called Cripplegate in the centre of the city. The intention was to create a formal park for recreation. Owing to 'the good offices of the Dean' it was reported, the Corporation was able to buy the land on 'extremely advantageous terms.'[2] William seems to have capitalised on the good will this engendered by subsequently lobbying

---

1. St Oswald's Hospital is a community of twenty-one residents. The present buildings, which date from the 1870s, are set around a central green square and have been described as a tranquil haven off a busy main road. Since the sixteenth century the Dean of Worcester has traditionally been the master of St Oswald's.

2. WCL scrapbooks, 'Meeting of Worcester City Council to Discuss the Freedom of the City,' *Berrows Worcester Journal*, 2 February 1934.

the Open Spaces Committee for one quarter of the new park (three acres) to be set aside for a children's playing field. Everyone recognised, he said, that outdoor spaces for play and games were essential for the health and vigour of our future citizens. Time and money were rightly being spent on the treatment of children found to be diseased, but would it not be more scientific to consider it a first duty to maintain and improve the health and physical development of all children? As ever he was abreast of the finer details of any new regulations which might usefully apply. The 1918 Fisher Education Act, he noted, was predominantly concerned with the expansion of continuing education but, he argued, it also allowed local education authorities to make provision for playing fields for elementary school children, in the interests of improving their overall development.[3] A short distance away from the proposed site, he observed, the King's School had ten acres for two hundred boys and the city's grammar school now had extensive playing fields for their 280 scholars. Surely it was right that the children of our state-maintained schools should have the same advantages? Their home surroundings and their lack of outdoor games demanded it, he said.[4] As a result there emerged, alongside the formal flower beds and public paths, a park that contained a significant space for children's games.[5] It was a much smaller park than that which exists today having gone through successive expansions and remodelling but it laid the foundation for what is now a multifunctional green space in the centre of Worcester, containing not only formally planted areas but also a children's playground, tennis courts, a bowling green and large grassed areas for popular events.

Another issue that sparked William's attention was the latest craze to arrive in Worcester's Foregate Street, the Silver Cinema. William was not initially against the cinema *per se*. In fact he rather approved of

3. The main provision of the Fisher Act of 1918 was for school leavers between the ages of fourteen and eighteen to attend continuation schools for vocational training. Other less prominent clauses, however, referred to outdoor games provision for younger children.

4. WCL scrapbooks; WME, letter to *The Times*, 2 June 1919.

5. Cripplegate Park was formally opened by the Prince of Wales in 1932 during his visit to the city when he also opened the newly widened Severn Bridge.

it, especially for the younger generation who, after the war, seemed to have become increasingly 'lost at sea.' One had to sympathise with the difficulties of the young, he said. 'Old barriers, customs and conventions had broken down and they were increasingly becoming like sailors driven out to sea, drifting in a storm, charts washed overboard, not sure that their compass pointed true.'[6] The cinema, he considered, was an important extension of the theatrical arts and a wonderful educational tool – but not on a Sunday and only if there was strict adherence to the requirements of the censor! In 1919, there had been much talk in the local newspapers about a proposal whereby the Dean would take over the Silver Cinema for a week in order to demonstrate the kind of films he considered suitable for the young, and others which would 'elevate and educate adults.' Unfortunately, he was forced to abandon the project when he was taken ill that year. By 1932, however, he had decided to lead a vigorous campaign to oppose an application from the proprietors for Sunday opening, a development which was already much in vogue in places such as Droitwich, Evesham and Hereford. 'I would rather have the young people of Worcester in well-lighted streets than in dark cinemas,' he said, adding that they would be 'far healthier in the open air than looking at films which tend to excite their sensual passions or watching representations of American crooks and gangsters.'[7] Against the odds he won his case and the citizens of Worcester had to wait for several more years to enjoy films on the Sabbath Day – unless of course they caught the train to a nearby town.

Perhaps William's greatest concern during this period, however, was the one that preoccupied the whole nation, namely the unemployment situation. William's response was a typically practical one. In 1933, at the request of Worcester's Chamber of Commerce, he prepared a report on the current operation of the city's unemployment centre. He raised serious concerns that the centre was 'not doing the work

6. WME, address at Hereford Social Purity Meeting, BNA, *Kington Times*, 26 September 1925.
7. 'No Sunday Cinemas. Worcester Churches Opposed,' BNA, *Birmingham Daily Gazette*, 17 December 1932.

it was intended to do and that those who frequented it did little else than play cards.'[8] He recommended that it be closed for a short time to allow it to be turned into an occupational centre with a manager who organised training in potentially useful skills such as carpentry, metal work, bricklaying and furniture making. Equipment and helpers would be needed, he said, and he appealed to 'all men of goodwill to assist.' With echoes of the welfare centres in the mining areas of the North East he further proposed that there should be a reading room, lectures, a concert room, and, with a nod to modern times, a wireless set. A grant of £200 was obtained from the council for the purpose. The centre itself was divided across a number of local sites, situated in drill halls across the county. This last suggestion apparently had come from the Prince of Wales who had discussed his own concerns about unemployment with William during his recent visit to open the reconstructed Severn Road Bridge. The establishment of the Occupation Centre was probably William's last foray into the world of working conditions and one that was entirely in character. The world had of course changed a great deal since he had begun his ministry in Alston and observed the ways of the Quakers, but in many ways, it seemed to him, the needs of working people remained essentially the same.

Given his involvement with so many local causes it is tempting to ask what effect this had on his ability to fulfil the requirements of 'the day job'. He was, after all, charged with the responsibility of running a Cathedral as well as fulfilling the normal duties of a clergyman. William, in fact, took these responsibilities very seriously. He was immensely proud of the old building and was determined to ensure that its memorials and furnishings were of high quality and its ancient monuments were well restored in a dignified manner. Many of the newer memorials in the Cathedral were directly related to the sacrifices of the war but in October 1930 he unveiled a bronze plaque to commemorate the life and work of his great friend Geoffrey Studdert Kennedy. Like many people William felt strongly that

---

8. 'Dean on Workless Centre,' BNA, *Birmingham Daily Gazette*, 15 April 1933.

Geoffrey should have been buried in Westminster Abbey. The Dean of Westminster, however, had been resolutely opposed to the idea of 'a socialist' being interred in the abbey.[9] On hearing this William, in a direct rebuff to the abbey, was adamant that Geoffrey's funeral should be held in Worcester Cathedral. And in the end it was perhaps fitting that Geoffrey should be buried amongst the people he loved and who loved him in return. It seemed the whole of Worcester had closed for his funeral. Shops were shuttered and thousands of people lined the streets in silence as the cortege travelled the mile and a half from the Cathedral to St John's cemetery. Today there is substantial monument marking his grave funded by a small part of the £7,000 raised immediately after his death to support his widow and children.

Later that year William turned his attention to a somewhat older memorial, the thirteenth-century tomb of King John. A proposal to renovate this generated a degree of controversy when local historians concluded that its Purbeck marble had probably been polished rather than painted in its original form. It had almost certainly been painted several times since then and William considered that to repaint it in the manner of its most recent renovation (in 1870) would make it look 'gaudy'. Much heated discussion ensued but William eventually won the day and King John's gilt coat was laboriously scraped off and his 'tin crown' was removed.[10] In 1933 William was presented with a somewhat different adornment for the Cathedral, a beautiful frontal of hand-made lace for use on the High Altar. It had been paid for by 'the women of Malvern' as a dedication to Miss Edith Todd, matron of the Royal Hospital at Woolwich which treated wounded soldiers during the war. Miss Todd also served on a hospital ship and was badly injured when the ship was torpedoed. As a result, she was confined to bed for the rest of her life but had begun work on the altar cloth before she died in 1930. She had always intended the frontal as a gift to Worcester Cathedral and on her death a skilled lace maker in Malvern

9. Dean of Westminster, William Foxley Norris, in office 1925–37
10. 'King John's Tomb: Discoveries During Restoration,' BNA, *Lichfield Mercury*, 19 September 1930.

called Mary Carter had taken over and completed the work. William dedicated it in a formal ceremony in October that year.[11] Meanwhile his love of history was such that he was always keen to discover as much as he could of the building's secrets. Sub-Dean James Wilson had spent some considerable time and effort in researching and re-organising the contents of the library and had unearthed a number of ancient treasures in the process. William had been delighted when James discovered an 'extremely old and exquisitely written book' which gave a detailed account of Benedictine music and services in the Cathedral in the thirteenth century. Displaying it at a meeting of the Worcester Archaeological Society he described proudly how the library was now 'in such excellent order that numbers of persons of scholastic distinction came from all parts of the country to inspect it.'[12]

William was also keen to introduce the contents of the building to the more general public and to encourage as many people as possible to visit. In 1924 he decided to follow the example of Chester Cathedral and discontinue charging for entry. Despite the fact that such charges brought about £500 a year into the Cathedral coffers, he thought it was wrong in principle to charge people to come into a house of God. He loved conducting tours around the various chapels and monuments, pointing out the stonework, the wood carvings and the memorials. Children were made particularly welcome, enthralled by his fund of dramatic tales about the people who had worshipped there over the years. A correspondent to the *Evesham Standard* was delighted by the whole 'visitor experience' writing that the Dean should be congratulated on 'making the Cathedral more accessible and providing excellent visitor information, including explanatory notices properly mounted and placed on all items of interest.' It gave an 'intelligent appreciation of the Cathedral,' he continued 'in contrast to Malvern Priory where, despite the long history, the visitor is left to roam about

11. 'Cathedral Gift: War Episode and Nurses Devotion Recalled,' BNA, *Birmingham Daily Gazette*, 11 October 1933.

12. 'Unique Discovery at Worcester,' BNA, *Birmingham Daily Gazette*, 3 November 1924. William was president of the Worcester Archaeological Society for the year 1919–20 and remained a keen supporter.

unassisted with the result that most visitors leave little wiser than when they went in.'[13] An American visitor had fulsome praise for the 'clean state' of Worcester Cathedral, compared with Westminster Abbey which he found to be 'full of very dusty and dirty memorials that seem to have got beyond the efforts of the charwomen and even the vacuum cleaners.'[14] One lady from Australia was similarly impressed by Worcester, writing on her return home in 1931:

> I would like to tell the Dean that Worcester is the most courteous city I have visited and the Dean and Chapter are to be complimented on their treatment of tourists; everything is most plainly marked and there are always vergers ready to show you round and point out any object of interest; there is no other Cathedral so wide awake to the wishes of the tourist![15]

The Cathedral may have been 'wide awake' but perhaps William himself was sometimes a little forgetful. On one occasion he remained behind after evensong to talk to an architect visiting from America and to show him some particularly interesting aspects of the building. So absorbed was he that only some time later did he realise that he had failed to put the master key to the Cathedral in his pocket and both were locked in. Fortunately the architect was younger and rather more sprightly than William and faced with the prospect of a chilly night in the Cathedral he managed to prise open the great oak doors of the north porch, climb over the fifteen-foot high iron gates beyond, and fetch the key.

13. 'Our Historic Buildings: Worcester Dean's Example Praised,' BNA, *Evesham Standard & Midland Observer*, 30 January 1926.
14. WCL. Scrapbooks. Worcester Herald, 19 November 1929.
15. 'Sung On Wireless in Australia,' BNA, *Evesham Standard and West Midlands Observer*, 27 June 1931.

Chapter Twenty-Eight
MUSICAL PASSIONS

One of William's particular responsibilities as Dean was to preside over the arrangements for the Three Choirs Festival, an event which rotated over a three-year cycle between the Cathedrals of Worcester, Hereford and Gloucester. The Three Choirs, which traces its origins back to 1715, is one of the world's oldest classical choral music festivals. Famed for its high-quality performances of both well-loved and new choral pieces it is a hugely important event in the music lovers' calendar.[1] During the 1920s and early '30s Worcester was particularly well endowed in terms of its musicians. Not only did it possess an internationally renowned organist and choirmaster, Sir Ivor Atkins, but also the support of the country's foremost composer, Sir Edward Elgar. Formally William's duty was simply to give his permission for the festival to be held in the Cathedral, but in reality the task was considerably more onerous, especially since 1914, when Bishop Yeatman-Biggs had withdrawn his support for the whole enterprise on the grounds that he objected strongly to some of the music selected. It was not, he said, suitable to be performed in a Christian church. Although it was not within his power to forbid it (that privilege lay with the Dean he conceded) he had nevertheless decided to have nothing more to do with the festival. As it happened, of course, the war intervened in this little local difficulty and by 1918 the Bishop

---

1. Until 2020 only the two world wars had prevented the festival taking place. Sadly, however, the festival due to take place in Worcester in 2020 had to be postponed for twelve months due to the national emergency caused by the COVID-19 pandemic. At the time of writing the organisers hope to resume the festival in 2021.

had removed himself to Coventry. The festival resumed in 1920 with William, enthusiastically occupying the driving seat.

Many people, however, continued to feel that the festival should be held in a concert hall 'not in a sanctuary like the Cathedral.' It was not a religious event they argued, but a secular one. When Bishop Yeatman-Biggs had resigned William had been forced to fend off a considerable amount of pressure to abandon the whole enterprise. When it resumed after the war with the additional challenge of a precarious financial situation the same questions began to arise again. William, however, was determined that the festival should continue in the Cathedral. To those who thought otherwise he preached a strong sermon on the matter in September 1923, taking as his text some words from Psalm 150. 'Praise God in his sanctuary. Praise Him with sound of the trumpet. Praise Him with the lute and harp. Praise Him with the timbrel and pipes. Praise Him with stringed instruments and organs.'[2] He was sure, he said, that the psalmist who wrote those words would have happily taken his place among the festival chorus and in doing so would have regarded himself as engaged in a true act of worship.[3]

There were four festivals held in Worcester during William's tenure, each one a triumphant success, but each creating its own special problems. At Christmas 1921 it became clear that, even in the capable hands of Sir Ivor Atkins, the music emanating from the Cathedral organ was not all it should be. On New Year's Day William was forced to issue a circular around the parishes to inform them that the organ had completely broken down. This was alarming news, for just eighteen months later Worcester was due to host the festival for the second time. Consultants Harrison & Harrison of London were called in to advise and pointed out that the experimental electrical action which had optimistically been installed twenty-five years earlier had failed to fulfil its earlier promise. It was now in an advanced state of decay. Their estimate for rebuilding the organ 'in a thoroughly satisfactory manner with a new

2. Psalms 150:3, King James Bible.
3. WME, 'Sermon in Worcester Cathedral,' BNA, *Birmingham Daily Gazette*, 3 September 1923.

electro-pneumatic action' would be £6,500.[4] Sir Ivor was unsurprised at this turn of events, remarking that during the last twenty-five years the middle keys had probably been struck between 25 and 50 million times![5] A meeting was called to consider how to raise the money and it was agreed that in the present difficult times it would be better to rely on a large number of small subscriptions. 'A few large donations could hardly be expected nowadays.'[6] Canon Southwell noted that, once restored, the organ would be worth £30,000 although how this helped the current situation was not entirely clear. Fortunately, Mrs Charlotte Broome of Areley Court in the Worcestershire village of Areley Kings came to the immediate rescue with a gift of a 'three manual organ' that she wished to donate in memory of her recently deceased husband. Mr Edward Broome. The wealthy owner of a wool spinning mill in nearby Kidderminster, Mr Broome had himself been a keen organist and an ardent supporter of the festival. Sadly, Mrs Broome herself did not live to enjoy the performance of her gift, dying a few months after her timely donation, but her daughters took over her legacy donating a further £400 to adapt the organ for Cathedral use.[7] It took a full three years to raise the money for a new organ despite some large donations from wealthier local benefactors such as Charles Dyson Perrins, owner of the well-known Worcestershire Sauce factory. William and Sarah gave £300 and the officers of each of the two Worcester regiments also gave generous amounts. The dedication ceremony took place on Sunday 12 April 1925 in an impressive ceremony where Sir Ivor 'played one of Bach's masterly fugues,' compositions which were apparently 'especially designed to test an organist's ability and to exhibit the resources of a great organ.'[8] The refurbished organ was to give stalwart service for just over eighty years, going out with a bang, literally, one Sunday in late February 2004 in the middle of

4. 'Worcester Cathedral Organ: A Collapse,' BNA, *Gloucester Citizen*, 6 January 1922.
5. 'Silent Organ at the Cathedral,' BNA, *Birmingham Daily Gazette*, 6 February 1922.
6. ibid.
7. ibid.
8. 'Cathedral Organ: Reopening Service After Restoration,' BNA, *Evesham Standard & West Midlands Observer*, 18 April 1925.

choral evensong. Much to the consternation of the choir, the organist and a large congregation, the organ 'exploded' as leather work within it gave way. This time the price of a replacement was just under one million pounds and the appeal fund took over four years. However, the new organ, complete with its twenty-first-century computer-controlled systems was formally dedicated by the Bishop of Worcester on the 4 October 2008 following which there was a recital by another internationally renowned organist, Thomas Trotter.

Things were not always sorted out so amicably. Finance for the festival, provided largely by subscriptions and donations was a continual source of argument. Several members of the committee were strongly in favour of paring the whole event down while an exasperated Sir Ivor decried having always to 'push against this persistent pessimism.'[9] They should embark on the preparations in a spirit of hope, he urged, resolutely refusing to compromise on the quality of the performers even if they proved to be increasingly expensive. He found a strong ally in William who always tended to err on the side of optimism, pointing out that in previous years the festival had on average raised £1,000 for distribution to various charities. In 1929, however, a problem arose that seemed to have completely wrong footed him. That year Miss Florence Austral, a world-famous Australian soprano, had been engaged to sing at the festival and her presence promised to be a considerable draw. Shortly before her arrival, however, it was announced that she would not be performing after all. The reason was duly ferreted out by the press. Miss Austral could not be allowed to sing in the Cathedral because many years earlier she had been named as a co-respondent in a divorce case. Her husband, echoing the general public outrage at this asserted that 'their action is a terrible indictment against the church – they have adopted an attitude reminiscent of the tyranny of medieval times.'[10]

9. 'Three Choirs Festival: Estimate of Expenditure Approved,' BNA, *Evesham Standard & West Midlands Observer*, 9 June 1923.
10. 'Ban on Singer Kept Secret: Husband Attacks Church Stand,' BNA, *Derby Daily Telegraph*, 12 September 1929.

As it turned out the judgement of Miss Austral was not only 'tyrannical' but also inconsistent, as many were quick to point out. The reason lay in certain events which had taken place in the Cathedral ten years earlier in 1919. That year Miss Lena Ashwell, a well-known actress, had created a considerably stir when she was allowed to read passages from the Bible in the Cathedral. The occasion was a fund-raising event for the Young Women's Christian Association (YWCA), composed of choral pieces interspersed with passages from the Old Testament. Miss Ashwell had worked for the YWCA during the war, organising popular concert parties for the troops and the idea of the Cathedral event had been suggested by William's friend, Earl Beauchamp. William had readily agreed, despite the fact that the involvement of a woman in something akin to a Cathedral service risked serious disapproval from sections of the church authorities. William and Sarah, however, were both members of the League of Church Militant (LCM), a successor to the CLWS, which by now campaigned for the ordination of women as well as universal suffrage. As such, they would have regarded Miss Ashwell's contribution to proceedings in the Cathedral as a matter of principle. However, Miss Ashwell was apparently the first woman in England to 'stand behind the lectern in an Anglican church' and this, together with the fact that she also 'occupied a Canon's stall within the chancel rails', provoked indignation in some orthodox quarters.[11] Meanwhile others wanted to know why, if an actress had been allowed to recite in church, the same privilege had not been afforded to Miss Maude Royden, a Christian orator of some note and a leading campaigner for female ordination. Miss Royden had recently been refused permission to preach at St Botolphs in Bishopgate. On a lighter note the international Roman Catholic newspaper *The Tablet*, no doubt basking in the prospect of several members of the ECU threatening to 'go over to Rome' in protest, had suggested that since Miss Lena Ashwell

11. 'Miss Lena Ashwell Recites Selected Scripture in Worcester Cathedral,' BNA, *Birmingham Daily Gazette*, 23 April 1919.

had now read the lessons in Worcester Cathedral the Dean should, in return, 'take a turn on the stage'.[12]

The event involving Miss Ashwell was a huge success, much enjoyed by the large congregation and ten years later it might be presumed that the furore over her appearance in the Cathedral had largely blown over. In fact, however, it remained a smouldering fire that was rapidly reignited by the proposal to invite Miss Austral. For by 1928 certain other information about Miss Ashwell had come to light which William may or may not have been aware of in 1919. Miss Ashwell, it appeared, had been divorced by her first husband in 1908 on the grounds of her adultery with the husband of a fellow actress. Opponents of her appearance at the lectern in 1919 were quick to capitalise on this revelation which might account for William's fear of similar shots being fired at him again. If, however, his rapid rejection of Miss Austral was intended to ward off a comparable outcry it was a serious misjudgement. Times and attitudes had moved on, at least in the minds of those unfettered by church doctrine and, even within the church, he was subject to highly critical remarks from various correspondents signing themselves 'A Christian'. 'Let he who is without sin cast the first stone' noted one, while another pointed out that 'if all sinners were to be condemned in such a manner the churches would be nearly empty on Sundays.' 'Can one wonder that the man in the street does not go to church,' opined a third. 'There is more Christianity in the open air than in the churches.'[13] Many people, both inside and outside the church, would of course have known (in the words of the aforementioned Humanitarian League) that the characters of numerous public figures 'did not bear scrutiny' when set against the social norms of the 1930s, and been well aware of the hypocrisy that lay behind many respectable facades. William's own views on the matter remain a mystery, not least because of his steadfast and uncharacteristic refusal to express them, a factor which only served to increase speculation in the press. Whatever his reasons,

12. 'Women and the Church,' BNA, *Westminster Gazette*, 22 May 1919.
13. op cit., 'Ban on Singer Kept Secret.'

however, he resolutely stuck to the decision to ban Miss Austral. Perhaps he genuinely shared the views of those who felt she should not be allowed to take a leading role in the event, for religious attitudes towards divorce were famously uncompromising during this period. Or perhaps he feared the consequences of providing more ammunition for those who campaigned relentlessly for the removal of the festival from the Cathedral. Yet in the process he provoked outrage in other quarters, particularly amongst feminist organisations, of which he and Sarah were such prominent members. Whatever discussions took place behind closed doors, however, it was not the festival's finest hour.

Music itself, of course, is rarely free from controversy. At different times its message may be politically, socially or religiously unacceptable to different sections of the population. Over the years the festival has repeatedly fallen foul of these different strands of opinion, a problem that has continued well into the twenty-first century. In 2019 a strong protest by Brexit supporters against the inclusion of Beethoven's *Ode to Joy* meant that audience numbers were somewhat reduced on the last night of the festival.[14] William it seemed had to spend a lot of time defending the programme from critics whose beliefs it was deemed to have violated. In 1923 the inclusion of *Parsifal* led to accusations from the *Church Times* that the Dean had surrendered control of the Cathedral to a committee of irreligious enthusiasts.[15] And in 1932, as discussion of the programme turned to the possible inclusion of William Walton's Viola Concerto, Sir Ivor noted that the young composer's cantata *Belshazzar's Feast*, first performed at the Leeds festival the previous year was enjoying phenomenal success. 'Why then not have Belshazzar?' William asked innocently. Amidst laughter from the rest of the committee, clearly more attuned to current religious sensitivities, Sir Ivor told him 'It is a work I would not recommend you have in the Cathedral. You may go to the Bible for the libretto, and still may not take the work to the

14. The final movement of Beethoven's Ninth Symphony is widely considered to be the unofficial anthem of the European Union.

15. WME, letter to the *Church Times* defending the inclusion of *Parsifal*, Wagner's opera based on an epic poem recounting the story of the quest for the Holy Grail by the Arthurian knight Parsifal (Percival).

Cathedral.'[16] Sir Ivor was right. The Synod of the Church of England continued to view this work as inappropriate for performance in a Cathedral until the late 1950s. It was not until 1957 that it was finally performed in Worcester Cathedral as part of the Three Choirs Festival.

Even the national anthem was capable of causing a stir. In 1931, a major argument erupted about the content of the second verse of the anthem, a controversy which William himself seems to have had a hand in fomenting. As preparations got underway for the festival in Gloucester that year William received an anonymous letter complaining about the words of the verse which variously appealed to God to 'scatter our enemies, confound their politics and make them fall, and frustrate their knavish tricks and save us all'. The writer felt that the singing of such words in a church was 'blasphemous and in a Cathedral a brawling obscenity.'[17] William sent the letter to *The Times* with a request to know whether such a change might 'commend itself to the people of Great Britain.' He cannot have been surprised by the uproar that ensued. By the end of the month an enormous number of alternative verses had been submitted. A selection of the worthier efforts was published in *The Times* whilst a very popular satirical one from A. A. Milne (author of *Winnie the Pooh*) appeared in the *Northampton Chronicle*.[18]

> O Lord our God arise;
> Guard our securities;
> Don't let them fall.
> Scatter all party hacks
> (Save those my party backs)
> And make the income tax
> Op-ti-on-al.

16. 'Praise for Concerto,' BNA, *Birmingham Daily Gazette*, 6 February 1932.
17. 'Is the National Anthem Obscene?' Correspondence in *The Times*, 'Comment,' BNA, *Burnley News*, 21 February 1931.
18. 'National Anthem,' BNA, *Northampton Chronicle*, 7 February 1931.

William himself favoured retaining the original verse of the anthem, not least because it was what he was used to, but with two crucial changes, 'scatter thy enemies' and 'frustrate *all* knavish tricks'.[19] Within a few years, however, it would become the custom to sing only the first verse of the anthem!

A few years after William was confronted with the problem of paying for a new organ he also had to face another expensive difficulty, the recasting of the Cathedral bells. As president of the Worcestershire Change Ringing Association, a position he held for twenty-five years, he had presided over many meetings which discussed grants of varying sizes to be awarded to struggling country parishes scattered across the county. And there had been numerous renovations at places that Bishop Yeatman-Biggs would have known well, at Claines, at Dodderhill, at Grimley, at Hinton Green, at Hanley Castle and at Offenham, as well as a more major restoration at St Helen's in Worcester. Bells, it seemed, were always requiring attention of some sort. Yet William was a dedicated supporter of bellringing which he considered to be a sacred act of worship. It was a divine service, he said, just as much as that provided by the choir. By the same token he didn't like people 'coming down from the belfry having summoned people to church and then just walking away'[20]. He was keen to emphasise, not only church attendance but also high standards, and he was pleased at the improvements from 'the old state of things' which apparently included 'dusty, cobwebby towers, belfries used as rubbish deposits, bells dirty and neglected, ropes clumsy and knotted, ringers half-fuddled with cider or at all events content to do only a minimum of rounds and call changes for a few weeks in the middle of winter.'[21] In 1924 he was delighted to report 'clean tidy towers and ringing rooms, bells and frames in good going order, ringers intelligent, interested and keen on their art.' Moreover, the numbers of members and people coming

---

19. WME, letter to *The Times*. 'Confound Their Politics: The National Anthem.' *The Times*, 12 February 1931.
20. 'Notes and Comments,' BNA, *Leamington Spa Courier*, 1 April 1921.
21. 'Improvements in Church Belfries,' BNA, *Tamworth Herald*, 26 April 1924.

forward to train as ringers was increasing year on year. In December 1927, however, he reported sadly that owing to the dangerous state of the fittings the Cathedral bells could not be rung to mark the passing of the year. For many years, he said, the people of Worcester have heard the Cathedral bells ring out the old year and ring in the new. It was time to launch yet another appeal. The sum required was £1,400 and he urged the people of the city to respond generously – and by Easter – in order to get the work done by the end of the year. It was hoped, he said enthusiastically, that by the end of 1928 the bells will be rehung, recast, and tuned to a deeper note, and to ring such a peal as was never before sounded from the Cathedral tower! Once more his optimism won through. By the beginning of April he was able to report that the response to the appeal had been so good that he had signed a contract for the work with the Loughborough Bell Foundry and he now confidently hoped the bells would be ready for ringing on Armistice Day. Charles Dyson Perrins had made a substantial donation, together with two people who described themselves as 'Lovers of Bells' while William and Sarah once more led the way with a donation of £200. The remainder came from smaller contributions from individual citizens. The Cathedral got its newly restored bells, and two more churches, St John-in-Bedwardine and St Aiden & St Eadburgha in the village of Broadway got small grants from the 'Belfry Repair Fund'. Moreover, the Cathedral got some loudspeakers, a very modern innovation in 1928.

Chapter Twenty-Nine
THE FRIENDS

Maintenance of an ancient building and its various accoutrements and activities inevitably required a great deal of money and as Head of Chapter William found himself endlessly preoccupied with financial matters. When he arrived in Worcester he found, as he described it, a complete lack of any system for raising money. No-one knew, he said, how much was spent on each activity and any enquiries about the organisation of diocesan finances were met with 'talk of difficulty, objections and the dead hand of lethargy.'[1] In 1913 he had attempted to set up a subscription system in each parish whereby every church member should be asked to contribute a minimum amount regularly to church funds if they wished to remain on the electoral role. The names of contributors were to be published each year in the parish magazine and, somewhat ominously, those whose names did not appear 'should be seen individually'.[2] Perhaps predictably this system was somewhat unpopular and never really got off the ground. After the war, however, the financial situation became even more acute. In 1921 the *Church Times* reported that, unless additional income could be obtained, Worcester Cathedral was likely to become bankrupt. Congregations were smaller, people were poorer and the tradition of giving by wealthy benefactors, which many churches had relied on in the past, seemed to be fading as a feature of national life. Added to this many Canons were living in large houses that were now well beyond their means, a problem that William personally understood

---

1. WCL scrapbooks, New Organisation of Diocesan Finance, 1913.
2. ibid.

all too well. Briefly in 1924 he had hoped that the Old Palace might be sold for conversion into a girl's school, but the negotiations came to nothing and he was reluctantly forced to remain in his palatial surroundings, however cold, draughty and expensive they might be.

During the 1920s a number of steps were taken in an attempt to reduce the Cathedral's outgoings. Notably the number of Cathedral staff was reduced, including the number of minor Canons while those remaining agreed to increase their period of duty each year.[3] And when Sub-Dean James Wilson retired in 1926 his position was temporarily suspended. Meanwhile William struggled to gain the necessary permission to sell or let any church property, something he considered would have made all the difference. It seemed to him that the machinery of the Church of England responsible for such momentous decisions moved at an impossibly slow pace. William was personally good at raising money. He was an inspiring speaker, he had good contacts amongst what remained of Worcestershire's wealthy and he and Sarah were always willing to contribute generously themselves, despite their own limited income. But he was all too well aware that the building he loved was endlessly draining the Chapter's limited resources. In 1931 he detailed some of the most glaring problems. Frost and smoke were eating into the fabric of the building and large parts of the stonework needed restoration. Some of the turrets were in a dangerous condition and if they could not be repaired they would have to be removed. Many of the problems he laid at the door of the Victorian renovation of 1870 which, he considered was beset by bad building practices and 'many mistakes.' There was also a need to replace gas with electricity to comply with new fire regulations, the retaining wall of the promenade and roadway to the north door needed repair and there was Death Watch beetle in the timbers of the library. One beam was so rotten, he noted, that 'you could put your arm through it.'[4] In October that year, therefore, he decided to launch the initiative

---

3. Minor Canons: clergy who are members of staff of the Cathedral but are not part of the formal Chapter.

4. WCL scrapbooks, *Berrows Worcester Journal*, 17 October 1931.

that seems to have become his most well-known legacy. He formed the Friends of Worcester Cathedral.

By the end of the twentieth century, it seems, everything from theatres and orchestras to animal rescue centres had 'Friends' and no programme or guide book was complete without an invitation on its back page to 'join the Friends'. The formation of a group of dedicated supporters whose primary focus was to raise funds for a particular organisation or building seems to have first been suggested around 1930. In the decade that followed scores of organisations took up the idea, especially those associated with ancient buildings that needed continual expensive repairs. By 1940 nearly every Cathedral had its 'Friends'. Pershore Abbey and Worcester Cathedral seem to have been the first religious establishments to venture into this territory, each launching their Friends in 1931. Predictably it was William who had the idea, for Cathedral finances always weighed heavily on his mind. The ancestral estates of Worcester Cathedral had been transferred to the Ecclesiastical Commissioners in 1859 at which point £800 per year had been allocated for the maintenance of the building. Whether or not this was a sufficient sum at the time it was certainly woefully inadequate by 1931. Aside from financial considerations, however, William had always wanted to involve more of the people of the city with the life of the Cathedral. In 1921, conscious of the fact that, unlike the parishes, the Cathedral did not carry out any formal pastoral work he had formed a society called the Cathedral Fellowship. Originally based on those who regularly attended the service on Sunday evenings the society was launched at a garden party held on a glorious sunny day on the river terrace behind the Deanery. (The area was presumably now recovering from its wartime function as a potato patch). The Fellowship developed into a form of friendship organisation with lectures, discussion groups and social activities and he may well have had this in mind as a basis for a fund-raising group. He called the official inaugural meeting of the Friends of Worcester Cathedral in the Chapter House on 12 October that year.

According to Lord Cobham who chaired the proceedings the

meeting attracted 'a goodly gathering'. William had in fact been very busy since February attracting potential members. Letters had been sent out to all those listed as private residents in Kelly's Directory of Worcester and five thousand circulars had been distributed around the county. By the end of September 511 people had already been enrolled in the organisation, including Sir Edward Elgar and the playwright Bernard Shaw. Subscriptions at this point amounted to £571.2s.6d and donations stood at £278.18s. Addressing the meeting Lord Cobham said, with laudable frankness, that the Dean and Chapter knew that since the war there were now fewer people with large amounts of money that they didn't know what to do with. As a consequence it was necessary to enrol a larger number who could afford small amounts. The Dean, he said, had already personally raised considerable sums for repairs to the organ, bells, cloisters and windows but nothing had so far been done to the fabric of the building which required considerable attention. The main purpose of the meeting was to show the residents of the county that many people cared about this magnificent Cathedral. They should all go out and tell their friends that their 5s and 10s would add up to a considerable sum.[5] William, who by now obviously had a reputation as a relentless fundraiser, then stood up and said, with typical charm, that he had heard that some people had stayed away from the meeting because they thought 'its a scheme of the wily Dean to get us there and then he's going to send round a hat and ask for an additional subscription.' But, he said, he was not going to send round a hat or ask for further money, he was going to give them something – a copy of the new guidebook – and then he was going to give them tea.[6] More seriously he emphasised that the Friends should be a body that was entirely independent of the Dean and Chapter. It was, he said, for the latter to come cap in hand and say they wanted to do such and such repair. The Friends would always keep control of their own money and they would decide what

5. WCL scrapbooks, 'First Meeting of the Friends of Worcester Cathedral,' *Berrows Worcester Journal*, 17 October 1931.

6. ibid.

they would spend it on. And by the way, he said, if they all brought one person to the next meeting they would have one thousand members.[7]

If anything kept William awake at night it was probably the stone turrets on the gable ends of the north and south transepts. He had long been exercised about their dangerous condition and at the first meeting of the Friends he argued forcefully that the removal of these precarious pinnacles should be the first claim on their resources. When the artist Turner painted the Cathedral in 1795, William said, he left the turrets out because he didn't like them! It was a somewhat questionable claim but the Bishop agreed. They were not part of the original structure, he said, and the Cathedral was architecturally complete without them. A recent report by Vernon Rowe had shown that the stones had split as a result of being held together with iron clamps. Years of exposure to moisture had caused a layer of iron oxide to form on their surface such that they had swollen to twice their original thickness causing the stones to crack. The meeting, suitably alarmed, voted overwhelmingly to remove them. The decision was not without controversy, however. A 'lover of old buildings', for example, wrote to William to protest. Removal of the fine perpendicular turrets would lose much of the architectural character of the building he said, adding ominously that the turrets were in fact important for the structure, adding weight to the buttresses as they resisted the weight of heavy stone vaults and arches below.[8] The fear of losing part of the building altogether and perhaps the lives of some of those within it held sway however and by the time the Friends met in June 1932 the task had been completed. Moreover, William had managed to reduce the cost by finding steeplejacks to carry out the work. Even in the 1930s, it seemed, the cost of scaffolding was prohibitive. Despite all this, however, the turrets lingered fondly in the collective memory of successive congregations and clergy who were never quite reconciled to their loss. In 1932, fully aware of these sensibilities, William agreed that the bases of the turrets should be left intact so that they could be

7. ibid.
8. ibid.

replaced 'if this was desired and if sufficient funds were available.'[9] In 2004, therefore, the Friends indirectly helped to reverse the decision of their predecessors by providing some of the funds for the Cathedral stonemasons, who faithfully reproduced copies of the originals. Today the turrets stand proudly in their old place, hopefully held on by rather more durable clamps.

Less controversially during their first year the Friends also funded the replacement of the three rotten beams in the library and the treatment of the others with a pesticide. And a year later William had a further shopping list of items to lay before them. These included the repair of the roof of the north cloister and the purchase of fifty new seats for the nave. The loud-speakers now needed updating and also, as ever, the bells demanded more attention, this time the renovation of their chiming mechanism. The Friends contributed £250 towards the cost of all these.[10] It was not all about repairs, however. In 1933 they contributed to the cost of two beautiful new windows in the cloisters designed by members of the Bromsgrove Guild.[11] The windows were the latest addition to an ongoing project to create the historical story of Christianity through the medium of stained glass.

Perhaps the most pressing concern of these early years, however, was beyond the resources of the Friends and in fact beyond their remit. This was the Edgar Tower, the fourteenth-century gatehouse to College Green, a building that was particularly close to William's heart. In 1910 he had launched a campaign to fund the replacement of its crumbling statue of King Edgar as well as the addition of new terracotta figures in the empty alcoves alongside. Although the Tower was not officially part of the Cathedral the figure of Bishop Bosel, the first Bishop of Worcester, had been largely paid for by the Chapter

9. WCL scrapbooks, 19 March 1932.
10. 'Cathedral Friends: What They Have Done,' BNA, *Evesham Standard & West Midlands Observer*, 29 June 1935.
11. The Bromsgrove Guild of Applied Arts was a company of modern artists and designers associated with the Arts and Crafts movement. It was founded by Walter Gilbert in the Worcestershire town of Bromsgrove and became well-known for its highly skilled work in glass, metal, wood, plaster, tapestry and other mediums. It received a Royal Warrant in 1908.

with William himself contributing £20. Now, in the spring of 1933, the Tower was in danger of falling down altogether, another victim it seems of substandard Victorian restorations. Immediate repairs would cost about £800 but the whole work to save the Tower was in the region of £2,000. William was well aware that he could not expect the fledgling Friends to meet these sorts of costs and set about looking for alternatives. Within a few months he had secured £250 from the city council contingency fund and £500 from a charity called the Pilgrim's Trust which had recently been established, with a two million pound gift from an American philanthropist called Edward Harkness. Mr Harkness, who was of British descent, 'felt himself bound by many ties of affection to the country.' He was, he said, concerned about the financial difficulties Britain had found itself in after the war 'having spent her resources freely in the common cause had since the Peace sustained a burden honourably and without complaint.'[12] Significantly one of the inaugural board members of the Trust was Worcestershire MP and leader of the Conservative Party, Stanley Baldwin, a friend of William who shared his love of ancient buildings and had personally paid for one of the terracotta figures placed in the Edgar Tower in 1910.[13] In 1933 William raised the remainder of the money, which eventually amounted to £1,716, from a public appeal and some of the very few wealthy citizens who still resided in the county. The work on the Tower was completed by May 1934. It was perhaps William's last major fund-raising effort on behalf of the Cathedral that meant so much to him. It did not, however, represent the final chapter in the restoration of the Edgar Tower which took place during the five years between 2015 and 2020 at a cost of £300,000. This time much of the money was given by a number of different charitable trusts but a significant amount was raised via a popular twenty-first-century fund raising method. In 2020, as the final tranche of money was sought, local people were asked to sponsor a stone at £50 each. Each person's stone was

12. H. P. MacMillan, *A Man of Law's Tale* (MacMillan & Co, London, 1952).
13. The Pilgrim's Trust remains today and makes grants of about two million pounds per year for the preservation of architecturally and historically significant buildings.

to be engraved with their initials and a short dedication of their choice. Worcestershire County Council led the way with the purchase of ten stones marked WCC. Stone purchasers also received a map which showed them exactly where their stone was placed in the building, as well as a certificate from the current Dean. William would, no doubt, have thoroughly approved.

The Friends of Worcester Cathedral celebrated their seventy-fifth anniversary in 2006. While the ongoing demands of the Edgar Tower have always been beyond their resources they have, since 1931, contributed more than a million pounds to the work and maintenance of the Cathedral and the scope of their work has expanded enormously. Not only have they continued to support the repair and preservation of the ancient building and its contents, but also the library and archives and, through scholarships and bursaries, the work of the stonemasons and the maintenance of the choir. Friend's groups now help with embroidery, with flowers, and with Cathedral stewarding and guiding. Even William with his boundless optimism and enthusiasm could not have imagined what would grow from the foundation he laid in 1931. What is certain is that he would have been delighted at what has been achieved and would no doubt have spent even more of his time proudly showing people around his much-loved Cathedral.

Formal photograph of William as Dean of Worcester (National Portrait Gallery)

Chapter Thirty
THE FINAL YEARS

For two weeks at the beginning of July 1934 Worcester took part in a nationwide initiative called the 'Cathedral Pilgrimage'. For the price of a half crown ticket (2s.6d) people could visit each Cathedral in turn, the money raised being sent to an organisation called the National Welfare League which helped those in extreme poverty in what were deemed 'derelict areas'. These were areas where large industries had closed down leaving the people unemployed and destitute. William, ever mindful of the situation of the miners in the North East, ensured that Worcester Cathedral played a full role, enthusiastically organising tours with lady members of the Friends who were enlisted as guides. The eleventh-century crypt beneath the building as well as the Chapter House were open to visitors and those interested in the library were able to view its ancient treasures. There were afternoon addresses by the clergy, special organ voluntaries and choral evening services each day. It was all extremely popular with more than two thousand people, many of them children, reportedly visiting in the first week. William gave one of his last official addresses as Dean during this event returning to a simple theme that had inspired much of his life's work. Creeds had their place and usefulness, he said, but the real test of Christianity was not a man's profession of faith but the way in which he showed by his actions the spirit of sympathy and helpfulness.

Two weeks later on 14 July he announced his retirement. The occasion was the prize-giving at the King's School. Twenty-six years earlier, he said, he had made his first appearance in Worcester at that very same event and therefore he felt this was an appropriate place to make the announcement. His normally strong voice reportedly 'broke with emotion such that it was scarcely audible except to those on the front row.' He described how he had been thinking about retirement for some time but had finally made his decision when recently his wife's health 'had broken down'.[1] William was by now eighty-five years old, reputedly the oldest Dean in England. Unsurprisingly he had recently been 'handicapped by muscular trouble' and intermittent bouts of ill-health that had kept him away from various meetings and events, but it is clear that he never really wanted to retire.[2] Rather he would, so to speak, have preferred to die in harness. For him, his work was central to his life and the Cathedral and the city had become central to that work. Years before he had missed Tyneside greatly and struggled to adapt to life in Worcester but now, he said, 'this is where we belong, our friends are in Worcester, our interests are in Worcester and the people of Worcester recently did me the honour of making me a Freeman of the City.'[3]

Earlier in the year, on 17 April at a formal ceremony in the Guildhall, William had been admitted as an Honorary Freeman of the City of Worcester. Recalling his grandfather's naval career he would probably have been rather interested to know that he was following in the footsteps of Lord Nelson who had received the honour in 1802.[4] More significantly, however, William himself was the first clergyman to receive such an honour and it was well deserved, for his long and dedicated service to the city as well as the Cathedral was unquestionable. As he delivered his address that day, he emphasised the fact that fundamentally, over the years since his appointment to Worcester, he had not changed, either in his persona, his politics, or his theology. He might have added that in his movement from parish priest to Cathedral Dean the nature of his activities had also remained largely the same. For this was a

1. 'Dean of Worcester Resigning,' BNA, *Birmingham Daily Gazette*, 14 July 1934.
2. ibid.
3. ibid.
4. Lord Nelson was made a Freeman of the City during a visit in August 1802. He and Lady Hamilton ordered a porcelain dinner service from Chamberlain's China Factory, the forerunner of Royal Worcester Porcelain, but failed to pay the bill!

Dean who had involved himself in every aspect of local affairs, from the grievances of the chainmakers in Cradley Heath to the appalling housing conditions in the city, from the food shortages during the war to the lack of playgrounds for small children. He had, it seems, served on every imaginable committee that was concerned with improving the lives of the ordinary men, women and children of Worcester. And, as much as he was able, he wanted to make the Cathedral the people's church, not the place where the workers coming off shift on a Sunday morning stood to marvel at the finery of those emerging from their religious observances. As his friend James Wilson once put it 'to him religion is not a matter of authority, or logic, or opinion; it is a life, a life of service, service to all around him based on Christ's teaching.'[5]

William's actual retirement took place in September 1934 when, as the Prime Minister had suggested, he had put his affairs in order and found a new home in the city. He and Sarah at last moved out of the Old Palace to a house called the Priory on London Road. They were now situated in the parish of St Martin's and William lost no time in offering his services to the church there, taking the Armistice service in November that year. The same month he chaired a meeting to discuss the form of a memorial to Sir Edward Elgar who had died the previous February. The original suggestion had been for a small window in the cloisters, but William was insistent that something much more elaborate would be a fitting tribute to the famous musician who had played such a prominent role in the musical life of the Cathedral. It was agreed, therefore, that a window illustrating one of his most famous works, the *Dream of Gerontius*, would be placed in the north aisle near the spot where Elgar habitually stood to listen to rehearsals for the Three Choirs Festival.[6]

The choice of *Gerontius* was in fact highly significant and reflective of both the close friendship that existed between William and Elgar and the composer's own strong attachment to the Cathedral. As a Roman

---

5. James M. Wilson, *An Autobiography* (Sidgwick & Jackson Ltd, London).
6. 'Memorial Window in Worcester Cathedral Approved,' BNA, *Birmingham Daily Gazette*, 19 November 1934.

Catholic from relatively humble beginnings, Elgar had frequently experienced feelings of rejection at the hands of both the Anglican church and the higher ranks of society. The history of his *Gerontius* is a particularly poignant one. The work had had its first performance in 1900 at the Birmingham Triennial Music Festival, an occasion that had turned out to be disastrous affair. The complex music proved to be far too challenging, not only for the somewhat under-rehearsed amateur choir, but also for the professional soloists. The situation was made worse by the sudden death of the chorus master who was replaced at short notice by an elderly musician who similarly found the score to be completely beyond him. Elgar, who always considered *Gerontius* to be his greatest work, was devastated by the event. The dreadful reviews brought to a head all his feelings of social and professional exclusion and shook his religious faith to the core. 'I have allowed my heart to open once – it is now shut against every religious feeling and every soft gentle impulse forever,' he said. This, however, was to be only the beginning of a long series of problems for *Gerontius*. Many Anglican clergy objected to references to Roman Catholic doctrine contained within the text. Even after Elgar had agreed to remove some offending verses such as those relating to 'purgatory' most refused to allow its performance in Anglican Cathedrals, a situation which would continue for many years.[7] In February 1902, however, Christian Socialist Charles Gore, an Anglo-Catholic by religious inclination, was installed as Bishop of Worcester and readily agreed to the work being performed at the Three Choirs Festival held in Worcester Cathedral that year. This time the occasion was a huge success. *Gerontius*, with a much more talented choir under the baton of Elgar himself, was performed to great acclaim. It was something that went a long way towards healing the hurt that Elgar felt so keenly and, despite his continuing feelings of rejection by the religious establishment, he always felt very much at home within the precincts of Worcester Cathedral. Many of his works would be performed there in future

---

7. As late as 1932 the Dean of Peterborough persisted with this ban.

years, notably *For the Fallen* in 1917, which he dedicated to the men who died at Gheluvelt. In 1932 he addressed a meeting of the Friends having become an enthusiastic member. He talked of how he had always found the building to be 'a place of rest, contemplation and refreshment in the highest sense of the word.' 'Having spent my life, with absences, in the shadow of the Cathedral,' he said, 'and having been born close to it and having come back as a truant to die under its shadow, nothing would give me greater happiness to know that its future improvement was secure.'[8] William, meanwhile, would always regard it as an honour to host works by Elgar. Both the Cathedral and the city were extremely proud of their famous composer.

Sadly, William did not live to see the unveiling of the Elgar window on the eve of the festival in 1935. He and Sarah enjoyed only a short retirement together. By Christmas 1934 Sarah's health was deteriorating rapidly. She was suffering from arterial sclerosis causing cerebral degeneration and was becoming increasingly confused and disorientated. She died at the Priory in early February 1935. Sarah had enjoyed a high profile in the work of the Cathedral, organising events, supervising much of the housekeeping work of the building and playing an active role in many of the initiatives pursued by William. Without her, he said, he could not have done many of the things he did. He once commented that he owed much to her personal care of him and for 'preventing him from saying and doing stupid things.'[9] Perhaps it was her strong Quaker connections which provoked this comment. William would have remembered from Alston the customary practice of 'reflection and discernment' that preceded any serious decision making amongst the Religious Society of Friends. Her funeral took place in the Cathedral on 5 February following a cremation a few days earlier, as was her wish. Eleanor's funeral, nearly twenty-five years earlier, had been a quiet family affair, for due to her own ill health she had

---

8. WCL scrapbook, 'Meeting of The Friends,' *Berrows Worcester Journal*, 25 June 1932.
9. WME, address in Worcester Guildhall on receiving the Freedom of the City, BNA, *Evesham Standard & West Midland Observer*, 21 April 1934.

struggled to play a significant role in the life of the Cathedral. In marked contrast Sarah's funeral, conducted by the Bishop, was a major event. The casket containing her ashes had lain during the previous night in front of the candlelit altar of the Jesus Chapel covered by a purple cloth, embroidered by the Cathedral Needlework Guild with the arms of the Bishop and Dean and Chapter. The following day her funeral, with a long procession of clergy and a full choir, was attended by a large congregation. Subsequently, however, her remains were laid alongside Eleanor's in the simple grave contained within the cloisters.

William struggled on alone for only four months. At the Priory on the evening of Sunday 2 June during a visit by one of his nephews he suffered a stroke and died shortly afterwards. His funeral, held a few days later, was again a major formal event, as befitted the former Dean of a Cathedral. The ten pall bearers were representatives of the various organisations with which William was 'specially identified' and clergy from all parts of the diocese were present. In William's case, however, there were, in addition to his extended family, hundreds of other mourners which, as the *Birmingham Daily Gazette* described it, represented every aspect of religious, civic, philanthropic and social life of the city. The service itself was, it was reported, 'mainly choral, and gained in impressiveness from its briefness and simplicity.'[10]

In 1931 the French scientist and philosopher Pierre Teilhard de Chardin wrote: 'we are not human beings having a spiritual experience; we are spiritual beings having a human experience'.[11] These profound and often quoted words seem particularly apposite when considering the life of William Moore-Ede. On the Sunday morning following the funeral, the Bishop, Arthur Perowne, paid tribute to William in a sermon where he addressed directly the question of spirituality within a ministry that had emphasised, above all things, the practical

---

10. 'Worcester's Tribute to the late Dr Moore-Ede,' BNA, *Birmingham Daily Gazette*, 6 June 1935.
11. Pierre Teilhard de Chardin, *The Phenomenon of Man* (Harper Perennial, 1976, first published in French 1955).

application of the Christian faith.[12] Basing his address on the text 'There are diversities of gifts, but the same spirit,'[13] he emphasised the essential spirituality that pervaded William's life:

> Dr Moore-Ede was a new and unfamiliar type when he came to Worcester twenty-six years ago. His bent was social righteousness and his soul was on fire with a passion for carrying the spirit of Christ into everyday life, outside the ordinary routine of Cathedral worship and devotion. No-one could ever accuse him of neglect of the public worship of this place. He loved the building and its historical associations and spent much time and energy and money in repairing and enriching it, making its beauties and its history known to others. He was anxious that the thousands who are visitors every year should feel the atmosphere of devotion and be drawn forwards by what they saw and heard as they wandered round and perhaps stayed to worship at the regular services. But his heart was in the application of the Christian ethic to daily life. He was a passionate believer in the possibility and the necessity of Christianizing our civilisation. It was this faith that inspired him in all his various social and economic experiments.
>
> How completely diverse from the Deans that went before him he was! How strangely different a form the Holy Spirit's gifts had taken with his personality! Not mystical, not contemplative, but practical was his type of Christian life. He was not content to preach about slums and housing. He started homes for aging miners in Gateshead and a housing scheme in Worcester, while others were only talking about it. And who shall say that such is not spiritual?
>
> He was a passionate believer in the League of Nations ideal. Peace and goodwill among men were to him a part of the message he was privileged to deliver both at home and abroad. His whole life was devoted to the service of friendship between people of different shades of belief, between

---

12. Arthur Perowne, Bishop of Worcester, in office 1931–41. Formerly the first Bishop of Bradford, he would have been much in sympathy with William's concerns for the poor in industrial towns.

13. Corinthians 1:12, King James Bible.

people of different stations, between the old and the young, the rich and the poor. With all his keenness for social amelioration and international relations, he was a loving friend. Is not that the fruit of the spirit?[14]

In the days that followed obituaries and tributes appeared in newspapers across the country and from all the various organisations to which William had belonged and contributed. Once more, however, it was the simple grave in the cloisters that received his remains, where they lie next to those of Eleanor and Sarah. And during the following year a small memorial window was added to those in the surrounding cloister walls.

The memorial window to William Moore-Ede in the cloisters of Worcester Cathedral. (Courtesy of Chris Guy, Worcester Cathedral.)

It is not known where Mary Jane Gray was buried. The graveyard at St Mary's, Gateshead, the church where her father had sought out William to tell him about the death of his daughter, had already closed in 1882. Most probably she lies in one of the large municipal cemeteries

14. 'The late Dr Moore-Ede: The Bishop's Appreciation at the Cathedral Service' (extracts), BNA, *Evesham Standard & West Midlands Observer*, 15 June 1935.

opened in Newcastle and Gateshead during the second half of the nineteenth century. For the population of Tyneside was growing rapidly during this period and by 1882 most church graveyards had already reached their capacity. These public cemeteries contain many splendid monuments commemorating the prominent and wealthy citizens of Tyneside but, like so many of the poor of the period, Mary Jane has no marked grave. We do not know if, ultimately, William paid for her coffin and the cost of her funeral. Perhaps he did, for it was the sort of thing he might have done. What we do know, however, is that he never forgot the death of Mary Jane. And in the years that followed he went on to devote himself unsparingly to the needs of the poor and the social conditions which blighted their lives. In the course of his own life, therefore, perhaps he created his own special memorial to this one defenceless victim of the society in which he lived.

AFTERWORD

This book has been written, no doubt like so many others, during the months of the COVID-19 pandemic of 2020–21 when the fault lines of our societies have been exposed as never before. Eighty-five years after William Moore-Ede's death people across the world are struggling to feed their families, pay their rent and heat (or cool) their homes. On our television screens in the UK we have been confronted with the sight of clergy in a northern English town reduced to tears by the poverty, grief and desperation of the people they are trying to help. And as the prospect of a life-saving vaccine appears on the horizon parts of the world have descended into conflict over its unequal distribution and supply. Yet never before has the mantra 'we are all in this together' been more relevant to our situation.

Today, in 'developed' countries, the twin systems of capitalism and competition have reached levels which would probably have dismayed William Moore-Ede and his fellow Christian Socialists, pervading every aspect of our commercial and cultural life. The Co-operative model which he so much admired now plays only a small role in a world where the divisions in society seem to grow ever wider. Meanwhile the catastrophic problems caused by climate change demand, more than ever before, that people work together to save the very planet we inhabit. Today's world, therefore, continues to fall far short of the one William Moore-Ede dreamed of. Certainly, in the UK at least, we have not so far 'adapted our social arrangements for the benefit of all in society.' Yet William, who in his later years often pointed to the social improvements he had noted during his long life, would not have despaired. He was essentially a practical man who always rose to the immediate challenges in times of crisis and it is not difficult to imagine his personal response to the individual tragedies of 2020–21. He would, however, have seen his own work simply as part of a whole, his particular contribution to an ongoing process towards the longer-term goal of social justice which, in good times and bad, would ensure that the needs of all would be met, that the vulnerable would be cared for and that everyone would have the opportunity to flourish. As a Christian he based this belief and this vision on the teaching of Jesus Christ. And as a student of philosophy he would, no doubt, have been familiar with the words of Edmund Burke. 'Nobody made a greater mistake than he who did nothing because he could do only a little.' Many in 2020–21 have not made that mistake and many, like William Moore-Ede, have done far more than a little. There have been many inspiring tales of generosity and self-sacrifice to brighten the days of fear and despair. Today, therefore, in the midst of what seems like a perfect storm of problems on an international scale, numerous voices are being raised which demand the need for a fundamental change in the way we organise our societies. Many express the hope that the pandemic which has wreaked such havoc across the world may signal a turning point in our collective lives. For William, and for Frederick Maurice who inspired him, the ills of our societies emanate from the emphasis on competition rather than co-operation as the defining element of human relationships. Ultimately, they believed, it was co-operation and mutual helpfulness that would always triumph in terms of producing a just and fulfilling society and that these were, in fact, intrinsic qualities of human nature. As William was so fond of saying 'Our social conditions are of our own making, they are what they are because of what we are. There is no law of the universe that says we should live like this.'

BIBLIOGRAPHY

Books

Armstrong, C. *Pilgrimage from Nenthead: An Autobiography*. Methuen, London, 1938.

Best, G. *Bishop Westcott and the Miners*. The Bishop Westcott Memorial Lecture, Cambridge University Press, Cambridge, 1966.

Brett-Young, F. *Far Forest*. Heinemann Ltd, London, 1936.

Bryant, C. Possible Dreams. Hodder & Stoughton, London, 1996.

Darwin, C. *On the Origin of Species by Means of Natural Selection*. John Murray, London, 1859.

Dickens, C. *Oliver Twist*. Bentley, London, 1838.

Edge, B. *History of Leadgate School*. Local Studies, Alston Library, Cumbria, 2009.

Edwards, D. L. *Leaders of the Church of England 1828–1944*. Oxford University Press, Oxford, 1971.

Grundy, M. *A Fiery Glow in the Darkness. Woodbine Willie: Padre & Poet*. Osborne Books, Worcester, 1997.

Gwilliam, B. *Old Worcester: People and Places*. Halfshire Books, Bromsgrove, 1993.

Jepson, M. A. *The Beginnings of English University Education – Policy and Problems*. Michael Joseph, London, 1973.

Johnson, R. W. *The Making of the Tyne, A Record of Fifty Years' Progress*. W. Scott, London, 1895.

Lawson, J. *A Man's Life*. Hodder & Stoughton, London, 1932.

MacMillan, H. P. *A Man of Law's Tale.* Macmillan & Co, London, 1952.

Manders, F. W. D. *A History of Gateshead.* Gateshead Corporation, UK, 1973.

Marrin, A. *The Last Crusade: The Church of England in the First World War.* Duke University Press, Durham, 1974.

Marshall, A. *Principles of Political Economy.* Macmillan, London, 1890. Reproduced by Prometheus Books, 1997.

Maurice, F. D. *Theological Essays.* Macmillan & Co, Cambridge, 1853. Reproduced by Scholar Select, no date.

Maurice, J. F. D. (ed.) *The Life of F. D. Maurice, Chiefly Told in His Own Letters,* vol. ii, Macmillan, London, 1884.

Moore-Ede, W. *The Hulsean Lectures for 1895: The Attitude of the Church to Some of the Social Problems of Town Life.* Cambridge University Press, Cambridge, 1896. Reproduced by Scholar Select, no date.

Moore-Ede, W. *Cheap Food and Cheap Cooking: To which is Added Hints for the Management of Penny Dinners for School Children.* Walter Scott, Newcastle Upon Tyne, 1884.

Moore-Ede, W. *The Cathedral Church of Christ and the Blessed Virgin Mary, of Worcester: Its Monuments and Their Stories.* Phillips & Probert, Worcester, 1925.

Mumford, E. E. R. *Through Rose-coloured Spectacles: The Story of a Life.* Edgar Backus, Leicester, 1952.

Neville, G. *William Moore-Ede, Dean of Worcester 1908–1934.* Office of the Friends of Worcester Cathedral, Worcester, 2008.

Nichols, T. L. *Penny Vegetarian Cookery. The Science and the Art of Selecting and Preparing a Pure, Healthful, and Sufficient Diet.* Franks & Co, London, 1888.

Paget, S. *Henry Scott Holland.* John Murray, London, 1921.

Patrick, G. A. *The Miner's Bishop.* Epworth Press, London, 2004.

Quennell, P. (ed.) *Mayhew's London.* Spring Books, London, 1969.

Raistrick, A. *Two Centuries of Industrial Welfare. The London Quaker Lead Company 1692–1905.* Kelsall & Davis, UK, 1988.

Rubenhold. H. *The Five. The Untold Story of the Women Killed by Jack the Ripper*. Transworld Publishers, London, 2019.

Satre, L. J. *Thomas Burt, Miners' MP. 1837–1922*. Leicester University Press, Leicester, 1999.

Sherard, R. H. *The White Slaves of England*. Fifield, London, 1897.

Sharp, E. *Hertha Ayrton: A Memoir*. Edward Arnold & Co, London, 1926.

Spence-Watson, R. *The History of the Literary and Philosophical Society of Newcastle-Upon-Tyne 1793–1896*. Walter Scott Ltd, London, 1897.

Teilhard de Chardin, Pierre. *The Phenomenon of Man*. Harper Perennial, 1976. First published in French 1955.

Welch, E. *The Peripatetic University*. Cambridge Local Lectures 1873–1973. Cambridge University Press, Cambridge, 1973.

Wilkinson, A. *Christian Socialism: Scott Holland to Tony Blair*. SCM Press, London, 1998.

Web-based references

British Newspaper Archives. www.britishnewspaperarchive.co.uk

Carlton, I. C. *A Short History of Gateshead*. Gateshead Corporation, 1974. https://www.genuki.org.uk/big/eng/DUR/GatesheadHistory

Calhoun, D. B. 'Bright Messenger of God: Bishop Handley Moule,' *Knowing and Doing* (CS Lewis Institute, spring 2012). Accessed via www.cslewisinstitute.org

Coming Home: Tackling the Housing Crisis Together. Commission of the Archbishops of Canterbury and York on Housing, Church and Community, February 2021. www.archbishopofcanterbury.org

Cook, A. J. *The Nine Days. The Story of the General Strike Told by the Miner's Secretary*. Co-operative Printing Society, 1926. www.wikisource.org

Duma, V. & Lichtenberger, H. *Remembering Red Vienna*. www.jacobinmag.com

Fielden, K. C. 'The Church of England in the First World War'. Master's Thesis, East Tennessee State University, 2005. www.dc.etsu.edu/etd/1080

Finch, A. *The Provision of School Meals since 1906: Progress or a Recipe for Disaster? History and Policy.* 2019. www.historyandpolicy.org

Gear, G. C. *Industrial Schools in England 1857–1933. Moral Hospitals or Oppressive Institutions?* University of London Institute of Education, 1999. www.discovery.ucl.ac.uk

People in Housing Need. National Housing Federation. 15 September 2020. www.housing.org.uk

Steel, R. L. *The Contribution of F. D. Maurice to the Christian Socialist Movement of 1848–1854.* Bachelor of divinity thesis, University of Oregon, 1971. www.core.ac.uk

The Accord Coalition for Inclusive Education. www.accordcoalition.org.uk

Woodroofe, K. *The Royal Commission on Poor Laws, 1905–1909.* www.cambridge.org/core

First World War Centenary: 1914–1918. Worcestershire World War 100. 18 May 1917–24 February 1918. www.ww1worcestershire.co.uk

INDEX

A

Abbot Memorial School, Gateshead   101, 133
Abraham, May   116
Aged Miners' Homes   147, 155, 194, 234
Albert Hall, London   198
Albert Hall, Sheffield   71
Aldridge, Henry   151, 154, 156
Allott, Alderman R. W.   57
All Saints Church, Ecclesall, Sheffield   59, 60, 70
Alnwick, Northumberland   108
Alston Moor, Cumbria   30, 31, 33, 38
Anchorage Working Girls' Club, Gateshead   137
Anglican Group for the Ordination of Women in the Historic Ministry   202
Anglo-Catholic English Church Union (ECU)   62, 63, 274
Anglo-German Friendship Society   207, 209
Anti-Sweating League   189
Armistice Day   226, 229, 231, 279
Armstrong, Chester   31, 37
Armstrong, Lord William   75, 76, 95, 96
Arnold, Dr Thomas   21, 25
Arts and Crafts movement   10, 58
Ashwell, Lena   274, 275
Asquith, Herbert   82, 117, 168, 198, 199, 202
Association for the Care of Friendless Girls (the Lodge)   127, 128, 129, 131, 132
Association for the Higher Education of Working Men   185
Atkins, Sir Ivor   270, 271
Auckland Castle, Durham   119, 120, 139, 162
Austral, Florence   273, 274, 275, 276

B

Bach, J. S.   272
Backworth, Northumberland   76
Baker, Joseph Allen   206
Baldwin, Stanley   226, 286
Band of Hope, Gateshead   90, 137
Barbourne College, Worcester   227
Barbourne Waterworks, Worcester   185
Barnards Green, Malvern   217
Barnes Court Amateur Gymnastics Club (Gateshead)   137
Barnes, Eleanor Pollard   145
Battenhall, Worcester   224
Baylee, Eleanor. *See Moore-Ede, Eleanor (first wife of WME, formerly Baylee, nee Cookson)*
Baylee, Eleanor (step-daughter of WME)   59, 174
Baylee, Laetitia Lucy (daughter of Eleanor Moore-Ede, formerly Baylee)   39, 59
Baylee, Mary (step-daughter of WME)   59, 174
Baylee, Reverend William Cecil   37, 38, 39, 40, 53, 169
Beauchamp, Lord/Earl (Madresfield Court)   175, 223, 225, 239, 274
Bede, Venerable   77
Bedlington Mutual Improvement Association (Northumberland)   88
Beethoven, Ludwig van   276
Belfry Repair Fund   279

Belgium 203, 209, 210, 257
Bentham, Jeremy 27
Berne, Switzerland 212, 220
Birdport, Worcester 171
Birmingham Cathedral 67
Birmingham Railway Station 257
Birmingham University 67, 238
Bismark, Otto von 88, 89
Black Country 171, 172, 187, 188
Black Friday 254, 258
Blockhouse, the, Worcester 172, 204, 223
Blyth, Northumberland 76, 150, 154, 155
Boer War 113, 199
Bolshevists 254, 255
Bosel, Bishop 221, 285
Boyle, Hugh 156, 157, 158
Boyle, Robert 144
Boys Brigade Home for Destitute Boys, Gateshead 137
Bradford, West Yorkshire 55, 294
Bradley, George 25
Brandling Street Club for Working Men, Gateshead 137
Brewster Sessions 91
Brexit 276
British Association 87
British National Peace Congress 207
Brockmoor parish church, Worcestershire 257
Bromley-Martin, Madeleine 219
Bromsgrove Guild 285
Broome, Edward & Charlotte, Arely Court, Arely Kings 272
Browning, Oscar 79
Brunswick Wesleyan Chapel 110, 112
Bryce, Margery 198
Bulmer, Frederick 223, 224
Bund, William 210
Burge, Hubert, Bishop of Oxford 252, 253
Burke, Edmund 27, 298
Burt, Thomas 1, 2, 3, 5, 42, 43, 62, 76, 87, 115, 118, 126, 208, 255, 256, 259

C

Cadbury, George 226
Cadbury, Richard 228
Cambridge, King's College 79, 224
Cambridge, St John's College 25, 27
Cambridge, Trinity College 48
Cambridge, University of 14, 19, 21, 25, 26, 28, 29, 31, 40, 44, 45, 49, 52, 56, 61, 64, 66, 67, 68, 70, 73, 79, 81, 89, 118, 123, 170
Canterbury, Archbishop of 170, 176, 186, 204
Caris, John 2, 115
Carlisle, Dean of 61
Carlton, Arthur 216, 226
Carrs Lane Church, Birmingham 177, 253
Carter, Mary 268
Case, Annie 116
Castleton, Derbyshire 61
Cathedral Fellowship 282
cathedral library, Worcester 14, 268, 281, 285, 287, 288
Cathedral Needlework Guild 293
Cathedral Pilgrimage 288
Cavell, Edith 210
Caxton Hall, London 251
chainmakers, chainmaking, chainmakers' strike 188, 189, 191, 192, 245, 290
Chapter House 282, 288
Chartist movement, chartism 15, 17, 18
Chester Cathedral 268
Choppington, Northumberland 76
Christian Socialist Congress in Strasbourg 252
Christian Socialists, Christian Socialism 6, 7, 10, 13, 16, 17, 18, 19, 20, 21, 27, 33, 64, 83, 86, 119, 169, 174, 179, 188, 203, 209, 231, 252, 291, 297
Church Congress 7, 61, 62, 72, 257
Church League for Women's Suffrage (CLWS) 198, 199, 200, 201, 202, 274
Church of England Men's Society (CEMS) 183, 184
Church of England Temperance Society (CETS) 90, 177, 220
Church Peace League 206
City Food Economy Committee 216
Cleadon, County Durham 91, 164, 165
Clifford, John 206, 251
Cobham, Lord/Viscount, Hagley Hall 175, 223, 224, 225, 239, 282, 283
Colville-Stewart, Mr and Mrs 226
Colwall, Herefordshire 177
Commission on Housing, Church and Community, 2021 243

communal kitchens 215, 216, 217, 218, 226
Conciliation Bill, 1911 198
Conciliation Boards 120, 121, 122, 255
Congregational Union 252
conscientious objectors 211, 213, 250
Conservative Party 286
Constance, Germany 208, 248
Cook, Arthur J. 259
Cookery College, Worcester 216
Cookson & Co 117, 118
Cookson, Eleanor. *See Moore-Ede, Eleanor (first wife of WME, formerly Baylee, nee Cookson)*
Cookson, Norman and George (cousins of Eleanor Moore-Ede formerly Baylee nee Cookson) 40, 117
Cookson, Reverend Edward (father-in-law of WME) 40, 53, 117, 118
Cookson, William Isaac (uncle of Eleanor Moore-Ede formerly Baylee nee Cookson) 41, 118
Co-operative Flour Mills, Dunstan 121
Co-operative Hall, Consett, County Durham 88
Co-operative Society 49, 52, 147, 151, 155, 224
Copenhagen, Denmark 252, 259
Coronation Day 185, 198
Cottage Tavern 91
County Cricket Ground, Worcester 220
County Hotel, Westoe 147
Coventry 171, 229, 238, 249, 250, 271
Coventry, Bishop of 169, 229, 255
Coventry, Earl/Lord (Croome Park) 175, 210, 231, 232
Cradley Heath, Rowley Regis 187, 188, 189, 190, 191, 193, 245, 246, 290
Cradley, Worcestershire 173, 187
Cramlington Pit, Northumberland 43, 259
Creighton, Reverend (vicar of Embleton) 80
Crewe, Cheshire 49
Cripplegate Park, Worcester 264
crypt, Worcester Cathedral 288
Cutlers Hall, Sheffield x, 56

D

Darlington, County Durham 78
Darlington Mechanics Institute 86
Darwin, Charles 27, 181
Dawlish, Devon 53
Deptford, London 22, 23, 108
Derby 48, 49, 51
Despard, Charlotte 198
Digbeth Institute, Birmingham 177
Discharged Prisoners Aid Society 176
district nursing 176
District Nursing Association 138
Dobson, John 75
Dream of Gerontius 290, 291
Dryden Centre, Gateshead x, 8, 9
Dudley 171, 187
Dunn, Alderman William Henry 154
Dunstanburgh Castle, Northumberland 80
Dunstan, Gateshead 8, 83
Durham Aged Mineworkers' Homes Association (DAMHA) 149
Durham Education Committee 163, 164
Durham Land and Labour Committee 152
Durham Miners' Gala 260
Durham University Extension Scheme 76, 81
Durham, University of 72, 81
Dyson Perrins, Charles 272, 279

E

Eadie-Reid, James 10, 54, 231
Earl Grey Square 225, 226, 233
Ecclesiastical Art Exhibition, Sheffield 61
Ecclesiastical Commissioners 147, 282
Economics Society 93, 95, 96, 151
Ede, Anna (first wife of Edward Ede) 22
Ede, Denzil (great uncle of WME) 22
Ede, Edward (father of WME) 22
Ede, Ernest (nephew of WME) 22, 218, 219
Ede, James (brother of WME) 24
Ede, John (grandfather of WME) 22
Edgar Tower 221, 285, 286, 287
Education Act, 1870 (Forster Act) 35–36, 96
Education Act, 1902 (Balfour Act) 99, 100, 160, 165
Education (Provision of Meals) Act 113
Edward, King 262
Electricity Works, Worcester 185

Elementary Education Act (1880) 46
Elgar, Sir Edward 220, 270, 283, 290, 291, 292
Elliotson-Symes, Eleanor (step-daughter of WME nee Baylee) 174
Elliotson-Symes, Reverend John 174
Elliott, Robert 153
Engels, Frederik 27
English Church Union (ECU) 62, 63, 186, 274
English Housing Survey 242
Exchange of Pulpits 257
Extension Scheme 19, 49, 69, 81

F

Fabian Society 118, 176
Factory Act, 1833 46
Fairburn, Richard 238
Fenwick, Charles 118
Field, Frank 261
Firth College 57, 67, 68, 69
Firth, Mark 56, 57, 64, 65, 68, 69, 70, 71, 73, 76
Fisher Education Act, 1918 264
Foster & Blacketts leadworks 2
Fownes Gloves 171
France, Reverend George 98
Freedom of the City of Worcester 11, 13, 263, 292
French Protestant Brotherhood 252
Friends of Worcester Cathedral 9, 28, 282, 283, 287

G

gambling 262
garden city movement 155, 223, 225, 233
Gateshead Board of Guardians 2, 104, 115
Gateshead Public Dinner Company 109
Gateshead School Board 8, 96, 110, 132, 161
Gateshead Select Vestry 102, 103
Gateshead Stained Glass Company 10
Gateshead Workhouse 102
General Strike, 1926 258
Geological Society 61
Germany 87, 88, 89, 203, 207, 208, 209, 210, 212, 254, 256, 261
Gheluvelt Park 227, 228, 229
Gheluvelt, Ypres, Belgium 209, 227, 292

Girls Friendly Society (GFS) 127
Gladstone, Mary 81
Goodwill 209
Gore, Bishop Charles 169, 172, 173, 176, 204, 229, 291
Gotha Canal 257
Gray, James 2, 115
Gray, Mary Jane v, 2, 3, 13, 115, 116, 255, 295, 296
Great Disruption 15
Great War 112, 209, 228, 246, 250
Grey, Earl/Lord Albert 76, 79, 156, 225
Guildhall, Worcester 13, 170, 210, 250, 289, 292
Guild of St George 59
Guild of St Matthew 174

H

Halifax 55
Halifax, Lord 186
Hamstead Road Baptist Church, Birmingham 257
Handel, George Frederik 220
Harcourt, Sir Vernon 115
Hardy & Padmore's iron foundry 171
Harkness, Edward 286
Harrison & Harrison, London (church organ consultants) 271
Harrow School, London 119
Hartlebury Castle, Worcestershire 172, 173, 230
Hartlebury Common, Worcester 185
Hartlepool, County Durham 78, 162, 168
Harton Coal Company 142
Haswell Moor 147, 148, 150
Haulbowline Island, Co Cork 24
Headlam, Reverend Stuart 174
Hegel, Georg Wilhelm Friedrich 27
Henry VIII 180
Hereford, Bishop of 186, 202
Hereford garden city scheme 223
Higginson, General Sir George 226, 231
higher grade schools 101, 165
Highfield Cocoa and Coffee House, Sheffield 70
Highfield Free Public Library and Museum Committee, Sheffield 71
Hill & Evans Vinegar works, Worcester 171
Hinscliffe, Reverend Claude 200, 201

Holland, Henry Scott   7
Hopper, Joseph   146, 149
Hop Pickers Mission   178
Horsley, Canon John   206
Housing Act, 1890   151, 152, 166
Housing Act, 1919   233, 242
housing committee, Worcester   234, 236, 237, 240, 241
Howard, Ebenezer   155, 159
Howick Hall   79
Hughes, Thomas   5
Hulsean Lectures (John Hulse)   27, 123
Humanitarian League   1, 2, 275

I
Ideal Home Exhibition   239
Independent Labour Party movement   7, 17, 44, 89
Independent Order of Rechabites (IOR)   14, 89, 90, 177
industrial school   100, 133, 134
International Arbitration League   208
International Peace Congress   206

J
Jack the Ripper   1, 129
Jarrow, Tyne and Wear   77, 78
Jesmond Dene, Newcastle upon Tyne   75, 76
Jesmond Vale House   75
Johnson, Joseph   146
Jowett, Reverend John (Carrs Lane Church, Birmingham)   177, 252, 253
juvenile street vendors   132

K
Keighley   55
Kelley, Hannah   134
Kelley, Samuel and Kate   133
Kennedy, Reverend Geoffrey Studdert   204, 205, 266
Kenyon-Slaney amendment, 1902   164
King James' Hospital   137, 263
King John's tomb   267
King's College, Cambridge. *See Cambridge, King's College*
King's College, London   20
Kingsley, Charles   5, 6, 184
King's School, Worcester   214, 264, 288
Kirkby Thore, Cumberland)   40, 53, 54, 118
Koenig's Tables   105

L
labour bureau   176
labour congress   190
Labour Day   256
Labour Party   17, 44, 176, 179, 213, 249, 251, 254, 256
Laing, Mrs   108
Lambeth degree   170
Land Nationalisation League   150, 151
Land Restoration Society   150
Land Tenure Reform Association   150
Lansdowne Road, Worcester   234, 237, 241
Lawrence, Elizabeth (sister of WME nee Moore-Ede)   23, 54
Lawrence, Reverend Thomas (brother-in-law of WME)   54, 200
Lawson, Jack   65, 66
Leadgate school   36
lead mining   30, 31, 116
lead poisoning   ix, 1, 2, 5, 43, 115, 116
leadworks   1, 2, 116, 117
League of Church Militant (LCM)   274
League of Nations   212, 213, 248, 249, 251, 253, 254, 260, 261, 294
Leeds   49, 51, 68, 256, 276
Leicester   49, 51, 52
Leonard, James   167
Letchworth garden city, Hertfordshire   157
Levy, Elizabeth   127, 128
Liberal Party   42, 43
Lightfoot, Bishop J. B.   49, 75, 83, 84, 118
Literary and Philosophical Society   x, 53, 75, 93, 95, 96, 151
Liverpool   68, 108, 134, 156, 182, 233
Lloyd George, David   202, 220
Lodge, the. *See Association for the Care of Friendless Girls (the Lodge)*
London, Bishop of   204
London Lead Company   33
London Society for the Prevention of Cruelty to Children   134
London Trades Council   208
London, University of   48

Loughborough Bell Foundry 279
Lucas, John 103, 104
Ludlow, John 5, 6, 21, 24
Lusitania 210
Luther, Martin 184

M

MacArthur, Mary 189, 190, 245
Mackie, Mr (Gateshead Trade Council) 153
Magic Breakfast Project 114
Malvern Priory 268
Manchester 68, 107, 156, 182
Manhood Suffrage Bill, 1911 198
Mann, Tom 192
Mansbridge, Albert & Frances 184, 185
March of the Women 197
Marine Training School, South Shields 41
Marlborough College, Wiltshire 25, 26, 46, 64
Marsden colliery 141, 142, 143, 145, 146, 164
Marshall, Alfred 14, 26, 27, 28, 52, 121, 123, 125, 181
Marx, Karl 27, 96
Mary, Queen 216
Masefield, John 74
Maund, Arrowsmith 236, 238, 239
Maurice, Frederick Denison 5, 6, 18, 19, 20, 21, 24, 27, 28, 31, 45, 48, 52, 58, 67, 119, 174, 181, 184, 298
Mayhew, Henry 23, 132
McBean, Thomas 192
McCarthy, Hannah 115, 116
Mechanics Institute 47, 48, 77, 86, 87
Methodism, Methodists 14, 15, 31, 32, 33, 35, 37, 38, 57, 63, 89, 100, 141, 177
Methodist Central Hall, Westminster 251, 256
Meyer, Lady Adele 198
Mill, John Stuart 27, 95, 150
Millwall White Lead Company 115
Milne, A. A. 277
Milner, Reverend John 39, 41
Milverton Coffee-House 177
Milward, Charles 235
Miners' Institute, Marsden 141, 142
Miners' Welfare Centre, Barnes Institute, Whitburn 145

Ministry of Health 237
Mission Hall, Marsden 141
Mission Room, Marsden 141, 142, 143, 144, 217
Mohonk, Lake 206
Monkwearmouth 108, 147
Moore, Billy (grandfather of WME) 22
Moore-Ede, Alfred (son of WME) 59, 130
Moore-Ede, Beatrice (daughter-in-law of WME) 173
Moore-Ede, Cuthbert (son of WME) 130
Moore-Ede, Eleanor (first wife of WME, formerly Baylee, nee Cookson) 10, 39, 40, 41, 53, 59, 70, 75, 76, 118, 127, 128, 130, 131, 145, 175, 193, 195, 197, 292, 293, 295
Moore-Ede, Elizabeth. *See Rivers-Moore, Elizabeth*
Moore-Ede, Laetitia (daughter of WME) 59, 70, 130, 174
Moore-Ede, Oswald (grandson of WME) 193
Moore-Ede, Oswald (son of WME) 3, 130
Moore-Ede, Sarah (second wife of WME, formerly Pattinson, nee Harrison-Wilson) 10, 194, 195, 196, 197, 199, 201, 202, 219, 222, 226, 230, 251, 255, 272, 274, 276, 279, 281, 290, 292, 293, 295
Moore-Ede, Stuart (son of WME) 76, 130, 174
Moore-Ede, William Edward (son of WME) 54, 173, 187, 194
Moore, Elizabeth (mother of WME) 22, 24, 25
Morpeth, Northumberland 1, 43
Morse, Reverend Francis (vicar of Nottingham) 57
Moule, Bishop Handley 142, 162
Mozart, Wolfgang Amadeus 220
Mundella, Anthony 56

N

national anthem 277
National Council for Adult Suffrage 201
National Housing Reform Council 151, 156

National Labour Federation   118
National Mission of Repentance and Hope   221
National Pension Fund   87
National Savings Investment Bonds   262
National Schools   35, 36
National Service Act, 1939   261
National Society for the Prevention of Cruelty to Children (NSPCC)   134, 136
National Union of Women's Suffrage Societies (NUWSS)   196
Nelson, Lord Admiral   22, 289
Nelson Street Restaurant, Gateshead   109, 137
Nenthead   31, 33
Newark, Nottinghamshire   44, 54, 55
Newbrough, Northumberland   81
Newcastle College of (Physical) Science   66, 72, 75, 84
Newman, Reverend Edward   60, 184
Nichols, Dr Thomas & Mary Gove   105
North of England Cottage Exhibition   158
Northumberland Miners' Association (NMA)   42, 156
Northwick, Worcestershire   238, 240, 241
Nottingham, Nottinghamshire   44, 45, 49, 50, 51, 52, 57
Nottingham, University of   49, 51

O
Occupation Centre   266
Old Palace   172, 173, 215, 230, 252, 281, 290
Open Spaces Committee   264
organ, organist   80, 270, 271, 272, 273, 278, 283, 288
Owen, Robert (New Lanark)   35

P
Packer, Reverend   153
Palmer Brothers (shipbuilders)   77, 78
Parmoor, Lord (Charles Cripps)   213, 250, 251
Paton, Reverend John Brown (congregational minister, Nottingham)   49
Pattinson, Hugh Lee   194
Pattinson, Hugh Salvin   194

Peace Conference, The Hague (International Federation of Trade Unions)   254, 256
Peace Memorial, Stevens Park, Quarry Bank   245, 246, 247
Peace Society   199, 250, 251, 256
Pearce, Reverend Ernest   230, 241
Pease, Edward   118
Penny Dinners, Gateshead   8, 104, 105, 106, 109, 110, 114, 216
pensions   6, 33, 88, 96, 146, 176
People's Dispensary, Gateshead   138
People's Museum, Sheffield   58
Permanent Relief Fund (miners')   146
Perowne, Bishop Arthur   293, 294
Peterborough, dean of   291
Phelps & Johnson (builders)   234, 236
Pilgrim's Trust   286
Plymouth   22, 24, 25, 53, 257
Plymouth Grammar School   25, 45
Poor Law   43, 88, 175, 176, 180
Prest, Archdeacon Edward   83, 98
Public House Trust   147
Public Worship Regulation Act   5, 62
Putney, Wandsworth   23, 180, 181, 183

Q
Quakers. *See Religious Society of Friends (Quakers)*
Queen Elizabeth   145
Queen Mary   216
Queen Victoria   18, 40, 65

R
Radek, Karl   254
Rattler (Marsden–South Shields railway)   141
Rawlinson, General Lord   227
Red Cross   207, 220
Redmond, Charles   98
Red Vienna   251, 252
Religious Society of Friends (Quakers)   33, 195, 199, 211, 245, 252, 266, 292
Riley, Reverend Henry   98
Ripon College, Cuddesdon   253
Rivers-Moore, Elizabeth (daughter of WME)   130, 174
Rivers-Moore, Henry (son-in-law of WME)   174

Robertson, Field Marshall Sir William 227
Rochdale 19, 49
Rowbotham & Son (builders) 238
Rowe, Major Vernon 226, 234, 284
Royal Naval dockyard 22
Royal Show 155
Royal Worcester Porcelain 171, 289
Royden, Maude 274
Ruhr, Germany 256
Ruskin College, Oxford 65
Ruskin, John 58, 59, 61, 85
Russia 251, 254

S

Sale, Reverend Thomas (St Paul's, Sheffield) 60
Salt, Titus (Saltaire) 35
Salvation Army 215
Scheu, Dr Gustav 251, 252
Scheu-Riesz, Helene 251, 252
School Attendance Act, 1880 46
Scott Holland 6
Seaton Delaval, Northumberland 76, 77, 79, 81, 82
Second World War 246, 261
Severn, River 172, 255
Severn Road Bridge, Worcester 266
Seymour, Reverend Charles 111
Shaftsbury, Lord 155
Shankhouse, Northumberlan 87
Sharow, North Yorkshire 40
Shaw, George Bernard 283
Sheffield Café Company 70, 90
Sheffield Girls' High School 71
Sheffield School of Medicine 69
Sheffield Technical School 69
Sheffield, University of 56, 57, 65, 69
Shincliffe Colliery 147
Sidgwick, Professor Henry 49
Silver Cinema, Worcester 264, 265
Simmonds, Dr Walpole 235
Skinner, Thomas 237
Smith, L. O. (Lars Olsen Perrson) 104, 105
Society for the Promotion of Working Men's Associations 18
Sound, Øresund Strait 259
Soviet Communist Party 254

Spratt, Vicky 242
Stallard, John (mayor of Worcester) 170
Standard Housing Company 239
St Andrew's Church, Marsden 142
St Augustine's Church, Alston 37, 39
St Columba's Church, Gateshead 63, 85
Stevens, Ernest 246
St Hilda's Church, South Shields 42
St Hilda's colliery, South Shields 42
St John's College, Cambridge.
    See Cambridge, St John's College
St Jude's Church, Sheffield 71, 72
St Jude's mission room, Newcastle 111
St Martin's Parish, Worcester 290
St Mary's Church, Gateshead 2, 84, 102, 111, 137, 139, 175, 194, 295
St Mary's Church Institute, Gateshead 62, 137
St Mary's Church, Kidderminster 3
St Mary's Church, Putney, London 23, 180, 181, 183
St Mary's Church, Warwick 180
St Mary's Heritage Centre x
St Mary's National School, Gateshead 106
Stockholm, Sweden 105, 257
Stockton, County Durham 78
Storey, Samuel 163
St Oswald's Hospital 263
St Oswin's Literary Society,Tynemouth 88
Stourbridge, West Midlands 197, 198
St Paul's Cathedral, dean of 251
St Paul's Church, Sheffield 59, 60, 61, 70
St Peter's Church, North Shields 110
St Thomas the Martyr Church, Newcastle 75, 179
Stuart, James 48, 49, 50, 51, 55, 56, 68
Sunday afternoon lectures for men 85, 137, 219
Sunderland 76, 78, 109, 111, 147, 179
Sunderland High School 131
Sunderland School Board 107
Sweated Trades Exhibition, London 188, 190
Sweden 104, 105, 257, 258, 259

T

Taft, President 206
Tarrant, Henry 226
Technical Education Act of 1889 101

temperance 13, 14, 70, 89, 90, 104, 105, 144, 175, 177, 178, 220, 262
Tenants Limited 154, 155, 225
Test workers 103, 104
Thomas, Emanuel 185
Three Choirs Festival 219, 231, 270, 273, 277, 290, 291
Thwaites, Sir William 205
Tillett, Ben 192
Todd, Edith 267
Tolladine Road, Worcester 224
Tomatoland 226
Toynbee Hall 173
Trade Council 153
Trade Dispute Act, 1906 260
Trades Board Act, 1909 189, 192
Trades Union Congress 190
Treaty of Versailles 256
Trinity College, Cambridge. *See Cambridge, Trinity College*
Trotter, Thomas 273
Troup, Edward 117
Turner, William 284
twopenny dinners 215–218
Tynemouth Aquarium 80
Tyne, River 1, 41, 74, 83, 122, 127

U

Unitarian, Unitarianism 3, 19
University College London 21
Urwick, Sir Henry 226

V

Vaux, Ernest 91
Vegetarian Society 105
Vernon, Sir Harry & Lady Georgina 175, 176
Victoria University 67, 69

W

Wade, George 246
Wages Board 120
Waifs Rescue Agency and Street Vendor's Club 132
Waldron, Arthur 206
Walker Homes 194
Walker, Newcastle 78, 157, 158, 224
Walker, Reverend (vicar of Cradley) 190

Walkerville, Newcastle upon Tyne 158, 159, 223, 234
Wallace, Henry 146
Wallsend, North Tyneside 108
Walters, Tudor 234, 242
Walton, William 276
Ward's chrome tanning works, Worcester 171
War Relief Fund 216
Warren Pot, Walker & Elmley 106, 108
Waugh, Reverend Benjamin 134, 135, 136
Wayfarers' Relief Society 176
Webb, Edward 171
Webb's chemical fertiliser factory, Worcester 171
Webb's horsehair carpet factory, Worcester 171
Weber, Max 27
Wellesley, HMS (training ship) 80
Wesley, John 32, 183, 184
Westcott, Reverend Brooke Foss 49, 118, 119, 120, 122, 125, 126, 138, 139, 146, 147, 152, 162, 255
Westminster Abbey 21, 197, 267, 269
Westminster, Dean of 267
Westminster's Central Hall. *See Methodist Central Hall, Westminster*
Whitburn colliery. *See Marsden colliery*
Whitburn Hall 140
Whitburn, South Tyneside 44, 138, 139, 140, 141, 142, 143, 145, 146, 154, 168, 177
white coal 259
White House 147
Wilde, Oscar 174
Williamson, Sir Hedworth 140
Wilson, Canon James 201, 218, 220, 222, 268, 281, 290
Wilson, John 146, 149, 152, 163
Wilson, President Woodrow 212
Windmill Hills, Gateshead 104
Women's Co-operative Guild 49
Women's Social and Political Union (WSPU) 196, 197, 198, 199
Woodbine Willie. *See Kennedy, Reverend Geoffrey Studdert*
Wood, Mrs Henry 221, 222
Wood, Sir Lindsay 141

Worcester Archaeological Society 268
Worcester Chamber of Commerce 265
Worcester Foresters 227
Worcester Grammar School 263, 264
Worcester Occupation Centre 266
Worcester School of Art 261
Worcestershire and District Association of Change Ringers 231, 278
Workers' Educational Association (WEA) 184, 185
Working Men's College 19, 21, 48, 58, 67
Working Women's College 48
World Alliance for Promoting International Friendship Through the Churches 208, 209, 212, 220, 248, 250, 252, 253, 257
World Brotherhood Organisation 251

Y

Yeatman-Biggs, Bishop Huyshe 169, 170, 172, 177, 190, 201, 218, 229, 255, 270, 271, 278
York, Archbishop of 62, 63, 203
York Railway Institute 88
Young Men's Christian Association (YMCA) 138
Young Women's Christian Association (YWCA) 230, 274

Z

Zion schoolroom, South Shields 88